Running off at a tangent

Steve Atherton

Running off at a tangent

Definition:

Go off at a tangent - To pursue a somewhat related or irrelevant course while neglecting the main subject.

Published 2021, in Great Britain,
Text Copyright © Steve Atherton 2021

All rights reserved. No part of this publication may be reproduced, stored in a retrieval system, or transmitted in any form or by any means, electronic, mechanical, photocopy, recording or otherwise, without prior written permission of the copyright owner. Nor can it be circulated in any form of binding or cover other than that in which it is published and without similar condition including this condition being imposed on a subsequent purchaser.

British Cataloguing Publication data:

A catalogue record of this book is available from the British Library

This book is also available as an ebook.

I dedicate this book to Ada, a true friend.

Contents

Prologue	Page 1
Introduction	Page 2
January	Page 5
March	Page 51
April	Page 65
May	Page 85
June	Page 96
July	Page 116
August	Page 138
September	Page 155
October	Page 194
November	Page 219
December	Page 248
Epilogue	Page 284
Acknowledgements	Page 286
About the author	Page 287

Steve Atherton

Prologue

What makes you get up in the morning?

We all like our bed and our bodies need rest, but just occasionally do something really special. Head to somewhere away from the town and be at one with nature; watch the sunrise at the start of a new day.

Better still; share the experience with your kids and those you love. When you do, you will have beaten the battle of the bed.

Introduction

It's Thursday 31st December 2015, at the end of a busy and at times, manic year and I am sat in the lounge at our home in Warwick on the eve of the start of another New Year.

I have some random and varied stuff on my bucket list, from being a pantomime dame to afternoon tea at the Ritz Hotel in London along with a myriad of other weird and wonderful items and like many people, I have trying my hand at becoming a world famous author to rival JK Rowling or Robin Sharma on my list too.

The original idea was a book based on my running year starting on New Year's Day and ending on the eve of the next year 366 days later, being a leap year, documenting in a diary form, my thoughts and sometimes sporting exploits of the period.

The title of my book started life simply as 'The Running Year', an obvious choice I hope you will agree. However, it soon became clear that 'Running off at a tangent' was a far more appropriate title, as when I started to write down my thoughts, the words that were going down on paper, had very little to do with running.

I did think about a blog, but it might be an age thing and call me old fashioned, but I do like a book! A bit like music, CD's and downloads are OK, but back in the day I used to love buying a new album on vinyl with a proper cover and everything – not unlike a book. I feel music downloads, like blogs, loose that physical interaction with the recipient so if I am going to try my hand at being an author, it had to be a book.

(Apologies if you are reading this on a kindle or an e-reader).

Steve Atherton

I have never been great with words, especially written and I am not one of life's great word smiths, but I hoped in my heart of hearts that my grade C O level in English Language would come in useful one day and if I decided to put pen to paper, I might be able to at least string a sentence or two together. I had a similar aspiration for the C's, the accumulated qualifications in the remainder of my school subjects.

I do think a lot (sometimes too much - always have), but some old habits die hard, so I hoped I would not be short of things to write about.

As with words, I am not a natural runner; at school, sport was something to be avoided and most weeks when games came around on the timetable, I arrived at school armed with a note from my mum; anything to get me out of anything remotely physical, but late in life I discovered running.

I joined the fitness craze in my twenties and dabbled at playing squash back in the Eighties, (like most men did) when gyms and sports centres became trendy. Coinciding with the arrival of TV fitness gurus Mr Motivator and the Green Goddess, along with Breakfast Television and junk food; maybe a little link there, I'll leave that thought with you.

I have always enjoyed the gym, but not running or jogging, this came to me late in life with my first race was back in 2005. The Regency Run, a 10km race in my hometown and this is where the story really begins.

I am not sure how I ended up entering the local annual event to be honest, but I did and after regular training runs with my work pal Kieran, race day arrived. As we walked up to the starting area, Kieran shook my hand, wished me well and headed nearer to the front (he was a lot better than me, and still is) and there I was, on my own, waiting for the race to begin. It felt like the first day of school with my heart was racing and I felt very, very alone. As I stood on the start line trying to blend in with hundreds of other runners, I crossed my heart, prayed for help from my late mum. This has become a race day tradition from that day and never run a race without a chat to my mum.

Running off at a tangent

The seconds ticked slowly towards the 9.00am kick off and my heart rate peaked at an all-time high. As the church bell chimed for the ninth time and in unison with the sound of the starting klaxon, the crowd clapped and cheered, and we were off and feel like I have been running ever since.

Before I put pen to paper and take you, whether you want to or not headfirst into a New Year and begin my journey, I warn you that I have left out peoples surnames and the odd bit of research is straight off 'tinter-web', so don't blame me if it's not quiet on the money.

JANUARY 2016

Friday 1st January 2016 - Let's get this show on the road.

With the arrival of the first day of a New Year, I begin the journey into the world of writing to document the life of a 'would be' athlete. Am I an athlete? Well that's a subject for debate, a desk job, good living and an appetite for all things bad for me; I soon concluded that being a good runner was always going to be a struggle. I realised that the odds were stacked against me, which was clearly not going to be helped by being born with big bones. It was clear that none of these things were ever really going to stand me in good shape to be anything but a jogger.

The answer to the question, if I am honest an athlete maybe not, but I do what I do with what I have.

New Year's Day and a bank holiday means no work today and with most of the drinking world nursing a hangover after successfully celebrating the arrival of a New Year, I had planned on having a lazy day today before returning to the rat race the following morning. But I thought you can't have a book based around the running year if you do not kick off with an outing on New Year's Day.

I knew I had to lace up them trainers and get out and do something, but I wanted today's run to be significant, meaningful with some relevance and as my family are very important to me as you will get to find out later no doubt, a run with a connection to my parents would be a perfect start to the year, as without them there would be no me.

As the baby of the family, being the youngest of three children, I wanted to somehow involve my late mum and dad in this new adventure and with this in mind I chose my route and destination. With that sorted and with a plan for the day, I headed out to St Mary Magdalene Church in Lillington to visit my parents' grave.

I have been coming to visit my mum's resting place since her death in 1992 at the far too early age of 64, but my dad is a new addition to the church yard joining my mum in July 2015 some 23 years later. The church is beautiful although Lillington has been swallowed up and has pretty much become a suburb of the 'Royal Borough' as I like to call it or Royal Leamington Spa as it is really called. The area around the church still retains that village feel and since the arrival of the first vicar back in 1252, the church has always played its part in the community and we always refer to 'St Mary Mags' as our spiritual home.

Although I shed a tear at the grave side, I know that life would have not been a lot of fun if either of them had they lived much longer, but I am sad that my girls never had a chance to know my Mum; she would have spoilt them rotten I am sure.

Rosina, or Rose as she was always known, suffered ill health most of her life especially in the later years and to be honest, my dad, Ron, stayed around far longer than he should have done or really wanted too.

When I run I often think of them, I was and guess still am, a proper mummy's boy and heading off to school in September 1966 at ripe old age of five was a massive shock for me. None of this slow ramp up to full time education that children enjoy nowadays with taster sessions and half days. Back in my childhood days, it was straight in at the deep end and I never really let go of the apron strings even in later life, but I did inevitably grow up.

During the slow progression from boy to man, both parents were very supportive and a great influence on me, albeit subtle at times, sowing the seeds needed to develop into the person I am today. Even now, I catch myself using the words of wisdom that my mum especially would share with my brother, sister and I during our childhood. You will get to hear some of them as the year progresses no doubt, so you have been warned.

Steve Atherton

Our parents met in the post war years, not really sure how but something to do with 'friends of friends' and penpals I am sure has been mentioned in the past. My dad doing national service in the navy, (which only ended in 1960, I was amazed to learn) travelling around Europe and stationed in the news office in Malta before returning home to marry my mum during the tough times after the Second World War.

With victory in Europe in 1945, with the end to the fighting in Japan later the same year, came a lot of hardship with rationing continuing until 1954, some 10 years after the end of the conflict. Our Dad returned to his old job at the Morning News, a daily one sheet local newspaper, once his service days were over. So it made sense for mum to leave her job in a textile mill and make home in the 'Royal Borough'.

My sister Linda was the first little Atherton coming along in May 1950 with my brother David joining the clan three years later in April 1953. With perfection taking a little time to develop, the family had to wait until 30th May 1961 before I made my appearance to become and remain the baby of the family.

As I have already mentioned, I say a few quiet words to my mum on the start line of every race and is a massive albeit silent part of my pre-race rituals, but it's only recently that I have thought more about my dad.

I never really saw him as a leader or a great statesman, but I was wrong. We always saw our mum as the driving force of the household with our dad doing with what he was told, but now I am not so sure. My dad had more of an influence on my character than I ever realised. Some traits are obvious, sharing the same sense of humour and love of the quick comeback, along with the inability to drink beer in any great quantity without losing the plot. But the greatest impact on me, especially in later life is that you do not need to be the boss or be at the front to make a difference and that leadership and support can come from within, be it a team, group or family; a great life lesson and has become foundation of my life today.

Oh yes, the run, from our cosy home on the banks of the River Avon in Warwick, over the border into Leamington Spa and heading to the north of town along the wide Regency streets to Lillington and back pretty much the same way and home to hot shower, a lovely roast dinner and a glass of something nice.

Happy New Year!

Sunday 3rd January 2016 - 'Look out of my window, still raining'

Just to warn you, I might occasionally throw in the odd song title or lyric, music is a big part of my life, but not my running but more about that as the year unfolds. You might recognise the song title above as a classic from the legendary Jonny Lang. Never had the pleasure? Check out this amazing blues guitarist from North Dakota, USA.

The year started off dull and wet and as the weekend continues, so does the rain. Today's run with my little running group Zero to Hero, more about this great group of people later. But this was a classic example of leading from the back, the very back of the pack with a bad back as it would happen. An overzealous shot during an impromptu badminton match during the previous week nearly ended my running career forever.

(Note to self, I must work on getting some more flexibility in this old body of mine - best put it on the list, I do like a list).

I very nearly didn't run today, but as I was already up and about, I did. I jumped in my car and headed to Kenilworth, the next town to where I live some five miles away, to say hello and to wish everyone a Happy New Year.
Although I had my running gear on I had absolutely no intention to run. I had planned to return home once I had done the pleasantries to a painkiller-based cocktail and a bit of

breakfast. However, I did not like the thought of seeing the group head off into the 'sunset', ok mist, without me and together with such a good turn out on such a shitty day, I revised my original plan and I stayed and ran.

I dug into the pack and managed to get a few painful miles in the bag, eager to hear the exciting plans from everyone for the New Year ahead.

I love the first few days of a New Year and the buzz of a clean slate along with all the hopes and dreams that come with it. You need to aim high if you want something, but with all hopes and aspirations, you must want it and a plan to make it happen.

New Years resolutions are nothing without a plan or better said 'An idea without a plan is just a dream!' A phrase an old manager used to quote a lot in the office but according to the internet, the actual quote is:

'a dream without a plan is just a wish' credited to Katherine Paterson, Chinese-born American writer best known for children's novels including *The Invisible Child*.

Although the shortest day has passed and the days are slowly getting longer, it does not seem to get light these first few days of 2016.

Roll on the longer days and better weather, for me this is when running is a pleasure, especially in the mornings; running at dawn is the best. Patience is not one of my best traits and with only just a few days into the first month of the year, I might just have to wait a little longer to have that pleasure. But until the spring, the warmth on the run comes from within the group.

Another common New Year's resolution for myself and most of the country I would image, is to shed a pound or two. With that thought in mind and to add to the misery of a wet morning and a bad back, today is the first weigh in of the year at our little 'fat club'. The result, although predictable, wasn't much better, five pounds on and a fiver lighter.

Running off at a tangent

I bet you are wondering what I am talking about?, I better explain then, some time ago we set up our own little Slimming World come Weight Watchers, aptly called 'fat club' to keep an eye on our waste lines. A weekly weigh in combined with the walk of shame with a fine for any increase in weight. It had worked so far but Christmas is never a good time reduce the calorie intact.

Not sure how the others managed to stay the same or only put a pound on over Christmas, I have no idea, bastards!! I reckon I must have heavy bones or is it something to do with the calorie laden calories that come with the brown food of Christmas.

I do like our little fat club, nothing like a bit of peer pressure to focus the mind. Setting our targets for January – mine, half a stone by the end of January, half a stone... I can do it!! What gets measured, gets improved, that's the theory and with that in mind, I need to keep focused and will be a lot easier when the house is bereft of the brown stuff!

I think Christmas food should all go out of date on the chime of Big Ben on New Year's Eve, I might just stand a fighting chance to lose a pound or two then.

I love it when all the great ideas and New Year's resolutions, are put on hold to allow the holiday season to come to an end and allows the New Year to start for real a few days later. I appreciate that it's all about the calendar and when the year ends, but New Year's Day was Friday this year so will make Monday a bank holiday, which successfully throws everything out of sync.

I am back to work on Tuesday, which allow me the chance to stay off the booze but that's seems like ages away so I might just have a have a drink today, one for the road.

After our run I grabbed a coffee with the runners, before heading home and once the sun was over the garden, my wife and I opened a bottle of something nice.

Tuesday 5th January 2016 - The Long Run.

The Long Run, did the Eagles have a song called that? Sorry, my feeble attempt at humour!
I ran to the end of the road and back, a very slow mile, but I did listen to my body. I didn't feel great this morning and my back still giving me some cause for concern so that's will have to do for today.

This could be the shortest book in history......

Friday 8th January 2016 - Back in the groove.

We have made it to the end of the first working week of the New Year. I always think that this is one of the toughest ones of the year after the traditional long and over indulgent festivities, it's hard to return to the grindstone but on the other hand, it does feel good to get back something like a routine and a chance to eat regular meals after the excess of Christmas and New Year.

I like running straight after work, it marks the end of the working week and heralds the start of the weekend. I am fortunate to have colleagues that like to run, giving a great opportunity to catch up on the gossip away from office.

With the start of a New Year and it looks like Team IAC is back on with a restart after a break. I ran with Roy this afternoon but checking the newly formed Facebook group, it looks like Mike and Ross have independently put their trainers on and gone for a run too. I can see this little Facebook group working a treat as it can be difficult to get everyone in the same place and time to run together, might just add a little peer pressure too. I will no doubt explain more about Team IAC as the year unfolds.

Saturday 9th January 2016 - Do you need a reason to run?

I feel a lot better than I have done for most of the previous week. With my dodgy back at last on the mend, or at least it felt like it thanks to a nice bottle of Rioja!

I think after taking three days off from putting the trainers on and a good night's sleep, I can see the light at the end of the running tunnel. But I think the main reason I am on the slow road to recovery is due to the red wine. I strongly feel that red wine IS the future or is it garlic bread?

People have a myriad of reasons to run and I am no different. Personally, keeping the pounds off is one of the incentives for getting the trainers on, although mainly I use running as a form of stress relief. Plus, I like to just run for the pleasure of being outside in the fresh air, especially as I have a desk-based job in an air-conditioned office. To be honest it's a bit of all the above.

Occasionally, I am a man on a mission, running for a specific reason and on the odd occasion it is not about running at all and it is all about the bike.

Today was a bit of both and this morning I was most definitely a man on a mission because I was going to do my own mini duathlon.

After was seemed an age, this morning, at last I was going to add a new vehicle to the Atherton fleet. It has got to be twenty years since I have bought a new bike and having lost my dad back in 2015 and I inheriting a few quid, I wanted to get something to remember him by.

A poignant choice having promised him on his death bed that I would follow in his footsteps, or wheels to be more accurate and cycle to Mow Cop. I thought a new bike would an appropriate and symbolic purchase.

I wanted to make the arrival of my new wheels an event, so what better way than to run over to Kenilworth to pick it up, although I did make a slight detour to check on the river at the Saxon Mill on the way.

Steve Atherton

I have always liked coming to this great place and the river was certainly making its presence felt on this special morning. I love the power of the water and I could stand on this bridge all day and loose myself in the currents and whirlpools of the rain swollen river Avon. The Saxon Mill is a really special place with an atmosphere that is magical. The former mill of Guys Cliff House was rebuilt as we see it today in 1822. It had produced flour on the same site since the 12th century and was in use as a mill until recently. 1938 to be more accurate and was then converted into a bar/restaurant in 1952. I would imagine this place could tell a tale or two.

The fields in and around the Saxon Mill and the path up to Saint James Church in Old Milverton have always been a favourite area of mine to explore with very fond memories of my childhood. Long walks with my parents on a Sunday afternoon and at the appropriate time of year, we'd stop off for a spot of blackberry picking, the product of which would enviably end up in a pie or crumble.

The area is still a popular place to run for me and many fellow joggers, but not a summers night when the restaurant terrace overlooking the river is crammed with people enjoying a drink or two. Then the place is best avoided as the desire to stop running and head to the bar is just torture, however, this will not

Although a pretty much road-based route taking a near straight line from my home in Warwick to the bike shop in Kenilworth, I had plenty to keep me occupied both visually and mentally. A good proportion of the run followed the annual Two Castles route from Warwick Castle to Kenilworth Castle which I have done many times since my first outing in 2005. The slow gradually climb still makes the legs work hard and brings a sweat on or is that just me?

The run does have some fun bits too and this morning included a little house looking or checking out the lovely little and not so little properties on route, this helps make the miles fly by.

Leek Wootton is a beautiful little village approximately halfway between Warwick and Kenilworth, little did I know that this place would become a great place to run in 2016.

I like the idea of a cliff hanger, the suspense, but don't get too excited.

The promise for a nice hot cuppa waiting for me at the shop, along with a nice shiny bike, was a great incentive and I was proper excited. I like to admire excellent customer service, and Mike Vaughan Bikes delivered in spade loads. A local family business providing great bikes to the cyclists of Warwickshire since 1961 (the year I was born – a bit of a coincidence) and now me!

However, today's activities were not just about the run or the bike. As the morning progressed on route, I discovered another 'hidden gem' that would soon become part of my life, an artisan bread shop.

I came across the little shop slightly off the beaten track as I headed back home on my shiny new bike, avoiding the main roads through town. I have never noticed the little bakers hidden in a little back street of Kenilworth before, but to be honest it was the smell that grabbed my attention.

It turned out that Nick, the owner and top baker at Crustum, the local artisan bakery in question was also in the running for a new bike. This coincidence would not become apparent until later the same day.

Such a nice guy, great bread and unknown to both of us, Nick and Crustum would also play many a part in 2016 – *double cliff hanger, more suspense!* Passing the shop, I vowed to return later in the day with my wife Julie who is a bit a bread aficionado.

The bike was great and I looked forward to spending many miles in the saddle in the months and years to come. I was already looking ahead to the adventure that would take us both, Ron, my newly christened bike and I, to Mow Cop to honour the promise I made to my dad in his last few hours.

Returning home with my new bike, a quick shower and I was ready for something to eat after a lovely five mile run and of course the same distance on my new shiny wheels.

Fed and watered, my wife and I headed back to check out the bread products. On walking into the tiny shop, I was met by a radiant smile, quickly followed by a knowing look. I must add that the almost immediate recognition was mutual and soon realised that the owner of the cheeky smile was Nick, who only the day before was at the cycle shop, as he was also in the running for a new bike. We made an immediate connection because we had a common interest as we test rode the latest and greatest offerings from Mike Vaughan the previous day and the guy bakes bread, we are going to be mates, I feel sure. What a small world!

Sunday 10th January 2016 - Deep and crisp and even (and not a pizza in sight!)

What a beautiful morning and at last some proper winter weather. A great turnout for the Sunday run today and good to catch up with an old running buddy. One thing that I love about our little running group is the way folks drop in and out without feeling any pressure to turn up every week. No guilt when life gets in the way and we all know that feeling when it does, the last thing we need is any more commitments.

I like having Phil, the old running buddy I mentioned, around and he is such a gent, some might say a little 'old school 'and nothing wrong with that. I haven't seen him for a while, so it was good to have a catch up. Phil and I go back a while, we met in the car park of the local amateur theatre when we were both on Dad's taxi duty.

At the time, Phil lived in Coventry and I lived in Leamington, so it made no sense for either of us to go home whist our offspring learnt how to be budding actors and actresses. The result meant we both had an hour to kill.

Sit in our cars we did not and we both had ways of filling the time. I would run and Phil would go out on his mountain bike then one night we were having a chat and Phil said he would join me for a run. I could see that Phil was a little older, but little I know that he was a racing snake! The guy's track record of running achievements was amazing and I enjoyed getting to know him over the years.

Like all good friendships, when we meet, we just pick up where we left off and always lovely to find out what he had been up too. Always good for a story is our Phil.

With such a great turnout, I was spoilt for choice with people to run along with today and walk a little too, whatever it takes.

Today was one of these days when it's a pleasure to get those trainers on, and again it's not always about the running. Out in the countryside, sometimes it's good to take time and just take it all in, and on such a beautiful day, a good chance to get to know fellow runners a bit better. I am not sure what I would do if I didn't run. I have never won a race, not even close and never one of the first fifty percent across the finish line, nearer the back if anything, but always in the thick of it. I have never yet started a race that I haven't finished, but it has been close. Well not that close to be honest, I am not a quitter.

What I do find most of all is that the people that inspire and motivate me are not the elite athletes or the racing snakes, but those folks who get out and just do it.

'Passion' is a word that when my day comes to leave the mothership, I would like that word to appear somewhere in my eulogy, although I can think of many other words that might make a guest appearance too. Stubborn, annoying, impatient are a few, but I am not in any hurry to find out for real.

'Marmite' as my wife calls me, not sure what that means but she does occasionally remind me that I'm an acquired taste, good job she likes 'Marmite'.

Live with passion, love with passion, run with passion.

Steve Atherton

I love music and just to warn you, I might drop in the odd lyric or two as the year progresses. I will listen to anything, but rock is my favourite and I am not a big fan of country and western. But when I run, especially on my own, my mind goes in a manner of all directions. So I have never really gone in for music on the move, even though I do have a pretty comprehensive collection of tunes.

On holiday or when travelling, I always feel the need a bit of a music, a soundtrack but not when I am running. The exception to the rule when music does come in handy is on those long runs , but then I generally opt for an audio book. Most of the time I am happy to run 'o'naturel', as there is always plenty going on around me and I like to take it all in.

When I'm in the gym and on the rare occasion I am working out on my own, then that's a different story – but another time for that.

Back to those thoughts when I run, I am a fairly half-full person, but in do get low and at times like these, I always find a good run can really blow the cobwebs away and lift my spirits. On those good days, the really special days, the stars align, and I get all my ducks in a row [Sorry I have been too long in the car industry]. When the thoughts all come together, I can set the world all fire.

Some of my greatest ideas and plans came to me when running. It's good to talk and when I don't have to have anyone with me to have a conversation with, then I am more than happy running along chatting away to myself. I must make a bit of a spectacle and no doubt raise an I brow or two, people must thing I am a little bit mad.

Morning is my time, dawn to be precise, this is when I like to run. The best dawn runs are the ones that start in the dark and finish with the light of a new day – so special. With these short days and dark mornings, I might just have to wait a while to enjoy this pleasure.

I am a pretty driven person, but this has not always been the case. I came to life late in the game and I feel I missed out on a shed load of opportunities, especially in my school days. I would love to have that time over again, with what I know now and maybe I would have made some better choices, who knows. Youth is wasted on the young they say and so very true in my case. I look back on my school days and I guess I would describe them as a curate's egg, good in parts. Never really understood what that meant, but I think it means there are good bits and bad bits. As I get older, especially in the last few years, I always say I have had a great life, with the chance to travel to some amazing places, sometimes paid for out of my own pocket but sometimes as part of my job and for that I am grateful.

I have met some amazing people during my life and some tossers too! I've made some great decisions and some absolute shockers, but I have never wanted to get to the end of my life taking my last breath with any regrets – if only!!

I do like a plan, but I try to live in the now. I heard this saying recently -

'The past is history; the future is a mystery and today is a gift, that's why it's called the present. '

Cheesy but true!

A work colleague Mat introduced me to Robin Sharma on a business trip to Belgium many years ago and since reading his bestselling book, 'The monk who sold his Ferrari' I was inspired to keep a journal, which not only keeps my life on the straight and narrow, but also helps keep my head relatively uncluttered.

In this crazy world we live in these days, I find any techniques that help with getting through the day worth sharing.

Steve Atherton

Monday 11th January 2016 - a learning curve.

When running is good there is nothing better, I run because I love how it makes me feel, usually at the end! However, when it's dark, cold and peeing it down with rain, I struggle to get motivated to head out and prefer my bed more – funny that!

What I don't like is when life gets in the way and I can't run, which is usually the time when I need to get out in the fresh air and to clear my head.

Today was very cold, but I did manage to get out early this morning to do a dawn run with my buddy Ian. I have ran with him for years and it's always an experience running with this guy and is never boring. We always put the world to rights, sharing life stories and occasionally I offer some advice to try and keep him on the straight and narrow. As I am a little older, I try to give him the benefit of my worldly knowledge – lucky for him he doesn't always take it and is still happily married. But maybe some of the less radical ideas and advice I offer will rub off on to him and maybe just help him a little and keep him out of the doghouse at home.

Seeing an insight into the lives of others sometimes shows up on our runs too. In this day and age no one should be without a roof over their heads, sometimes when we run through town, we come across someone asleep in a shop doorway or a person with everything they own, walking the streets.

We were running the canal today, which dissects the Royal Borough, mid run as Ian and I were having a good old rant about the trials and tribulations of home, work, life in no particular order, when we ran past someone curled up in a sleeping bag under the shelter of a canal bridge. The bridge affording at least some protection from the rain but providing relief from the cold on this freezing morning, surrounded by their worldly belongings. Our conversation ends and we continue on our run in silence ...

This particular run will stay with me and those thoughts filed away for something in the future maybe – the seed is planted and lay dormant ready for the time to start to grow. Its only January but today's run is going to change my life, you are going to have to wait until the end of the year to find out more but remember today, I certainly will.

The one good thing about running with others is the commitment, what's in the diary generally gets done and it's oh so easy to lose the battle of the bed when no one is waiting on a street corner. I love running with others, not only for the company as I love people, but also for the commitment.

It has got to be something serious for me not to show up, but a different kettle of fish if I am running solo. Without that promise of showing up, I will look for any excuse to stay in bed. But once I've put those trainers on and got out there, I am always glad I did; same goes for exercise of any shape or form.

You have got to love those endorphins; the best part of exercise is when it stops!

Saturday 16th January 2016 - A new place to run.

I love to travel and one of my greatest running pleasures is when I get the chance to go out and about and explore somewhere new or different. I never go away from home either for work or pleasure without my running kit, just in case I get chance to go for a little trot somewhere new.

Today was just great; a weekend away in a lovely little cottage in Ashbury and a bit of us time with my lovely wife. Plus, it also gave me a chance get my trainers on and do what I love in a very beautiful part of the country.

Arriving late afternoon the previous day at the aptly named 'church yard cottage', it was dark, so once we had settled in we only ventured as far as the pub for a lovely meal and a few beverages.

The cottage was old and although fitted with all mod cons, warm it was not, which made getting out of a cosy warm bed after a good night's sleep much harder.

After a nice cup of tea in bed and the early signs of the arrival of the new day, I ventured out of the cottage following the local knowledge imparted by the helpful owner. I was straight out the door, through the little church yard and up onto the Ridgeway.

The previous evening, the owner of the pub, told me all the details I needed to know about what is described as 'Britain's oldest road' having carried travellers for at least 5000 years. Armed with the information, I was practically a local, this was going to be good fun!

After climbing the short incline to the Ridgeway, I had two choices, left would take me to some culture or right to the pub… On a cold Saturday morning and the temptation of a nice glass of something and an open fire, not much choice to be honest, but it was 7.30am and the chance of the pub being open for business was pretty slim.

So, with that in mind, I reluctantly opted for the left route which would take me towards the Uffington White Horse and back to the Iron Age or late Bronze Age.

The horse, some 110 metres long in chalk, filled trenches carved on the upper slopes of aptly named White Horse Hill. It is the oldest of the white horse figures in Britain and is thought to represent a tribal figure and might be connect to a nearby castle. Why would you do that, go to all that trouble to etch a huge equine shape on the side of a hill, something on really seen from the air? These primitive people had only just started to make tools – bronze ones I guess (was never good at history!) and you go to all this effort.

This started me thinking of the early man evolving, still dressed in fur and getting a tad more sophisticated, so he thought. I can just imagine the conversation: 'I know we haven't got a telly yet, so let's carve a big fuck off horse into the side of this hill and people can watch that when passing in their ……..'What ? - space ship? I don't get it, think I must of be missed something! Far too much from history that we don't know.

Running off at a tangent

Have a read of Eric Von Daniken's cult book 'Chariots of the Gods'. Was God an astronaut?

Plenty to think about when I was running along, especially when a short detour took me to Waylands Smithy, a Neolithic long barrow, or collective chamber tomb very close to my route.

Doing a bit of research post run on Waylands Smithy, I discovered that Archaeologists have established that the monument was built by pastoralist communities shortly after the introduction of agriculture to Britain from continental Europe. The later mound was 185 feet (56 m) long and 43 feet (13 m) wide at the south end. Its present appearance is the result of restoration following excavations undertaken by Stuart Piggott and Richard Atkinson in the early sixties. They demonstrated that the site had been built in two different phases, a timber-chambered oval barrow built around 3590 and 3550 BC, and a later stone-chambered long barrow in around 3460 to 3400 BC.

I get a bit bamboozled by all the history facts and figures, but it was a very strange place and my mind went into overdrive .This was not helped when, within minutes of leaving the burial site and passing the time of day with a local dog walker (after the less friendly of his two dogs barked at me) punctuated the morning pleasantries with an off the cuff comment that did nothing for my state of anxiety.

'On your own?', he asked, going on to add 'you need to have some protection up here'. What that did he mean by that?

Feeling a little spooked, I upped the pace and ran a tad quicker, retracing my steps on the return to the cottage.

It was a beautiful morning and was great to see the sunrise on another great day. So cold this morning, that my IPhone, my electronic running buddy and life companion decided that it did not like the cold and went into hibernation in the final stages of the run leaving the route untracked. Never mind, I got it logged in the memory. A great run and some great photos too.

Sunday 17th January 2016 - Grey!

All change, what a difference a day makes, yesterday the dawn was stunning, crisp and bright, today was a different story.
A very murky, dark morning and after going left on the Ridgeway the previous day, I obviously went the opposite direction today. It was not that exciting to be honest and I ran 30 minutes before heading home. The morning - muddy, cold, windy, bleak. I heard voices but saw no one, spooky, but did take a great picture of a lifeless tree.
I promised myself a bath when I returned back to the cottage. I had my eyes on the big deep bath in the corner of the bedroom as soon as we arrived. I rarely have one at home, usually having a quicker, more efficient but less relaxing shower, so to take a bath would be a real treat. Pity the cottage was a little chilly for a leisurely soak, I like central heating. I resisted the urge to post the 'bath shot 'on Facebook. I have done this once before and did get a bit of stick from my friends, so this time I thought better of it, but I did enjoy my bath though.

Tuesday 19th January 2016 - Baby it's cold outside.

It's minus four degrees Celsius, minus four! and 5.45 in the am. The alarm went off about 35 minutes ago and I am up and ready to head out. I must be mad, but I don't think I am to be honest.
Plenty of time to sleep when I am older and a run before work is just the best way to kick the day off. Although my bed did have a good go at hanging on to me today, but if I did stay in bed, I would regret it for the rest of the day and so would my colleagues as I would be a grumpy so and so.
On a cold day like today, I love it when, after I return home post run, I can get back into a nice warm bad after my run with a nice cuppa. A treat reserved for the weekend so today alas

that was not going to happen and in the words of the seven dwarfs - 'Hi ho hi ho it's off to work we go.'

Thursday 21st January 2016 - *What shall we talk about?*

What do people talk about when they chat on a run? That's got a bit of a ring to it, what a great name for a book… I can hear the whoosh as that went over everyone's head. I was alluding to great book by Haruki Murakami with a similar title. Not sure where I am going with this it so I will quit while I am ahead, but just in case you do fancy a read, the proper title is *'What I talk about when I talk about running'*. If you do buy it, put a word in for me, he is one guy I would love to meet.

I think non-runners reckon that all runners talk about on a run is trainers, races and personal best's or PB's to get the lingo correct. Well some do for sure, but it never ceases to amaze me the topics of conversation that get covered as the miles fly by.

We talk about woman, well the lads do, work, music, lesbian camping (yes really), food (always a favourite), memories of youth, old age, food and work life balance… did I mention food?

Food is always high on a runner's mind, especially on a long run. Tonight, we did a detour to avoid the smell of the chippy, I am sure there should be a law against delicious and tempting odours wafting on to the streets.

One of my oldest and closest running buddies or RB's as us athletes like to call fellow running partners, is Sue. Our children grew up together, and over the years she has become a great friend and a good listener. To be honest I am not sure why Sue runs with me, in ability terms Sue is the polar opposite to me. She is a pro, wins races and everything, but run with me she does and for that I am extremely grateful.

A few years younger than me, only a few and her body weighs about the same as one of my legs. Sue is great company to run with and at the end of a few miles pounding the streets, I am red faced and sweating like a rapist (as my old buddy used to say) and Sue is fresh as a daisy. How does that work, it not rocket science to be honest. I do have a weight and age disadvantage, so a bit a sweat should not come as a surprise to be honest.

We put the world to right, as well as chat about crap. Sue is helping run a little 'fat club' that I mention earlier. Sunday is 'weigh in' day and Richard, Ian and I are looking for a good result after the excess of Christmas, so fingers crossed at Sundays weigh in. We've got trackers, charts and everything, I know it's sounds like a bit of a cliché but so true- what gets measured gets improved. It's not just about recording the fluctuation in our weight, as any gains hit the pocket by way of a fine. But all for a good cause and losing a fiver for gaining a pound or two is always a good incentive and the money goes to the guide dogs for the blind too.

As I was away last weekend, I missed the previous Sunday's call to account and also failed to witness co fat club member Ian gaining a few pounds, serves him right for not being a bloater in the first place. I bet you are wondering who all these folks are?

I am glad you asked. We have already met Ian before and is one of my regular dawn running partners and the victim to my life advice, as I mentioned before.

Richard is Sue's husband, who is consistently slimmer of the week and is making some great progress, nearly two stone lost so far, always so focused and a great guy. He is also Ian's boss so well what can I say? I hope you are keeping up with all this.

Richard is one of life's gentlemen; I guess we make unlikely friends, but a great friend he is and although very different types of people, it works. The one thing that Richard and I have in common is that we are a soft touch and cannot say no, which is how we meet when we became active members of our daughters PTA and before long, Chair and Treasure, obviously leaving the money side to Richard.

We used to run together in the past, that's how I met Ian, but Rich hasn't donned the trainers for a while. We changed to bikes some time ago opting for something a little more sociable, but we are both fair-weather cyclists. The last bike ride was a bit of a disaster to say the least, more about that later maybe or maybe not...

Like myself, and I'm sure Richard wouldn't mind me saying, neither of us are not natural athletes in both build and ability. He is a great swimmer, but once sport involves running, the laws of physics come into play, especially power to weight ratios and all that clever stuff, where every pound and extra pound in our case makes such a difference. We both like our food and share a fondness for cheese, never good for the figure.

I remember running together with Richard some years back, it was a dark night and as we closed in on a fellow runner, who remarkably was going slowly than Rich and I, from behind him so to speak, the guy jumped out of his skin. To our amazement he had not heard us coming up on the rear. 'I thought he would have felt us coming 'exclaimed Richard! Such was our heavy-footed running pattern combined with 40 stone of ballast. It did make us chuckle.

I miss running with him as was always good company and I live in hope that he will be back running again so the fun can restart, in the meantime we can carry on enjoying our allotment which we share.

Saturday 23rd January 2016 - The Bun Run.

Running on a weekday morning is good, but going for a run at the weekend is different. I love not having to worry about watching the clock and not going to work after is a proper treat. During my Saturday run (usually on my own unless Libby, or Olivia as she was christened, my oldest daughter is home from University) I ponder food – most importantly what am I going to have for my breakfast.

Not a quick refuelling breakfast like it is on a weekday, but at the weekend especially on a Saturday, I can enjoy the pleasure of something nice to eat. Eggs are the usual weapon of choice and tend to feature somewhere in the meal plan on a weekend, a really treat after a hot shower and a change of clothes. Today way no exception.

Engrained in my brain from my childhood, breakfast in the Atherton household was the most important meal of the day and skipping the first meal of the day was not an option especially for me as the baby of the family. Whatever was put out was rarely a choice, you got what you were given from the traditional bacon and egg, porridge, eggy bread and a bit of a favourite as a child, fried bread and sugar. Really, try it - it's a heart attack on a plate, but delicious.

The plan for my run today was with a purpose. As I had missed the gym during the week, I decided to combine my morning run with a short visit to the fitness room at my local tennis club.

A short muddy stretch along the river, then up onto the canal and a short jog to the gym. It's usual at the weekend for the gym to be busy, especially after Christmas, but today the place was empty with the exception of an older gent engrossed in the future plan for a knackered old running machine.

During the week a sign on the treadmill happily announced the arrival of a shiny one on Monday along with some other new kit that I have already forgotten, so with that in mind the old machine had to go.

The gent in question, after some chit chat, had been given the small task of getting the old model out of the room. I just knew I was going to be drawn in; I could tell by all the tutting and head scratching that there may be trouble was ahead.

I tried to carry on with my training regardless and took my place on the multi-gym and began my routine. 'Reckon this will go through the door? 'he said, I looked and said 'No 'carrying on lifting my weights. 'I thought that too', was the reply. I'm involved now aren't I, so I stopped and wondered over.

I thought a straight 'No 'needed some data to back it up, so a yoga mat became a makeshift rule, taking a measurement from the running machine and then against the door opening provided evidence to my negative response.

More head shaking followed from Mr Shifter, 'what about on its side?', 'No 'and he shared my wisdom along with my vast knowledge of trigonometry and furniture moving! I felt contented when with no further data, he rang his mate.

With the extraction project on hold temporarily it seemed and as he had put an end to my work out, we struck up a proper conversation and put the world to rights.

I don't know how we made the quantum heap from the extraction of a redundant running machine to the habits of the youth of today, but we did. We touched on a couple of pet hates of mine -Why do the lads who train at the gym never put anything away?

My gym buddy, Tim, thinks it's because they are used to their mothers doing everything for them - good point well-made I thought. We agreed that, we pity the women who end up with a less than man about the house in later life and continuing the conversation from inept lads, to a great conversation about social media, Facebook in particular.

Love it or hate it, it's now part of our lives for sure, but to some people the virtual world is everything! ... 'Just putting the bins out'- (I don't give a shit!) 'I'm having a bad day','what up babe','message me – 'Please! For God's sake!

Whist you are subconsciously drawing me in your constant bullshit, I am missing all the good stuff that social media can offer. Positive posts, great information and fun things too and I really don't give a monkeys that you have put the bin out or you are shopping at Asda - get a life people.

I am convinced some couples only talk via social media, and god only knows if they ever come across a place with no Wi-Fi! Forget the food, ambience or the service, get on trip advisor and slag off a place when you get home if it doesn't have good connectivity to the rest of the world! Really!? People need to get a life, a real one.

I do wonder when I see families in restaurants, those that obviously do have Wi-Fi and with the parents are on their phones and the kids glued to their tablets, when do these kids ever learn any social skills, I worry about the future of the human race if the next generation cannot get on with life for real. A 'like 'will not swell the population and I fear we are all doomed.

So having put the world put to right and the running machine wheeled back in its original location with no exit plan in sight, my new friend and I parted company, not before he took a selfie, tagged me and posted it on Facebook!! Like!

Not wanting to waste the gym visit, I returned to the multi gym and finished off my reps, upper body today before headed back out into the cold and a for home.

The second item on today's agenda was bread products, buns to be precise. My youngest daughter, Millie, although she's nearly sixteen, is still my baby and has me wrapped around her little finger.

So much so, many of my morning runs includes a detour to the shop to buy her something sweet for her breakfast. Millie likes her food in shades of brown and today's request was for a chocolate chip muffin, hence the Bun Run and so she doesn't end up with a bag of crumbs, I tend to make the purchase as close to the end of the run. I run the last half a mile or so like Haile Gebrselassie with my newly purchased buns or cakes held close to my chest, just like this great runner would carry his school books back in Ethiopia.

Successfully returning home with the spoils plays havoc with my running pattern, but I don't mind as it is always appreciated by Millie when she appears from her slumber.

I like to run with a purpose and the 'Bun Run 'does make it interesting. I did enjoy my eggs when I got back, but I did mix it up a little and have them poached eggs for a change.

Sunday 24th January 2016 - Sundays are for running.

Everyone seems obsessed with running further today! the usual Sunday runners managed a respectable, enjoyable seven miles, leaving the 18 miles to the professionals and with no marathons in the diary for me this year, thank the Lord, I was more than happy to go short.

I have done a couple of marathons in the past and I have promised myself that I will do one more.

There is something very rewarding about a long run, but the main issue for me is the time and OK fitness plays a part too, but sometimes there is just not enough spare hours in the day. To grab an hour to run is generally not an issue for me, but to try a find two or three hours, that is a different story.

I am fortunate have a very understanding family; in fact, they encourage me to go out for a run. I think that's because I am better, calmer person post run, funny that.

My wife, Julie, has on more than one occasion asked, 'you are going out for a run today, aren't you? 'and if I'm particularly stressed, almost pushes me out the door. To take on a long run and to disappear for a couple hours or more takes a bit of planning, then there's where to go!

I like to run with a mission, a purpose and not just run aimlessly plus I like a route that ideally takes me somewhere with minimum opportunity to short cut back home.

When the time comes for a long run, usually a couple of weeks before a half marathon and the panic sets in, I have a few favourite routes in my kit bag, out early and back with the dawn is always the best for me. That's always my plan A, getting my kit ready the night before, alarm set for the crack of dawn and an early night. But even with a robust plan, the battle of the bed can be tough one to win.

Then of course there is dilemma of a pre run cuppa which comes with the trade-off between hydration and mid run bodily functions, which needs a double dose of thinking about. Two hours is a long time and all of these things need to be considered before heading out to pound the streets for what feels like a lifetime.

Nutrition is another consideration that needs thought about and over the years I have tried many mid run food options. Unless you have the benefit of a support crew, which I do not have the luxury of, whatever I need, I have to carry.

I usually end up with energy gels as the preferred option, but I am not a big fan. The first hurdle for me is getting the dreaded goo into my body. A little un PC but the texture and technique of getting the gel down your throat always brings the thoughts of oral sex; sorry to put picture in your head, I should have warned you!

The chemical cocktail from the squidgy pouch also has a happy knack of giving me the trots, never nice running with the cheeks of your backside clenched together for a couple of hours.

I do have local knowledge and know when to find a loo if I am in town, a lot less of an issue if running in the countryside unless it's a bigger job as one says. I do keep persevering with gels if only to sample the weird and wonderful flavours that they come in and all-natural ingredients you know, said very tongue in cheek...

No feet up for me after today's run as I need to pack, off to Sweden later, but before I head nearer to the arctic circle, let me introduce our little running group to you.

The initial shoots of what would eventually grow into our little group called 'Zero to Hero'. Like many good things in life, the idea first appeared when alcohol had been consumed. Over a beer and a regular catch up with qualified personal trainer and lifelong friend Allan, the idea took its first breath. As we talked, it seemed we both wanted to do something that would combine our life skills and training to help the good people of Kenilworth to achieve their potential.

The obvious focus was the annual Two Castles event, a 10k run from Warwick Castle to Kenilworth Castle in the diary June 2012. The plan to take new to running from the coach to 10k in ten weeks. Enlisting Allan's friend Steve to the fold, sharing common ethics and visions and after a few training runs together, we went public and by Sunday 1st April, the first run of the 10 week plan, we had willing people looking for a challenge.

Within a blink of an eye, we found ourselves on the other side of the finish line and the ten weeks were over, mission accomplished and the project complete.

That was then and as I look back on what was only ever going to be only a ten-week project, the Run England group is going strong. A website, logo and merchandise along with a spin off cycling contingent who favour sitting down exercise and we have become one big happy family. Supportive, caring and a little dysfunctional at times, the project continues and is a core part of my life.

Monday 25th-27th January 2016 - Another new place to run.

I'm very fortunate that my job gives me the opportunity to travel from time to time and I always take advantage of a chance to run in new places. This week Gothenburg, Sweden was the destination.

I knew it would be cold after talking temperatures with my colleague over the weekend. I played -4°C in England against Henrik's -20°C, so it's a lot colder in Sweden, but it's a different sort of cold I kept telling myself, but it's still bloody freezing!!

With the benefit of advance local knowledge, I packed according, for both the workday and the inevitable run before the day started. Meeting rooms at the plant are of a premium, so for our business system team meetings, we stay in a hotel out of town with the bonus of conference facilities. With all we need in one location, we would have no need to leave the hotel for a couple of days, but I would soon get a little stir crazy.

The hotel perched on the headland at the mouth of the river Göta Älv afforded dramatic views out to sea. With my alarm set for an early get up, I headed out into the cold dark morning and on the side of the roads, white mounds gave clues to the snow fall in the previous days. Enough to bring England to a standstill, but with heavy snow the norm this far north, the Scandinavians just get on with life. Every car is fitted with snow tyres; I think these get fitted about October in preparation for the long winter ahead.

Although the Arkan Hotel generally meets the business needs, the location on the edge of the industrial area of Gothenburg, unfortunately it does not make for the most scenic of place to run. It's dark too so I was limited as to where I could go, more about blowing away the cobwebs in readiness for the busy day ahead.

The sea was close which was a bonus so with a little short cut through the labyrinth of office blocks all carrying the Volvo logo, but I could at least get to the water's edge before heading back for a shower and a healthy breakfast before getting in to work mode and the job at hand.

It never seemed to get light at this time of year and although I do love coming to Sweden, I am not sure a life in partial daylight for a good proportion of the year would suit me.

Although the absence of the sun is a negative to making this place home, the approach to work life balance is second to none. These guys work hard but family is everything, at the top of every plan and to do list; family is always number one. As a colleague told me once, life's priorities - first the family, then the family, followed by the family. I got the idea.

Every morning, before breakfast, I did run, each time a variation of a theme but it always included a look at the sea. I always find water a draw wherever I am. Certainly kick started the day although I was happy to return to the hotel with it warm open fire in the reception welcoming folks in from the cold.

Sunday 31st January 2016 - 'It's raining again' – Supertramp.

I think today will be a very wet run. I never usually find getting my trainers on a problem, but today was tough. I planned to do a longer run today, I had 13.1 miles in my head, but the weather had other ideas. Cold, wet and windy! I am ok with cold and wet, but not a great fan of the wind. I find it very unsettling. I planned to meet some of the group thirty minutes early. If you are going to run on a lousy day, I was going to need company, I got it today!

Once I am warm from exercise and have a running buddy, I'm all set and don't mind the weather as much. I kind of switch off from the outside world focusing on the moment and enjoy putting the world to rights. Anne is good company on a run and the chat is always varied, we do like to share memories of Michigan, with Anne as a Native American and myself purely a visitor back in the Eighties. Time passed super quick, where did we run? – not a clue, but happy to get back to the car. Might be an age thing, but once I had been cold, I didn't really seem to get warm for the rest of the day. Unfortunately, the 'Weigh in' that followed the run did not go well, with no weight loss between the three of us. With Ian on the scales, the digital readout hinted at a gain, but the reading settled on a stable result.

Still licking our wounds like a bunch of kids we got out the tape measure. What did make me smile was three grown men trying to take each other's measurements, maybe some positive progress could be had in size reduction rather than weight loss.

Sue was off marathon training so not around to officiate the end of month statistics.

What a bloody performance, deciding that we would be much better with the old tape measure; the staff of the Seventies sitcom 'Are you being served' had nothing on us!! Good job it was only waist and chest, measuring our inside leg would have pushed us over the edge and would have resulted in counselling or therapy of some kind. We recorded some results, but I feel a remeasure will be required when the fat club leader is back from her run. Productive, no, entertaining, oh yes!

February 2016

Sunday 7th February 2016 - It will be ok in the long run.

Today was a game of two halves as I wanted to get a few extra miles in before meeting up the main gang again at 8.30am. Another long run! When I say long run, I mean a couple of extra miles before the main Zero to Hero gang meet up and head out for the main run.

Today got off to a shaky start, work has been manic of late so although in my running gear, I headed off in my car on autopilot heading completely in the wrong direction towards the office rather than to pick up my buddy Sue. I know where my head is at, at the moment and clearly a run would do me the world of good, always does.

Meeting at 8.30am at the weekend I can do week in, week out but 8am is just a push too far on a Sunday, especially in the winter. But at least it had stopped raining and it was a nice morning.

I was surprised that we had a good turnout for the extra miles at 8am and happy to say that my pace is improving - get me! I still have a long way to go but happy with the progress and all this is almost starting to feel a little bit like training. I blame Mike and the very small but work in progress IAC running group. There is nothing like a bit of peer pressure combined with good old Facebook to provide some much appreciated motivation.

The IAC running group or Team IAC sounds rather grand as it's only the three of us at the moment, but it works and I will elaborate more about IAC group or Team IAC later, but enough to say the peer pressure was working its magic.

Steve Atherton

With a few extra miles in the bag and after a very short rest whilst we waited for the regular group to assemble, it was time for the second half. Having had the luxury of an extra thirty minutes in bed, the turnout at 8.30 was very good today. The cyclists won in terms of numbers, which did surprise me as the air was a little moist but appear they did. What the athletes [as I always call the runners, in front of the cyclists to wind them up a little] lacked in number, they made up for in style.

The rain had at last stopped, leaving plenty of wet stuff around on the roads and fields, but I was happy that the sun was out even if it was a little chilly.

As the gang assembled, we swap wet weather tales (got to love the Brits and our obsession with the climate). Another great subject of British conversation is sport, but not wishing to offend anyone especially in light of England's recent victory in the Six Nation tournament and with our eclectic group having the generous quota of Scots, rugby was kind of glossed over as I did not want to rub the 'Sweaties' * noses in it as they say.

For those not up to speed on the old Cockney rhyming slang - sweaty sock = jock. Apologies to any readers from north of the border.

As we started the run, the school boy came out in me and I wanted to take a short detour to check out the ford in Kenilworth, which with the slightest hint of rain, rises enough to cover the road. The swell of Finham Brooke inevitably closes the road with predictable regularity so much so the authorities have invested in a very elaborate sets of warning lights to deter would be 'deep water waders' getting stuck in the swollen stream. With today's downpour, we had to go down towards the castle and check the ford out, joining the growing crowd eagerly waiting for some deluded driver to go for a swim; there is always one!

The local council have invested £52000 in a wing ding early warning system with actual knobs, whistles and flashing lights. Although it is actually the general public always providing a knob who will insist in checking out the depth of the water for themselves.

As we headed away from the floor show, my close buddy gave me some bad news or the inkling of bad news about a mutual friends' wife and as we ran, the horror of the issue became more apparent, so sad to hear things that will change people's lives. It's always good to talk and running is good for that, you can talk and share thoughts and get shit aired.

Today's run was all about support, that's what I love about the group and running with others, you can vent off and share your life. No one judges or whatever, but you get the ear for free and one thing I have learnt over the years is everyone has a story.

An added bonus, we managed to get back before the rain comes again. I wonder if the cyclists got wet?

Saturday 13th February 2016 - A bit of a catch up.

I occasionally run alone, with my thoughts, rarely with music, especially when I have thinking to do, but to have company is the best. If get something in the diary and you are committed. I don't like to vague or tentative arrangements, I love a plan as my family know too well, and loose arrangements I hate. I was really fortunate to have some really close dependable running buddies who always show up, on time and in the right place. What more can a man ask?

When you run and chat the miles fly by. I love running in new places, but I also like to run in familiar places at different times of the day. To run through town in the early hours of the morning when the streets are just starting come alive is just magic. Unfortunately, along with the magic, comes the less than glamorous side of the 'Royal Borough' is on show, the homeless in sleeping bags in shop doorways. I have said before that this should not happen in our day and age, it's so wrong but does put my charmed life into perspective.

What never cease to amaze me is that whatever time of day I put those trainers on, the streets are never deserted, always someone on the move. Where are these people going, where have they been and why are they not snuggled up in bed?

So many questions without answers, I have never been a great fan of unanswered questions and what does my mind do – make up some plausible and maybe some unlikely responses with the reality being not that exciting...

I love running with people and especially on a long run, you can get to know someone. People open up and what's on a run, stays on a run as they say. I have always thought of counselling on a run, would be a good thing to get into as when you are out with nature and running, people let it all out.

I always pride myself as the coach who works on the muscle between the ears, the hardest one of them all! I was a pretty half full person, but I do have some moments and talking on a run is very much a two-way process.

Over the years, I have had so much help from others and for that I was so grateful. You don't always have to have a real running buddy or someone who is only there in the flesh, I sometimes have a virtual running partner too.

So as promised, more about Team IAC which is currently just three of us. All colleagues from the office but people I would also class as friends too. I have known these two guys for years - Ross, too young and healthy for his own good but a great guy; and Mike, the VP at the company and my old boss but a great good ear at times as well. I remember when I first connected with Mike in a running capacity. He knew I ran but when he suggested that we should have a run together, I thought was a little awkward as Mike was the Engineering Director at the time and was my bosses, bosses, boss. When I thought about the potential implications of running with him, it could go very wrong and what would people think, but I should not have worried.

To alleviate the potential tricky situation, I was thinking safety in numbers, so I suggested a group entry to the

Birmingham Half marathon, that was back in 2010, and the rest is history.

We started training in small groups mainly driven by workload and availability rather than ability. After a few weeks of training we were ready, taking our positions on the start line in our Team IAC tops with our surnames blazoned across the front; we looked the part. Everyone who started the race, finished and building on the success of Birmingham the fun continued.

In 2011, Team IAC went international as five of us headed for Paris for the half marathon. What a weekend! For the Birmingham Half, we had classy but understated grey and white running tops carrying the IAC logo and our surnames, but for Paris we let Mike pick the colour of the tops; big mistake.

Bright pink is not a flattering choice of colour for a man of my age or above average stature, but no one could say we didn't stand out. With our christian names emblazoned on the front this time along with the IAC logo we got noticed!

The addition of matching headbands did not help improve the image and somehow I managed to become separated from mine before the start of the race, never mind hey!

The Paris Half Marathon coincided with the European championships and our hotel was full of real athletes. The banter and camaraderie was excellent providing some lasting memories and who knew that Australia was part of Europe. Maybe not, after exchanging 'G'days' we soon realised maybe it was Austria and not Australia; easy mistake to make!

As the teams gathered in the hotel lobby, the atmosphere was electric and very infectious. The warmth was overwhelming as we shook hands and wished each other well for the days events before jumping in a couple of taxis and heading for the start.

The run should be piece of cake having walked pretty much the equivalent distance the previous day, probably not the best plan.

Thirteen point one miles later, Team IAC - Dan, Ross, Dean, Mike and I all safety crossed the finish line. As the last man in (being twice the age and weight of Dan -the baby of the group) I posted by best ever half marathon time of 2 hours 9 minutes and 20 seconds (the seconds can make all the difference).

Armed with our medal and t shirts, we headed to the bar for some food and the inevitable beer or two before a shower and a chill at the hotel ahead of heading into Paris for post-race celebrations. The celebrations introduced me to Desperado's, a tequila enhanced lager and after a few of these my face joined the rest of my body in a state of numbness. I cannot drink a bottle of the deadly combination without thinking of Dan, but a night out did add the icing to the cake on an amazing weekend.

Returning to the office the following morning we were greeted by an almost celebrity home coming. Team IAC were now an international running group and a great event to be part of, plus we raised a few quid for Birmingham Children's hospital as well.

The momentum continued later the same year, with Team IAC taking part in another event, a little closure to home this time. Helped along with a growing relationship with a local charity who were doing an amazing job dealing with terminal illness, gave a local connection and helped raise the company profile in the area.

Ray Woods from the John Taylor Hospice and I became great friends and come race day, the massive entry of around thirty-five colleagues and friends proudly wore their yellow tops to take to the streets as part of the Sutton Fun run.

Bringing together a great cross section of the IAC work force at Coleshill with friendships that would stand the test of time and the start of helping needy causes as we got a little fitter.

Although not a runner, the late great Tony G. was an avid supporter of Team IAC and was always happy to help with a donation or two. But most of all a smile and a genuine well done at the end, always first at the bar to buy the runners a drink.

We sadly said goodbye to Tony in March 2015, this true gentleman was a great inspiration to myself and many others and also a good friend. In the garden of our Warwickshire home, we have a tree that we planted in Tony's memory and still touch base with Tony's daughter Helen, from time to time and I still miss his cheery face around the office.

Mike and I often chat about these days and reminisce fondly of the events, our outing in Paris always a favourite and lasting memory for both of us.

Sunday 14th February 2016 - Saint Valentine's Day.

Violets are blue,
Roses are red,
It's time to run,
So, get out of bed!

Not a classic example of poetry I appreciate, but I did try my best and it did raise a smile with the group.

The weather provided a beautiful morning to celebrate Saint Valentine's Day, chilly but dry and being a Sunday, it made it perfect for a nice long run!

I planned a longer route than usual today with the Coventry Half Marathon looming ever closer and with my healthy eating regime paying off I was starting to see a definite improvement in my pace of late, so I'm a happy bunny!

Today's run took me to Ashow. A favourite place of mine, ours actually as my eldest daughter Libby loves the place too, as does my wife. I have always said that if I ever go missing, the bridge at Ashow would be the first place I would suggest to look. It's just a magic place with so many memories, both the good and not so good.

In a previous life, I would run from Kenilworth, down Rocky lane through Glasshouse Spinney, skirting Thickthorn Wood and then on to Ashow. I would imagine that before the

Steve Atherton

A46, (the Warwick or Coventry bypass - dependent on which end of the dual carriageway you live) Rocky Lane would have just been a farm track from Kenilworth to Ashow. Today it's only suitable for two legs or bikes and maybe a horse; definitely not a vehicular thoroughfare.

As soon as you cross the footbridge over the A46 and head down the lane and under the stone bridge alongside the wood, you sense the rolling back of the years. Feeling as if by passing through the moss covered arch, you enter some sort of time portal and travel back to a time when the horse and cart ruled the roads. Along with the present, the noise of the traffic stays on the other side of the divide and running down the tree lined cutting a sense of calm descends.

Memories of our rescue dog, Basil, come flooding back. He loved Rocky Lane and the elevation the root entwined bank gave him, a sense of being top dog. Being brought up with cats as a child and have cats today, Baz was the only dog I had.

Reaching the end of the lane with thoughts of a great companion and member of the family, we made the slow return to the twenty first century as the muddy narrow track becomes a road. You cross a busy road before making the gentle descent into the village of Ashow. A beautiful little place with an eclectic mix of houses general getting older, the closer you get to the village club and charming church, conveniently located next to each other. The Church of the Assumption of Our Lady is an early Norman gem built circa 1078 situated in the most idyllic and peaceful setting perched on the banks of the river Avon.

After a moment or two on the bridge to enjoy the tranquility of the babbling river below, we retrace our steps before returning along Rocky Lane and back through the arch returning to 2016 again.

Thursday 18th February 2016 – Under pressure.

Been a long few days at work, tough at times with lots of pressure, but this seems the same for everyone at the moment and a common point of discussion on many a run these days. A regular subject is work life balance and it seems that regardless of people's occupation or position in the pecking order, the pressure is the same. Tight deadlines and unrealistic demands with everyone wanting everything yesterday and sometimes technology does not help.

I was not thinking internet speed or robust IT or systems but the opposite. I was thinking more along the lines of communication technology especially smart phones. Nowhere to escape from the office these days as your work effectively travels with you.

My wife Julie will smile when she reads this because my mobile phone is never more than an arm's reach away from me at all times…just in case! I understand that mobile technology is now the norm and you are never going to stop progress, but wouldn't it be nice just occasionally be 'offline' and maybe replying to that email might just wait until the morning…

I guess I could turn my phone off but then there's the expectation of always being accessible plus there's F.OM.O of cause, Fear Of Missing Out. It might be an age thing and I know I was in the minority, but wouldn't it be nice to be occasionally 'out'?

Tonight's run was quite emotional with lots of talk of parents who've past and the pros and cons of seeing our loved ones in the chapel of rest. An unusual tonic of conversation but it certainly made the miles go by as we ran the beautiful streets and backwaters of the Leamington. The Royal Borough as I call it, is the town I was born and spent most of my early years, good old Leamington Spa or Royal Leamington Spa to give its Sunday or official name.

It was 1838 when it was given the Royal blessing and has given birth to some famous people over the years, Norman Painting,

Steve Atherton

Anne Diamond, Randolph Turpin, Russel Howard, Nicolas Ball, Kelly Sibley and Sir Frank Whittle to name but a few plus my good self of course!

Leamington has been home to many other famous people over the years Dion Dublin, Roberto Di Matteo, Trevor Harrison aka Eddie Grundy from the Archers - the list goes on.

Leamington has been featured in numerous television series - Keeping up appearances, Dangerfield along with the re-make of the series Upstairs, Downstairs all filmed in and around the area and regular visitors to the town, the legendary Chuckle Brothers.

Leamington is a great place to live, the contrast of the stunning Regency townhouses and the less grand architectural products of the sixties that happy sit side by side. The eclectic mix of cultures, extremes and of cause, copious lashings of history which is why I love this place and I was very proud of the town I was born.

De-stressed after a good run and back home for some home cooking – always the best part of any run.

Friday 19th February 2016 - Run Forest run!

Team IAC seems to be back up and running with a vengeance again (excuse the pun), with the Facebook group keeping the pressure on, with the three of us running on a Friday!

Justin reckoned I was IAC's Forest Gump which made me smile, I do know that life is like a box of chocolates, but I know what he means. I love to see ideas start out as a seed and grow into something – I know more will come from our Friday runs, tiny steps.

Sunday 28th February 2016 - Race day - Coventry Half.

Something special about race day, whatever the distance, whatever the event, it's always feels different. I rarely sleep that well the night before, even if I've had more than enough to drink. I do like a pre-race bottle of something the night before to help me sleep and calm my nerves, (maybe that's what I was doing wrong?).

The twinge in my _____, (insert any limb or muscle) always makes an appearance come the day of the race, something will always hurt but obviously all in the mind.

Getting out of bed far earlier than I need to, I was up and about; got to make sure I have been to the loo at least twice as needing the toilet during a run is my number one (or should it be number two) worry especially as the start time draws ever closer. Sorry, I was not doing a Paula Ratcliffe.

In contrast to emptying the tanks; I also need to take on fuel too. I don't want to be hungry mid run, although my body fat stores could keep me going for days without any fear of running out of carbs and hitting 'the wall'. Lots of science about all this and sure the purist athletes do their homework, but not for joggers like me I think.

For today's breakfast, I opted for toast with marmalade, a change from my usual porridge, but have taken a real liking for artisan bread in my old age - but that's another story.

Trying to keep myself busy as I make light work of my breakfast, I check social media and my emails. So glad I did as I had a great email, just what you need before a race - *'prepaid funeral plans for just a fiver a week'*! Talk about motivational and a little scary to be honest, I best not tell my wife, she is not a big fan of race days.

It's the third time I have entered Coventry Half Marathon but only the second time I have made it to the start line. The first time, back in 2010, a spell in hospital put play to any plans of running this particular event. I was what is known in medical circles as 'a former 'and I was prone to kidney stones - the pain from these bad boys apparently is the closest a man gets to that equivalent of child birth.

I was in good shape for the event, I had done the training, put the time in the trainers but a few weeks before race day, I became aware of the early signs of trouble.

Not for the first time in my life, the unpredictability of the little blighters resulted in an ambulance ride to hospital after giving my eldest daughter Libby, who was only 14 at the time, a bit of a fright.

Stepping up to the plate, she calmly called 999 to get me help, chatting to the controller and shortly after, a couple of medics arrived and together we headed off to hospital. Then as now, she takes life in her stride and I was so proud of her.

After a few days in hospital, escaping the knife for the second time, I remember asking the doctor on discharge day if I could still take part in the Coventry Half Marathon. I could tell he was also a runner and with a knowing smile, he told me that after days being filled with pain killers and laying in bed, running might not be one my best ideas, so reluctantly I cheered Ian home on the finish line.

I have always fancied taking part in this event and planned to run today with fellow Zero to Hero runner and local GP Shazli. It has got to be a good idea to have a medic on a run at my advanced years and always glad of the company.

I do love the start of the race, any race. I seem to go into panto mode, taking on an almost alter ego, a little bit larger-than-life.

After over ten years of running, you start to see some familiar faces at the start, one such guy, Usingh Bolt always makes me smile and is such a lovely guy. Alongside Mick and Phil, these guys are absolute legends and what running it all about.

It was good to see Mick and Phil, I first met these gents back in 2015 whist running the Stratford half marathon. These boys are legends and familiar faces at events up and down the country. Who are these guys, I thought I let the words from their website *www.micknphil-marathonlads.com* tell their story.

Running off at a tangent

Our names are Mick n Phil, Marathon Lads from Stratford On Avon. My Dad (Mick) is a very experienced long distance marathon runner. Occasionally, Dad has had to break off from running because of personal circumstances, myself (Philip), as I was disabled, suffering from Cerebral Palsy and Sodium Valproate Syndrome. Now a days, Dad pushes me in my wheelchair around the circuits we race at. This is because I was at my most content when on the move. My mobility is extremely limited and I was completely dependant on my Dad for all my needs. Because of my disability my whole family has been affected and has not been without its challenges, mainly because I have no speech and my mum also suffers from poor health.

Mick Says... Nursing Philip through the years have driven my wife and I to mental breakdowns. She now is no longer able to cope with Phillip's extreme needs, but that is not to say she has not a remarkable job over the years, bringing him through his severe illness which almost cost him his life.

My wife gave me an ultimatum in early 2002, 'either take Phillip in his wheelchair running with you, or pack it all in as, as I cannot cope any longer'. Well, I can tell you now, I thought it was the end of things, so I had a long hard think. Would the wheelchair stand up to it? Would Phillip like it? and most importantly, could I do this whilst pushing him? Running is hard enough at times no matter what standard you are. This was make or break, all or nothing. We started with a 2 mile fun run, taking 17m 45s, moved up to a 10k clocking 46m then tackled a 10 miler in a time of 1hr 48m. The final test was the full marathon where we achieved a time of 4hr 12m. This was fantastic, we were both loving it and quite simply, having the time of our lives. The rest they say, is history.

We then started taking on tougher, hilly races mainly of half marathon distance. The toughest to date is Great Langdale in Cumbria. We have now completed this twice with a best time of 2h 45m.

Our thanks must go to all the fellow athletes who support us in every way with kind words of support and their ideas for our racing. All the adaptions to Phillips wheelchair and even the idea for my vest has come from other athletes on a travels.

So far we have completed 947 races which include 500 half marathons. I feel it is most important for me to say that none of this have been possible

Steve Atherton

had it not been for the race organisers and thousands of fellow runners. We appreciate it all very much.
YOU HAVE MADE A CHRONICALLY SICK LAD AND HIS DAD VERY HAPPY !!

A true inspiration and they always cross the finish line way before me, but running is not about the winners or the elite athletes in my opinion, but about real people pushing the boundaries and stepping out of there comfort zone.

I have never been a big fan of the organised warm up at big events like this one, I much prefer to save my energy for the 13.1 miles that lie ahead. But I generally make a token gesture, making some movements not unlike a singer surrounded by professional dancers, I take on the spirit of the warm up without actually doing a fat lot.

I like the build up to the start, but it does feel like we have been standing around forever today and I will be glad to get on my way. I think I have already established that I was not a fast runner, but this does have it benefits.

On a big event like the city half marathons with phased starts, I like to let the elite and club runners go ahead and warm the streets and giving chance for the crowd of supporters to line the route. The atmosphere in the back pens is the best; this is where the fun happens.

Normal people doing amazing things, leaping out of their comfort zone to make a difference, maybe raising money for some well deserving charity or maybe taking part in memory of a loved one.

The T shirts tell the stories and can be very emotional. I like running with people, I was very much a people person and feel very much at home running with the pack, maybe it's safety in numbers. Preparing to start and with my pre-race ritual done with a quick pray to my mum to keep me safe and to look over me, I was ready.

The horn goes off in the distance, the pack 'bob 'and we are on our way, inching slowly toward the start line and the start of our individual race.

Running off at a tangent

One thing I notice today is that the timing mats did not squeal as us athletes pass over the red carpet to trigger the imbedded timing chips, I love that sound, it's all part of the experience.

The crowd lining both sides of the road in the city, more than made up for silent mats and support always helps but when someone shouts 'Not far to go now'.What!, I think there might be...

MARCH 2016

Thursday, 3 March 2016 - Remember me?

It's Thursday already and I haven't run since last weekend. I had every intention of running earlier in the week, but with my dawn running buddies all other wise engaged I lost the commitment and the bed won. However, I had a feeling that today would be different even before I had a chance to wipe the sleep from my eyes.

The morning arrived a little earlier than normal, making tea at 4.30am for my restless wife (what a good hubby I am!). I checked my phone whist waiting for the kettle to come to the boil and was greeted by a surprise message, it read:

'Hi Steve, you may not remember me, but I ran the half marathon in Stratford upon Avon last year. You helped me through, and I never really said thanks. I am running again this year, might see you there, however a massive thank you for helping me finish last year. I tried to find you straight after the race but couldn't, so I checked Facebook but no joy. I remembered you saying you were a member of a running club in Kenilworth, so I made some calls, again with no joy. I also had a picture with your race number on, so I found out your name off the race times using your number. I had almost given up but checked all the members of members of all the Kenilworth running group Facebook pages and found you that way. I can honestly say that I was close to giving up on the run and feel that without your help, I would not have finished which is why it is so important for me to say thank you to you'

Thanks Melvin, you have made my day!

I have to say, this early morning message made me feel great, life is a journey for sure and it's things like this that make all the difference. I never go looking for praise or thanks, that is not what I am about, but sometimes it's nice to hear that in some small way, you made a difference.

Did I run today, you bet I did!

Friday, 4 March 2016 - Time for new trainers.

You have got to love new trainers and I do get through a few pairs in the year mainly because I'm big boned and I give them a run for their money. I go for the heavy-duty ones these days but if I can, I opt for some in bright colours; so I might be seen as well as heard when I come stomping down the street.

Today was the day for a trip to my favourite sports shop and once the deal was done, I did not plan on wasting any time. As soon as possible I was proudly taking my new bad boys out for a test spin around the park and even though they had been out of the box a matter of minutes and I had already managed to get mud on them!

I am a bit of a creature of habit when it comes to my sportswear. T shorts, happy to wear those from the post run goody bag. Shorts, online as a rule but trainers, I always go to the same shop, Essential Sports in the Royal borough, where Mick and Moz have looked after by feet for many years.

In this age of online shopping, call me old fashioned, I like to buy off a person and I like a town with independent shops rather than soulless chain stores. I am not a big fan of 'out of town' retail parks which are successful at turning town centres into ghost towns and don't get me started on Primark.

It's what the people want apparently. Money talks, so no point trying to stand in the way of 'progress' and after all it is way above my pay grade. With my trainers officially broken in, the weekend could begin.

Friday 11th March 2016 - And another new place to run.

Where did that week go?

At last after much talk of relocation to new premises for work, it has final happened and the team are on the move. The new location is closer in miles to home but takes longer to get to work; not quite sure how that works.

It has taken a while to make the transition to the new building, but a hidden benefit is that we get new places to run and explore after work, plus it's near the airport which I can see coming in handy.

The old office location was a little industrial, although once away from the main roads and the eclectic selection of businesses, the area was pretty and I'd recently found some great new routes, just a little too late.

I will on occasional return back to the old office in Coleshill so will still have chance to explore and it's only a few miles down the road so no big deal.

The new office is by Birmingham Airport and the NEC, and when I say by the airport, I mean by the side of the runway. It's great for plane spotting and watching lucky buggers heading off on their holidays.

I am not familiar with the area so I have invested in a Ordnance Survey map of the area with the intention of doing a bit of research and planning to map out some interesting routes. Or maybe I could just do the bloke thing, forget planning just put the trainers on and set off in a likely looking direction and see what happens, letting the route just develop. Who needs a map! Bit like self-assembly instructions, what waste of paper.

Just two of us out on the run today, bad backs and conference calls reduced the size of the group, but with the sun shining, sky blue and the shorts on, Justin and I were out there – trail blazing!

Skirting the perimeter fence of the airport, close enough for a few lung fulls of aviation fuel fumes (I wonder what the human body does to the gallon?) and then across the bridge over the A45, one of the main arteries into Birmingham, England's the second city.

A glimpse of a sign out the corner of the eye saved the day as were just about to head to Birmingham down the side of a busy duel carriage way. All part of the adventure and it was as if we had planned it, the route took us away from the hustle and bushel of the airport and into the beautiful little village of Bickenhill. This was proper England, straight off the chocolate box but alas no sign of a nice little pub and oh so very quiet.

It has to be said that with my new trainers on, this part of the route was a little muddy and already my nice new clean footwear had lost the showroom appeal. Oh well!

As with most runs with others, I love the varied topics of conversation and today with Justin, we had some crackers.

Discussions about end of life plans, old flames and the office totty, all helped to make the time fly by to the point that neither of us sure how we go back to the office and I am not certain if I could find the route again as we were so engrossed in discussion.

The main topic, end of life planning or the exit plan was an interesting subject and has come up on a few runs in the last few weeks; must be an age thing. This deep and meaningful conversation piece has got me thinking though, do I want to be buried or cremated. I don't fancy either option to be perfectly honest, another alternative I am not a big fan of is being buried at sea as never been a particularly strong swimmer.

I am ok with a funeral, either in a church or at the local crematorium but it's the presence of the coffin that I don't like. I realise that it is an obvious feature of the process and I know you need to have the chance to say goodbye but I prefer the idea of a remembrance service, a celebration of life but do you need the coffin?

For me it kind of gets in the way, like the skeleton in the room, nearly. I think the presence of the newly departed puts people under added pressure especially the loved ones and don't get me started on the whole curtains or no curtains if the crematorium option is the chosen method of departure.

I love it when folks say, oh I don't care or I'm not bothered what you do with me– tell someone that you're not bothered either way, it's a tough enough process as it is without debating what they would have wanted!

Have got your exit plan sorted? Have you written a will? Give it some thought and get it down on paper, the love ones you leave behind will thank you, but no surprises and confessions from the grave as it maybe not the best time to let out one of your best secrets or announce the slept with your wife's mother.

And then there is the whole eulogy discussion, do you leave this final statement, the last summary of your life in the hands of a member of the cloth to trot out some potted life history created from a generic script or hand over the burden to a close friend?

I reckon I want to write my own, not sure I can trust anyone else to find all the right words or is that part of the fun.

Of late, I have been on a bit of a mission to bring this tender subject to the top of peoples to do list but have I sorted my end of life plan out? The answer is no, but it is on my list...

Did you see how I completely overlooked our conversions about ex-girlfriend's and the office totty? What's on the run, stays on the run.

Saturday 12th March 2016 - Here comes the rain again.

I run regardless of the weather, come rain or shine but when I run in the rain I have to be in the mood. Sometimes I can find the experience quite liberating with a sense of freedom, skin is waterproof right? But other times, it can make putting on the trainers a real chore.

Today the rain was relentless with part of the route I had intended to take falling foul to the rising water levels of the river Avon. This left me with two options - turn back and retrace my steps adding a few miles to the run or just go for it and get my feet wet, what is the worst that could happen!

The rising water levels brought back memories of the great flood back in the late nineties and as it happens, coincided with my first encounter with kidney stones. Back in 1998, those painful little sods had an impact on me but not on my running as back then I hadn't been bitten by the running bug. Kidney stones did put me in hospital for a few days not only making me miss an opportunity to go to Japan but also witness the impact of the river Leam on the town I was born in.

A local website describes the event:

In the early hours of Good Friday, April 10th, 1998, the River Leam burst its banks and flooded the centre of Leamington Spa, effectively cutting the town in half. The Parade, Leamington's main street, with the river flowing right across it. The current was so fast that one woman who attempted to wade through the floods was swept off her feet and saved herself by grabbing a lamppost. She was marooned clinging to the lamppost for some time because the torrent was raging too fast for rescue boats.

Leamington's beautiful gardens disappeared under the swirling muddy water. In the Jephson Gardens, the ornamental lakes and the river merged into one mass of water which covered the lawns, paths and flower beds, and flowed across the Parade into the Pump Room Gardens, leaving the famous bandstand marooned. Miraculously the flowers were not washed from their beds and were soon blooming again. Within days it was difficult to imagine that the flowers had spent a day on the bed of the river.

Reading the encounter of the lady, maybe I should have retraced my steps rather than opting to stick to the planned route and getting my feet wet, all adds to the fun though!

Steve Atherton

Sunday, 13th March 2016 - A venture to the 'dark side'.

Although it's Sunday, I fancied a change from running and opted to have a sit down for a change, so today it was all about the bike.

'It's a beautiful day, don't let it get away' Thanks U2.

Very apt although I did miss judge the weather as it was a little on the chilly side.

Clothing choice is a little different when heading out on a bike, you do not warm up as quickly on two wheels so need to be canny with the wardrobe selections. I was a little underdress for the start of my ride but by the time I arrived in Kenilworth, I had managed to get the body temperature up enough to enjoy the rest of the ride.

For me, life is all about people in most things that I do, whether work or play, I rarely enjoy doing anything on my own and today was no exception.

I cycled from home over to Kenilworth, the meeting point for today's ride with David, someone from the running group I had known a while but never really had a proper chat with. Mainly because he is a cyclist and never runs so before having a catch up with the rest of the group, we seized the moment.

I love people, I could never be a hermit or a crab for that matter, mainly because I would need a bloody big shell.

I am without question a pack creature and I do like a crowd or an event so today I was in luck. I will confess, it wasn't luck as I had signed up to ride the annual Mike Vaughan ride for Myton Hospice.

The sportive was organised by the shop from where I bought my new bike from, so I thought it would be a well organised ride and a lot of fun raising funds for a local charity.

I stopped off on route to say hello to the runners and to make sure they knew that my venture to the dark side was only temporary and I would be back in the trainers running the following week.

The turnout at the sportive was amazing, with the road outside the shop closed to cars allowing bikes to take over the area. The growing crowd, mainly blokes to be honest, although a few of the fairer sex, but lots of MAMmaLs (Middle Aged Men in Lycra).

After the short ride over, I was ready for a pre-race coffee and a bit of cake together with the chance to catch up with some old faces. I was careful, very careful who I stood next to as lycra is never flattering unless you have the body of a Greek god and I definitely do not have the body of a god unless its Buddha.

I remember buying my Genesis cycling top in readiness for my epic London to Paris cycle outing in 2014 and on its arrival and I eagerly paraded around the house in my new outfit to be greeted by my youngest daughter grinning face with the comment 'Did they not have your size Dad?' You have got to enjoy the honesty of youths and I do look a little snug in lycra to be honest! But for my sports, running or cycling, it's a must and I am sure I do not look the worst, well in my head at least.

I did ask Steve, an old friend and work colleague from the past to stand somewhere else as he was making me look a bit like Mr Blobby as he did have the body for lycra. Don't you just hate people like that?

I had no inclination or the ability to be at the front so with that in mind, we waved the proper cyclists off on their way. My plan was to stay with fellow Zero to Hero riders today, a real mixed bunch of riders and very strange to be on two wheels for a change.

The new bike was performing like a dream and on a very pleasant and well thought out route with only one problem.

For very good reasons, the route basically headed out from Kenilworth for approximately five miles like a spoke of a wheel before commencing the start a circular orbit around the start point. The problem as we travelled the circumference of the wheel like route, signposts constantly reminded me that home was only five or six miles away, which I found a little tough on the mind and motivation.

This was yet another bike ride where I carried a selection of energy gels along for the ride, just in case. I will use them one day but not today and my tummy was not feeling that great so the last thing I need was anything that could make it worse.

As we complete the final stage of the route and heading towards the outskirts of Kenilworth, a sign post indicated that the distance to the finish was identical to the distance to home, this information got the better of me and with the magnificent landmark of Saint Mary's Church Warwick to guide me, I headed for home – thank you very much!

What a lovely ride, a great event and some great company reminding me that Warwickshire is such a beautiful place to live.

Sunday 20th March 2016 - Today is a good day!

Spring Equinox, my wishes are coming true and today is one of my favourite days of the year. This is the day when the hours of daylight are the same as that of darkness and best of all, from tomorrow the days get longer. Shorter nights and better dawn runs – bring it on!

Today was a good day to run, perfect conditions, dry and not too cold with no wind and some blue sky.

Wednesday 23rd March 2016 - a different view of running.

Such a funny story and too good not to share.

I do like a routine and the general format of my work week is generally the same with set days when regular things happen. One such activity involves picking my youngest daughter Millie up from her mums on the way home from work a couple of days a week, generally Tuesdays and Thursdays, but for some reason today was a Wednesday evening and Millie was in the car with me.

My mobile phone rang and on answering the call, hands free of course, it was my great friend Sue calling to arrange a run later on in the week.

The conversation was upbeat and chatty as always, Millie sat quietly with a look of amazement on her face. As the call ended, she turned to me with her face showing a combination of bewilderment and her trademark cheeky grin. 'How can you be enthusiastic about going for a run Dad?' she exclaimed 'running is the sport of the devil!'

Saturday 26th March 2016 - home.

My first born is back for Easter, still focused and quietly working her way through uni, I haven't seen Libby since Christmas and it's lovely to have her home.

As she is also a keen runner, we take advantage of the time in our trainers to have a proper good catch up. We have some 'must do 'routes that we try to run when we get together dependent on the starting point. Old Milverton, Ashow - all favourites but the locations are immaterial, in all about quality time together.

I am very fortunate that because of the relationship that I have with both of my daughters, and the girls know that they can talk to me about anything and they do.

No subject taboo and the advice and support is definitely reciprocated. My children are my world and a chance for Libby and I to run together and put the world to rights is the best, not always easy conversations with at times some challenging subjects, but by the end we are both the better for the time together.

A different method and not in trainers with my youngest daughter, with Millie we usually do our therapy over a nice dessert, same rules and varied conversation but with the results are the same.

Sunday 27th March 2016 - Easter Sunday Run.

Trying to get folks to turn out for a run on Easter Sunday can be a tricky and the attendance can be little hit and miss. The first national holiday of the year with the kids off school which traditional becomes a family-based weekend with many folks taking the opportunity of a long weekend to grab a holiday, a bit of winter sun or time at home.

Since I started our little running group back in 2012 and I have always tried to do something to make the group smile and Easter is a perfect opportunity to do just that.

Armed with bunny ears and a bag of Cadbury cream eggs, I become the Easter bunny and who can resist a bit of chocolate.

A good turn out today and always a diverse selection of topics of conversation from the love of sweet things to religion, both have their place in our lives but neither as history and data shows, are always good for you. I might just leave it there before I get a little controversial.

Monday 28th March 2016 - bloody typical...

It's Bank Holiday Monday and the weather of course is as predictable as ever. Julie and I have taken advantage of the extended weekend and booked into a nice little pub for the night, which gives us both a chance of a change of scenery and for me somewhere new to run.

A day full of good intention but it turned out not to be a good day to run or to run in the morning at least. The odds of me running this morning were stacked against me:

a)   We were staying in a country pub in the middle of nowhere, country lanes with no foot paths.
b)   It was windy and I do not like the wind.
c)   It was peeing down with rain.
d)   My trainers were in the car.
e)   It was proper cosy in bed!

However all was not lost, as today was a game of two halves and after a hearty but not deserved breakfast, we headed home to find, once we arrived in Warwick, the rain had stopped and grey cloudy skies replaced bright sunshine.

Seizing the opportunity and with the trainers and my kit handy, I managed to get out later in the day.

Not a run that will go down in history as I felt like someone had taken out my batteries as I had no energy, every step a chore. So decided to make it a short one and headed to my local park.

Bad idea, the place was rammed with the impromptu appearance of the sun and a bank holiday so folks were out in force. What are all these people doing in my park?

It felt like a Sunday with the park full of all my pet hates. Young kids on scooters who just wanted to get in my way, magnet toddlers who were on a mission to catch me out like an unpredictable druggie staggering in my path and something I would imagine most runners hate, retractable dog leads.

These bloody things should be band, the number of times I have nearly literally fallen foul to these pieces of shit! Serving no purpose than to indiscriminately up end anyone in the radius of the nylon cord. As for controlling a dog, not a hope in hell.

I gave up and after successfully managing to escape all manner of potential traps, I did a circuit of the park and headed home, safe in the knowledge that there was sure to be a James Bond film on the telly later, well it is a bank holiday - tradition!

Tuesday 29th March 2016 - What a difference a day makes.

Awaking to such a beautiful morning and even though it was a Tuesday, I did not have to go to work. Working in the car industry attracts a few quirky working practices, we do not work Friday afternoons. However, Good Friday is a normal workday, ok half day (did I mention I don't work Friday afternoons?) and as a result we get the Tuesday off instead - bonus.

Polar opposite from the previous day, I really enjoyed my run today and decided to head for Leamington for a change, although I had to skirt Warwick park just to make sure everyone had gone home!

The Royal Borough looked stunning today and after posting a few photos on social media, Paul, my old school mates quoted, 'always impressed by our hometown'. So true I love Leamington and proud to call it my hometown. I want a plaque on the wall of the house I was born in...

Today's run was all about water, the river side path hugging the meandering course of the River Avon, then along the Grand Union canal, past my old school, past my old house in Edmondscote Road, where I was born in fact, then along the banks of the River Leam, past number one Dormer Place, my Dad's childhood home and back past Mid Warwickshire College of further Education. All the places from my youth, a great run.

A solo run for a change and unfortunately my mind was going into overdrive, I had plenty to focus on this morning as I have a pain in my nether regions and to be honest, is giving me a little concern.

The Jephson Gardens were, as always, amazing, the smell of the hyacinths was breath taking so I had to stop and tell the gardeners what a great job they do.

Wednesday 30th March 2016 - spring forward.

With the end of the winter in sight, comes a change to the clocks. So not only did we lose an hour in bed at the weekend, but the time change makes the morning darker again.

I hate it when they piss about with the clocks! Double checking my notes for this book to see what I said about the clocks going forward and although I had a moan, I did not make half as much fuss when the clocks went forward, losing an hour in bed, boy did I kick off! Something to look forward to readers.

5:45am - cold, dark and I was spark out when the alarm went off! But meeting up with the gang at what felt like the middle of the night, the reward was good spirits from my morning running buddies and some great banter on the run today- all about Easter eggs and John in the dog house.

A quick shower, a spot of breakfast then I jumped in the car for a regular visit to a sister plant in Scunthorpe and meet a fellow runner Wendy; great hearing her passion. She is new to running and is loving it!

Gives me a warm feeling when I hear folks talk about running, not PB's and races, but getting out and living the dream, which for me, that is what running is all about.

APRIL 2016

Friday 1st April 2016 - So the jokes on me.

What a difference a day makes, 24 little hours- can't remember who sang that one but so true. My run after work was shit! Slow and I had no energy, so I was not a happy bunny. I had to get out and blow the cobwebs away, but I was definitely running on empty this afternoon.

I am not keen on boring you with stats but really... I want you to see what I am talking about.

1.38 miles, 15 mins, average pace 11.01 min/mile.

I could barely put one foot in front of another, so with that in mind, there was only one thing for it, and I finished the week off with a bottle of red! Not sure it will do anything for my performance but it's the weekend and tomorrow is as they say, another day.

April fool's day was one of my Dad's favourite day of the year, especially in his younger days. He loved to play a prank, the more elaborate the joke the better and working on the newspapers, he was always liked the pranks that the television and daily papers dreamed up, spaghetti trees, Big Ben going digital et al. Dad's pranks were not limited to one day a year or needed to be complicated, my sister often went to work with a peg on the hem of her skirt - a particular favourite.

Saturday 2nd April 2016 - If it ain't raining, it ain't training.

I had a great night's sleep, a rare treat these days, I think the intake of wine helped. I had planned to go for a run and although I was out of bed and into my gear, the weather was pants and because I could, I revised my plans, hoping the weather might improve. Staying in my running gear, I headed over to Kenilworth and fetched my bread ready for my egg and soldiers.

Returning home and with no improvement in the weather, I just did it, headed out, it still raining but pushed myself. I was really on a mission today, head up and no deep and meaningful thinking, just focused and got the job done.

Boom! 3.5 miles, 32.54 mins, 9.23 min/mile, all the effort is worth it when you get the results you wanted.

Back home, showered and breakfast, to the victor, the prize, the egg and soldiers and I must say, they tasted the best.

Sunday 3rd April 2016 - Mixing it up.

Where possible, I try to do different things as it's good to mix it up a bit on our Sunday group runs, after all, variety is the spice of life.

Even on a run, sometimes it's good to take time out and cheer on others and today we had the chance to do just that. It's the Warwick Half Marathon today, the annual fund raiser for British Heart Foundation with the start and finish in Warwick (obviously) and skirting the edge of Kenilworth, the usual base of our little group, gave us the opportunity to combine a fab run with a chance to offer some support to fellow runners. The best of both worlds.

With our route following that of the race for part, we managed to be snapped a couple of times by the official race photographers, with the images inevitably destined to end up in the 'runner not identified, no number visible 'folder.

The route for the Warwick Half is a combination of other local events, with parts of the Two Castles, the middle part of the Kenilworth Half, both events that I have taken part in over the years.

Keeping to the side so as not to get in the way of the race participants, we headed on our way taking a few minutes to cheer on a few runners before returning to Kenilworth, before we got too cold.

As this was the first Saturday of the month, that meant just one thing, a visit to the local coffee stop post run and a chance for a natter.

My youngest daughter, Millie, who does not run with the group but takes no persuading to join us for a post run hot chocolate. She even has a Zero to Hero mug with the group catch phrase 'Sunday's are for running 'customised to with 'running 'crossed out to declare 'Sunday's are for hot chocolate'. You have to admire her style and she is always welcomed as an honorary member of the gang.

Saturday 9th April 2016 - Such a good quote.

'If you want to do good things, surround yourself with great people.'

Taking full advantage of Libby being home, I welcomed the company on my usual solo Saturday morning run into town.

I am pretty much a creature of habit when it comes to the weekend especially when it comes to Saturday, when my run generally involves a trip to a shop.

As always, Libby and I are never short of something to talk about, we chat about the past and exciting plans for the future. I never tire of listening to the hopes and dreams of my daughters with their lives ahead of them and a big wide world to explore. The opportunities are endless, unlike an old fart like me but nevertheless, I have hopes and dreams too and I am not done with this life just yet.

Not sure how we got on to the subject but Levison Wood came up in conversation. I like this guy, former soldier in the Parachute Regiment becoming a writer, photographer and explorer sharing his journeys walking the length of the Nile, the Himalayas and the Americas brilliantly documented in a number of series on Channel 4.

Julie and I were fortunate to spend an evening with Lev back in 2017, along with a few hundred other people when he visited the 'Royal Borough'. One of the things he said really resonated with me and little did I know at the time, but these words of wisdom would guide me in the weeks and months ahead into an exciting period of my life.

We sat, engrossed in the intrepid traveler's life story from around the world and once Levison left the stage, I used my inside knowledge of the theatre where I used to work, to grab the opportunity to meet up with him for a quick chat and a photo or two.

Running with Libby in Warwick on such a beautiful morning is priceless, feeding off one another's enthusiasm our ideas took another step to becoming reality and we were both energised and ready to take on the day.

Logging the run on Strava, pretty much Facebook for athletes giving all the data you could possibly need including where we had ran. The route we had taken had successfully drawn a dog.

Friday 8th April 2016 - Can you keep a secret?

What's on the run stays on the run, I love that phrase. It is true though, on a run with someone, side by side, there is a tendency to open up a talk about things that I guess if you sat face to face with someone you probably would not talk about.

I was running with a mate from the office today and you would not believe the myriad of subjects and people that get discussed, hence the phrase.

The new location is giving us a variety of new places to explore but the glass sided office building does leave us wide open to a bit of shorts-based banter. Good job we are both thick skinned and I reckon I haven't got bad legs for a man of my age!

Sunday 10th April 2016

I wasn't feeling my best today, reckon I had a touch of man flu and we all know how serious that can be, don't we ladies?

I wanted to get a bit of fresh air and although medical advice would recommend that you don't run if you feel off colour, I was working on the 'kill or cure 'principle. But just in case, I opted for an out and back route so the fast runners could run further and faster, meeting me on the way back. Plus giving me the option to turn back when I thought I stood a chance of returning to finish point at roughly the same time.

My calculations worked out perfectly and as we regrouped and we were within sight of the end, I thought maybe a spot of spontaneous training might be in order and I had just the drill in mind.

A little routine that was always a favourite of my good friend Phil when he was trying to prepare a few others and I for longer distances.

His efforts and training regime wasted on me unfortunately, but his sessions did leave me with the great training idea affectionately called 'bus shelters'.

As the name suggests the routine involves running from one bus shelter on Bridge Street, which is at the bottom of Rosemary Hill, up the grueling incline, periodically increasing the pace and arriving at the second bus shelter which is alas, not at the top of the hill but cruelly located around the corner on top of Abbey Hill, just when you think the torture is over, the session asked for just that little bit extra.

The session guaranteed on leaving everyone breathless at the second bus shelter and today was no exception. Today's impromptu training session attracted a few choice comments from some of the group before heading back to the finish, I am sure they enjoyed it really.

I survived the run myself and felt better for getting my trainers on.

Returning home, post run and taking the opportunity to catch up on my emails, I followed a link from recent correspondence from the race organisers of the annual Regency Run, which took me to the event website.

A quote caught on the page caught my eye, *'success is not final, failure is not fatal. It's the courage to continue that counts'*

Takes me back to my first race back in 2005, but I told you all about this at the start of the book.

Wednesday 13th April 2016

After a couple of days of taking it easy, I'm back in the groove. If I am not firing on all cylinders, I am usually not down for long and today I was on fire.

Which was just as well as this morning's run turned into a full on 'crack of dawn' life coaching session with the deluxe addition of the 'work-life balance' module. The latter seems to be a regular subject on many runs these days and was top of the list this morning, so I had to pull out all the stops and get all the tools from the toolbox! (I bet you are thinking, how much crap can you get in one sentence?)

I listened then rolled out all the good stuff. When I hear about people working ridiculously long hours and we have all been there I am afraid, I get folks to do the maths.

When they break down their contracted hours to an hourly rate and then compared with actual hours worked and the new hourly rate, you see what the true hourly rate turns out to be.

This simple calculation really does focus the mind for sure and can give you a good reality check.

Time has got to be the most precious commodity in our lives and all the money in the world cannot buy any extra, once it's gone it's gone. Time with your kids is priceless and once our children grow up, one thing is a definite, they never become kids again and rewinding the clock is not an option.

Looking back at 9/11, the calls made from the doomed aircraft, passenger laden bombs on route towards the final history defining target of the 'Twin Towers' in New York City, were not to the office but to love ones. Doesn't that speak volumes.

I remember a conversation at an old colleague's funeral when work life balance again raised its ugly head. If you think about the average life span for a man is three score years and ten - seventy years old. Now compare the life of Mr average to a week, with each day of the week equaling 10 years. End of Monday equals ten years passed, Tuesday night twenty years gone and so on, most of the folks in the conversation were in our late forties at the time, we only have the weekend left and we all know how the weekend flies by!

To focus my mind and as I start to write this book, I am fifty-eight, Saturday night then - bloody hell! It might be Sunday before it sees the light of day the way its going.

I bet you are wondering if my crude attempt at life coaching worked?, Only time will tell, but you have to want to change and want to break the habit to make alterations to our routine, life is not a rehearsal.

On a related but not related subject, I have no clue what's happening in our little running group, the posts on the Zero to Hero Facebook page along with enquires via the website were coming thick and fast. This can only be a good thing and we must be doing something right.

Friday 15th April 2016 - Inside out.

I like going to the gym but I do not like running on a tread mill, I would rather poke my eyes with a sharp stick and much prefer to be outside. But I was under pressure from Mike via our work Facebook group, posting his running stats so I had to throw my hat in the ring and reciprocate the honours.

If I was to stand any chance of giving Mike's figures a run for their money, I needed the best possible set up and I thought a flat treadmill was the answer.

Unlike running outside, stopping to take a breath is not so easy as the belt keeps on coming, unforgiving and constant. I gave it my best shot, 5k running on the spot and I was done, posting a pretty respectable attack to end the week, bring on the weekend.

Saturday 16th April 2016.

With the time for my first born to head back to Leeds for the final push to summer and the end of another academic year fast approaching, we were keen get a run in together.

The price you have pay for being together are the farewells and with that in mind, the destination was pretty obvious. One of our favourites and a route that we have ran many times over the years.

Even though we had picked a pretty rubbish day weather wise, cold and wet, neither of us seemed to mind. We were off to Ashow, this quintessentially English village is 'our' place, so a natural place to head.

As always, we were not short of conversation, but we dwelled on the random subject of making an 'end of life 'plan. Not really sure how we end up on such a deep and meaningful subject but it's one that needs talking about at some point as one thing that is certain is you will eventually pop your clogs.

Having lost both my parents, I know their wishes are very important when the time comes. I know people say, when I go

Steve Atherton

I don't care what happens to me because I am dead, but that does not really help those you leave behind.

At a time when you have just lost a loved one, trying to guess what they would have wanted is a pretty thankless task as you are sure to upset someone.

If you leave your wishes written down, the problem goes away as no one messes with the dead. The written wishes are the ace card and takes away all the guess work.

As we ran, I shared my thoughts with Libby and what she would want once I head off on the last great adventure. A headstone can be a focal point for grief but from experience after losing my own parents, a headstone can be a distraction.

Libby was open and very mature about the subject, I just want somewhere I can go and connect in my thoughts and as we ran, the bridge at Ashow feels like a perfect place to have my ashes scattered. A very positive and meaningful run, I just need to practice what I preach and get my exit plan on paper.

My Dad's life was relatively steady and predictable up to the death of my Mum, when his world was turned upside down.

During the initial period of being widowed, life carried on as it was when Mum was around albeit a little repetitive with each day from meals to the daily routine, the same day in day out. He was a lost soul which I can fully appreciate, spending time at her grave side. In the churchyard is where he met a similar lost soul sharing time together, but it came to nothing before Dad starting his succession of moves.

From his house, to sheltered housing to care home finally followed by a number of nursing homes before ending his days just around the corner from where we lived and the home in which I was born.

It felt like he had come full circle and with each move, the number of possessions decreased until final the worldly goods of Ronald Atherton resided in a cardboard archive box. In the infamous 'exit box' along with a lifetime of memories was a letter.

The contents of this letter were Dads final wishes even down to the music he wanted and the request that the service be as short as possible.

I remember sitting in the garden at home a few days after he died, before the house had woken up and in the peace of the morning with a cup of tea and the exit box.

All the important documents were together along with the letter, He could not have made it any easier, thanks Dad.

Have I made you think, have I touch a nerve? I hope so, don't leave this the task to those you leave behind.

Sunday 17th April 2016 - Memory Lane.

A very special day today, you will remember that in the open few paragraphs of this book I talked about the very first event I took part in back in 2005, the Regency Run, and today I get to run again where it all started.

I felt very nostalgic and so much has happened in the last eleven years. Back in 2005, I was new to running and hardly knew anyone, very different today when I feel very much in the thick of the local running community.

A good turn out from the Zero to Hero family which made for a great atmosphere as we hovered around the start line. What to wear on race day always needs a little thinking about and I went for a shocking pink T shirt this morning with 'Steve 'printed in big letters. A legacy from the Paris Half Marathon with Team IAC back in 2011 and no way would I not be spotted today.

With town notoriously busy on race day, I opted to park well away from the event and had a slow jog down to the start, meeting others on route.

This was becoming a real trip down memory lane this morning, parking in Lillington, in North Leamington near our old flat, we ran past a beautifully restored Georgian town house looking like it would be not out of place gracing the glossy pages of Warwickshire Life.

This stunning house I alway affectionately call 'Running HQ'. If I ever won the lottery, I dream that I would buy this house and from this stunning residence, I would coordinate my running world and the rest of my life of course. I best keep dreaming and maybe actually doing the lottery might increase my chances of ever winning.

The weather had been pretty wet of late but this morning it was fine with no rain, although the legacy of the previous days down pours would sure to have left the first half of the route a tad on the muddy side.

I have run the Regency run many times but for one of our group, today was their first 10k. I know that feeling and Fatema's emotions were clear to see, excitement, fear, anticipation, apprehension along with a myriad of others, but I think having friends around clearly helped.

Before long, just like back in 2005, the klaxon sounded and we were on our way. The support was brilliant and the marshals ready with a smile and positive comments, this makes such a difference especially to us 'fun runners'. Maybe the athletes at the front don't feel or need the support as much, I might just find out?

Back in the 'Royal Borough' and I am on home turf so I know many of the marshals, many of them are Spa Striders. The Leamington based club has been associated with the Regency Run since the first event back in 2004. In addition to setting up the course and providing most of the marshals, keeping us runners safe on the day, the club also do a lot of the pre-race activities too such as goody bag packing.

Without volunteers, many events would not take place and I occasionally take a break from running and do my bit. I love marshalling, always great fun, but today I run.

As predicted, the route around the common was muddy, made increasingly worse by the assistance of thousands of trainers. Fortunately, the latter half of the run is on paths and a chance to shake off the acquired mud from the first 5k.

The support in town was the best, it looks like the whole of Leamington had come out to cheer and I was in my element.

Today Trish was my wingman, rarely far from my side at many events over the years. We keep each going and I am sure Trish secretly likes the attention that I seem to attractive.

As the number of supporters swell in number as we head towards the last few kilometres, I go in panto mode and do my best to make every run an occasion.

Approaching the finish line, the welcome face of my old buddy, Mali. This guy played a massive part in my life and is such a great friend, coming to my rescue at a real low point in my running journey along with some good stuff too.

One event that I always say I would never take part in again is a local race call the Summer Six. Organised by Stratford upon Avon AC, described as an undulating six-mile evening road race, starting and finishing at Mary Arden's Farm in Wilmcote, Warwickshire.

I had no intention of taking part in the first place but a good friend of mine, Kieron, who got me into running in the first place had a place in the annual race in 2006 but for some reason, he could not take part and offered me his place.

The timing was perfect as I was trying to kick start my return to fitness so was happy to take his place. Back then, my life was not dull putting it mildly and I was on a self-inflicted roller coaster ride and my personal fitness had taken a bit of a battering so to put on the trainers was a big ask.

I knew little of the event but as I stood on the start line, it soon became apparent that this was a serious event. The start, in the village synonymous with Mary Arden, William Shakespeare's mother, remains a blur as once the starting horn went off, within seconds, I was running on my own.

The field, 99% club runners who were on a mission were off into the sunset leaving me to spend the remainder of the six miles pretty much on my own.

A pretty route but I was not in the best frame of mind to enjoy it, although it was a beautiful summers evening. I dug in and just focused on putting one step in front of another and longed to be reunited with my lady at the finish.

This is where Mali enters the story, we have known each other for ages, sharing a parallel running path. Both members of Spa Striders, one of Leamington's running clubs but also a member of Spa Hash House Harriers, the two groups could not be any different to each other.

To reinforce the difference, I will quote from the two organisations promotional material.

From Spa Striders website:

'We are a friendly running club based in Leamington Spa. If you want to train for a marathon, compete in races, get a bit fitter, or just meet some new people then browse around a bit to check out what we do, how to find us and what you need to know about joining.

The club is for anyone who enjoys running. Take a look at our events calendar to see which training sessions are best for you.

If you are already running regularly then you will find plenty of runners in the club who will be able to help you push that bit further and faster. Most new members improve pretty quickly. Joining a club such as ours is the best way to get faster and make friends while you do so!'

As you can see, the focus is all about faster and further.

In contrast, the objectives of the Hash House Harriers as recorded on the club registration card dated 1950:

- To *promote physical fitness among our members*
- To *get rid of weekend hangovers*
- To *acquire a good thirst and to satisfy it in beer*
- To *persuade the older members that they are not as old as they feel*

I would imagine at this point, I might be just about to lose you so let me explain a little more about Hashing.

Running off at a tangent

The Hash House Harriers, HHH or H3 as its sometimes known originated in December 1938 in Selayang Quarry, Selangor, then in the Federated Malay States (now Malaysia), when a group of British colonial officers and expatriates began meeting on Monday evenings to run, in a fashion patterned after the traditional British paper chase or 'hare and hounds', to rid themselves of the excesses of the previous weekend.

These weekly gathering continued before taking a break for the second world war, today the hash house harriers is very much alive and kicking with currently almost two thousand chapters in all parts of the world, with members distributing newsletters, directories, and magazines and organising regional and world hashing events.

Are you keeping up?

At a hash, one or more members ('hares') lay a trail, which is then followed by the remainder of the group (the 'pack 'or 'hounds'). Little mounds of flour are usually used to mark the trail and periodically ends at a 'check 'and the pack must find where it begins again; often the trail includes false trails, short cuts, dead ends, back checks, and splits. These features are designed to keep the pack together despite differences in fitness level or running speed, as front-runners or FRB's (Front Running Bastards) as they are affectionately known, are forced to slow down to find the 'true 'trail, allowing stragglers to catch up.

Members sometimes describe their group as 'a drinking club with a running problem, 'very different to a traditional running club.

I have only touched on the surface of hashing, so here is a little homework for you to go and find out more or better still, give it a go and let me know how you get on.

So back to the Summer Six, I am still trotting the country lanes of Warwickshire, passing the occasional marshal giving me welcome words of encouragement but secretly wishing that I and the remaining few stragglers would hurry up so they could all pack up and go home or maybe to the pub.

Julie, still at the finish, patiently waiting for her man to return and this is where Mali enters the story and something for which I will be eternally grateful.

'How did Steve get on? 'Mali asked Julie.'He is not back yet... 'came her reply maybe with just a tinge of concern in her voice.

With that, Mali was off, armed with refreshments grabbed from a table aside of the finish, he was retracing the route that he ran some time before to find me.

Totally unaware of help on its way, I was done, my legs had given up and my spirit was lower than shark shit. I had about a mile to go to the finish line end of this torture, but it felt like a mile too far.

The village was on a hill, well it would be wouldn't it! So the final section was up a rather steep road, although I could have quite easily stopped in the side of the road and cried hoping that someone would take pity and drive me to the finish, I had to do this.

Taking a deep breath, I draw on every last drop of energy I had left and pushed on up the hill. Staring at the ground most of the time, periodically glancing up to review my extremely slow ascent.

As I did, I could not believe my eyes, heading towards me with a cup of water in each hand, was my knight in shining armour, Mali. I have never been so pleased to see another human being in all my life. Refreshed and with my spirits lifted, we headed for home. Mali by my side until just before the finished when he peeled off and became a spectator and cheered me over the finish line.

A night I will remember for the rest of my life, gratitude to a true friend and the love of a very special person who face at the finish line was the icing on the cake and who's faith kept me going.

It was fitting that years later we both went back to school and obtained formal running qualifications. Initially completing a short Run England course to become a 'leader in running fitness' then progressing through the intense training to become a fully qualified coach in running fitness, from which the Zero to Hero group was born.

Today is the groups fourth birthday and we would celebrate later with a curry and a beer or two. As part of my little speech, I was delighted to have the chance to congratulate Fatema on completing her first race, defiantly a hero!

I hit my bed looking back on a great day with some very special people.

Sunday 24th April 2016 - London calling.

Today is the day of the annual London Marathon, been there done that, got the T Shirt!

I always love the day of the London Marathon, I am not running today but takes me back to when I did.

I love to watch real people doing this event and every year I enter the ballot along with tens of thousands of others, but I have never been successful in getting a ballot place. However, in 2013, thanks to a club place from Spa Striders, I did take my place on the start line at the most iconic mass participation event in the world.

I had watch the event on the TV like most of us for many years and back in 2003 I was actually in London on race day, keeping busy whilst my first born was preparing to dance at the Albert Hall and by accident I did have the privilege to watch the thousands of people pound the streets of London.

A very emotional day, proud to see Libby dance with the bonus of seeing this iconic race in person and I promised myself that one day I would be one of those runners.

The seen was sown and what stuck in my mind was the determination and passion of these amazing people. All shapes and sizes from the complete spectrum of life, all with one thing in mind, to become a marathon runner and complete the 26.2 miles.

As my friend Kieron said at the end of my first marathon :-

'there are runners and there are marathon runners, you are a marathon runner'

That was back in 2013, my first London Marathon, with the event was overshadowed by a terrorist attack in Boston a few days before sending shock waves through the running community. The last thing you expect to happen to you as you cross the finish line in any event is to get blown up.
Speculation rose as to whether the event would go ahead in the days after this awful atrocity, but with the world and the organisers of events all wanting to make a clear statement and standup against terrorism, almost deviant, the race went ahead albeit with an increased level of security and clear presence of police and army on the streets of the capital.
As a symbol of solidarity and respect, every participant was given a black ribbon to pin to their race number along with a minute silence at the start.
My then partner, Julie, was left with the tough job of keeping two relatively young children occupied as I ran the 26.2 miles from Greenwich to the Mall to the soundtrack of police sirens, not good for the mind or body for that matter.
Every year, the London marathon is all about normal people doing amazing achievements, but the 2016 event also brought sadness. For Captain David Seath, aged 31, the marathon dream ended 3.2 miles from the finish near Southwalk Bridge when he collapsed after a cardiac arrest and later died in St Thomas's hospital.

What happened next summed up runners for me, as the running community worldwide, with the help of social media, followed the lead from David's army colleagues and either in groups or in private, ran the 3.2 miles in the Afghanistan veteran's honour to finish his marathon.

With a tinge of sadness and grateful for my good health, I did my 3.2 miles the following day on a beautiful frosty April morning.

No comparison with what the family of David have to deal with at the moment, but never the less a difficult time for me at the moment so today it was good to get out and run with a purpose and as always a great stress buster.

This one is for you RIP Captain David Seath. 1985 - 2016.

Thursday 28th April 2016 - Happy Birthday Mum.

There was only one place to run to today and that was to St Mary Magdalene to visit my Mums grave. I like having a focal point to go to but it's more symbolic than spiritual. I hate looking at that granite headstone, it feels so cold and clinical.

I much prefer to remember my Mum with a wall full of heavily scented roses, rather than a head stone, I feel closer to my Mum then. I don't like to think of her buried in the ground, she was so full of life, for me she will always be on the scent of a rose and in my heart.

Friday 29th April 2016 - Open wide!

I love days like this, shame they do not happen that often but when they do, I make the most of them.

I had a dental appointment this morning (that's the bit I don't care for) but like most dentists including mine, they seem not to be so keen on an early start, but it gave me a chance to start work a little later and the chance to run a little further than on a school day without the need to get up at the crack of dawn.

Today's run was perfectly timed as had to include a bun run and the route this morning took me along the canal. One of my favourite places to run, away from traffic and peaceful but not so keen when on two wheels. I did forget my gloves and my hands were a little on the chilly side to start with so into the sleeves they went.

I must have looked a right knob but not for long, I soon ended up with sweaty hands. I love running in the morning as you do meet 'morning people', if that makes sense?

Folks who just love to be up and about and making the most of the best part of the day, maybe I should get a dog...

Saturday 30th April 2016 - Home run.

It's Saturday and great to see my home town of Warwick come alive, I love the weekend and all the good things that come with it.

Fortunately, it's been a long time since I have had to work on a Saturday, so the arrival of the weekend gives a welcome opportunity to recharge the batteries a little.

If I run locally at the weekend, I am a bit of a creature of habit. I like to take a look at Warwick castle, I never tire of this iconic view. Then running into town through the square before heading away from the hustle and bustle of the local market and into the peaceful sanctuary of Priory Park. I love this time of day, with people out enjoying the best part of the day.

Pausing my Garmin, I took time to enjoy the tranquility with an old gent, sat on a bench at the top of the hill over looking Leamington. 8.30am in the morning and this lovely man sat with a bottle of wine. We talked and was nice to have the time to enjoy each other's company, a bit early for me to be having a drink but why not? The sun is over the yard somewhere in the world I am sure.

The conversation made me think, I like a drink and sometimes it's all you need to access your soul and discover one's inner self.

I could have sat there all day and was tempted to go and get a bottle from the One Stop and dig in for the day, a nice idea but not sure that would end well.

I did stop to admire the bluebells a little longer that I had intended and ended up with a copy of 'The watchtower'. A charming old lady was waiting to ambush me and saw me as a potential addition to the Jehovah's Witness flock, coming away from our brief encounter with a little light reading.

I love living around here, I wish the sea was closer but sometimes when I run, I pinch myself. The contrast between the town and countryside, the regal splendor of Royal Leamington Spa, with its majestic sense of grandeur, wide streets, stunning parks and gardens along with grand houses and a matter of a few miles away, medieval Warwick with its quaint narrow streets, timber frames houses and a bloody great castle.

Sometimes the history overwhelms me and my mind goes into overdrive. I think back to what life would have be like during the years.

Especially in Warwick, some of the streets off the beaten track freak me out at times. The past almost crawls out of the walls, add a foggy cold morning into the equation and that does get imagination working overtime and as for goosebumps ...

Steve Atherton

MAY 2016

Sunday 1st May 2016 - bluebells.

One of the many things I like about England is the seasons. Ok maybe not as well defined these days, but as April turns into May, nature celebrates with the arrival of bluebells, or Hyacinthoides non-scripta to give them their Sunday name.

I love bluebells and this time of year winter has pretty much left the building. The signs of better weather and longer days are starting to make their presence known.

Bluebell season only lasts a few weeks and around the beginning of May I try to arrange a Bluebell run. I should have been taking part in the Litchfield Half Marathon this morning but to be perfectly honest, I could not be arsed and decided to head off to the woods with Sunday gang instead.

We are fortunate to have numerous woods that we can run in locally and today we opted for Crackley Woods. Infamous as it's known locally for dogging rather than jogging, but it does have nice established paths and bluebells.

When I look back on the first bluebell run with the group back in 2016, I always smile. As we left the greenway and headed into the woods, I knew the subject of dogging would raise its cheeky head.

One of our regular Sunday runners is from Egypt and she had never heard of this bizarre outdoor pursuit and I waited with bated breath for the inevitable question - 'What's dogging?', I knew it was coming and I found myself running alone with the curious question-master. You try to explain this strange activity to someone from a different culture! The more I explained, the more puzzled Fatema became.

By the time we left the woods, I had done my best to provide a factual, but sympathetic answer without embarrassing either of us. With the explanation done, I was more than a little exhausted. Can I have a question on sport now please?

We had a new runner with us today and as always, they are always better than they think they are and today was no exception. As we headed back to Kenilworth, I was ready for a coffee.

First Sunday of the month and predictably, my youngest Millie, turns up for a hot chocolate.

3rd May 2016 - *Sharing the love.*

Sometimes you don't have to be in the same place to enjoy a run together. Today with the aid of social media and cross platform messaging, I managed to feel the support of others even though I ran alone.

My regular dawn running buddy, Ian was taking in the early morning sights of the capital, beating the battle of the bed to run along the river Thames. My love of running in new places must be rubbing of on him as he took his trainers on a business trip to the big smoke and managed an early morning run, setting himself up for the day - good lad!

I love running in London, especially before it has properly woken up and the streets become a mass of people going about the day.

Ian 'living the dream' down south. Libby, my eldest daughter who is studying Psychology at Leeds University is out and about too and had found a new place to run in her new home town and was keen to share it with me.

Away from the buzz of the city, Libby had found a lovely little running sanctuary in Meanwood Park and it went on to become one of her go to places to run as her Uni year progressed.

To complete today's hat trick of virtual running partners, Mike, my old boss, was in Sweden and posted a picture of his run. I was very jealous as he had managed a run that took him across the 933 metre long Älvsborg bridge, affording amazing views over the city of Göteborg.

This is on my bucket list so I would be keen to check out his route to see how he managed to get from the hotel at sea level, to the walkway some 45 metres above the river Göta älv. I best have a chat when we are both in the office and find out the local knowledge.

Sunday 8th May 2016 - Summer is on its way!

The bluebells are still out so our Sunday gang took advantage of another run in the woods. A different location this week, but a carpet of bluebells, nevertheless. It was just one of those mornings, the summer is on its way and todays run was top drawer.

A beautiful morning, Thickthorn Wood delivered the wow factor and running on down to Ashow with a great group of people, the conversation flowed.

My description of the traditional sprint to the finish as 'going balls out 'apparently conjured up a disturbing image for some of our ladies! Maybe it was the wrong choice of words for describing the mad dash for the finish line.

Wednesday 11th May 2016

Our usual mid-week dawn run was a bit moist this morning. Ok it was raining, I did try to pretty it up a bit, but I don't mind the rain.

The best part about running for me is the people. If truth be told, the best part about life is people. I do love running with so many different people, I am lucky and never short of conversation. On a run, its clear men talk about completely different things to woman and from my experience of runs with the fairer sex always end up talking about bloody sports bras.

What do men talk about? That would be telling, whats on the run stays on the run and it definitely is not sports bras!

Friday 13th May 2016 - Today is a good day!

It might be Friday the 13th, but unlucky it certainly is not. After starting at the Kingsley School in 2004 as a tiny tot, today marks Millie's last day at senior school and the start of her exam study leave.

Leavers assemblies are the best and dependent on how exams fall, maybe the last time this year group will be in the same place.

Tears will be shed by the girls and parents alike, teachers will prepare for the next batch of young ladies and as tradition would have it, the school gets a bit of a makeover.

Kingsley do a great job of the last day and the whole school gathering that goes with it. Always a good teacher's song or video production to send the over excited bunch on their way.

A surprise for Millie was that Libby had managed to come home for the weekend to take part in the celebrations and a sneaky chance to catch up with some of the teachers and old friends too and for me, my first born home.

As I took a day off work, Libby and I seized the chance to have a catch up and a run down to Ashow. Where else?

Following the advice, I received from my own parents, I encourage my girls to lead their own lives as there is a big old world out there. But I do miss having them around and love to hear all about what they have been doing and their future plans.

I find it really exciting and makes be so proud, very apt as Millie closes one chapter and prepares for the next.

As predicted, the leavers assembly was a bit of a tearjerker, with only a hand full of girls that had done the full stint from prep to the end of seniors. The screen showed the journey with memories a plenty. Boy do I feel old! I love to see my kids growing up. My family is everything.

Saturday 14th May 2016 - upping the anti.

Felt good in my trainers this morning, I wanted to up the pace and push myself a little. The weather has been a little mixed of late, but today the rain stayed away, the signs of spring are very apparent. The world seems to have changed from the monochrome of winter to glorious technicolour that comes with the arrival of spring and I like it.

I had no time for pleasantries this morning, I had the need for speed and decided to keep it simple and local with a few spritely circuits of the park. I felt good. What's for breakfast?

Sunday 15th May 2016 - keeping the momentum.

Ashow has a magnetic effect on me, it's such a special place and a great place to run too. Always a favourite with the gang too, so never a problem whenever I suggest a trot down Rocky Lane.

This morning was just stunning and helped keep up the momentum; a good run had by all. With the weather so nice, I managed to get the bike out too in the afternoon and so completed my own little duathlon.

Friday 20th May 2016 - looking back on the week.

With all talk about work life balance of late, I try my best to keep it level. Unfortunately, my plan to do just that got ever so slightly screwed up this week, but I did manage a couple of runs.

Tuesday saw a break from the norm on a dawn run for today. I ran solo, the significant difference was that I had to motivate myself, which meant getting up and out at 5.30am.

I did and it was just brilliant. To run alone made a nice change, a time to catch up with my own thoughts, which can be a double edge sword and today was no exception.

With not a particularly great week behind me, my outlook on life today was always going to be a little tainted. But as always, a few miles in my trainers and the world was a better place.

Midweek I grab the opportunity to run in the evening. Sue and I managed to beat the rain. I did not want to get wet as that would not have helped my state of mind, but our timing was perfect, just missing the rain.

Some really strange conversations with Sue tonight, felt a bit like being in the confession box. But that's what talking on a run is all about. What did we talk about? That would be telling, what's on the run, stays on the run.

I did have a lovely email from a colleague in a sister plant in Scunthorpe.

'Morning Steve, I read a lot and on occasion I like to read about peoples inspirational stories, especially on subjects that interest me, such as running. So there I was reading such a book and it mentioned a person, I thought 'hey this guy sounds familiar' and as I continued I felt sure that I did know who the book was referring to, with a bit of research I did manage confirm that it was you. Way to go, that is pretty cool!

Tell me about it next time you are in Sunny Scunny!'

I knew exactly what Wendy was talking about...

If you want to find out what Wendy was talking about too, checkout a great book called 'The reason I run' by Chris Spriggs.

Friday and with the weekend in sight, I did manage to get a run in before heading for home. You cannot beat a lung full of aviation fuel! After a tough week I was so glad to get out for a run straight after work with Justin. The wind was obviously blowing in our direction and working so close to the airport, a lung full of aviation fumes is an occupational hazard.

We did find a new route, who knew all these great routes existed! Well obviously people did, but it was new for us and what fun we are going to have checking out the neighborhood.

Saturday 21st May 2016 - A funny old day.

I had the day all mapped out and their seemed to be so much going on today it was untrue. I didn't know where to begin.

The main activity of today was to go public about my planned bike ride to Mow Cop. But before I did anything social media based, I planned to get out and stretch my legs.

The park is full of runners with the same idea. Many it seemed doing circuits of the park, but unfortunately in the opposite direction. Very confusing to my sleepy head but it did give chance for some subtle competition without anyone ever needing to know. It all about where on the perimeter of the park you pass them!

In between doing the laps maths and fighting for breath, I was deciding what I was going to have for my breakfast. A trip to Crustums maybe but that would involve getting into my car. So many decisions and today was not the day for more things to consider.

I did relent and post run, I headed over for some fresh bread from Crustums and the rest of the day went pretty much as planned. I did my Facebook post and from then on the day developed in to a normal Saturday, until I had a call on my mobile from a number I did not recognise.

Answering the phone, the voice was familiar. On the other end of the phone was Paul, the brother of one of my oldest friends Adrian, or Ada as will always call him, with the bad news that he had been admitted to Myton, a local hospice. The prognosis did not look good and the family thought I should know.

Talk about recalibration of the day and my plans, I made a couple of calls and the rest of the day was a blur.....

Sunday 22nd May 2016 - deep in thought.

Joining the heroes for our regular Sunday run, my mind was elsewhere. I was not my usual happy go lucky self, very somber, but I really appreciated the company and a chance to get out in the fresh air.

Today would be a long day and Elton John's hit song from the Lion King, 'the circle of life' was buzzing around my head. The poignant and meaningful words of this great song seemed very apt for my mood today ...

'From the day we arrived on the planet
And blinking, step into the sun
There's more to be seen then can ever be seen
More to do than can ever be done

Some say eat or be eaten
Some say live and let live
But all are agreed as they join the stampede
You should never take more than you give.'

It's the last line that always make me think. I love the sentiment and in this self-centred world we live in these days, it's something that we should all think about. The lyrics from this great song always reinforces the fragility of life and the never-ending cycle.

Back in the late seventies, fresh out of school and ready to take my place in the big wide world, I opt for an apprenticeship with a local engineering company. Thinking that after 11 years at school, I have left education behind me, but the integral part of the apprenticeship was going back to school or college to be more accurate.

The location for my chosen centre of learning was very handy as Mid Warwickshire College of Further Education was five minutes walk from home, giving me no excuse to be late.

It was here that I met Andy, who was on the same course and as our friendship developed along with my knowledge of engineering, so did my circle of friends. At one of Andy's parties, I met two old school friends of his, Allan aka Jobbit and Adrian.

Our friendship blossomed and the four of us became inseparable during our late teens and early twenties. So having known these guys for most my of life, the news of Ada's terminal illness hit us all hard.

Having suffered from a stroke some years before, I always thought Ada had been dealt a shit hand and to now to be given more bad news of the recent diagnosis of bowel cancer must have been the final straw.

I had lost touch with Andy and Allan back in the early nineties, I still kept in touch with Ada and in more recent years, I had linked up again with Allan too.

It was Allan I called first, with the news soon spreading to other old friends and ex-girlfriends. On the phone we immediately agreed to head to the hospice the following afternoon to see our old friend, so my thoughts during my morning run surrounded contemplating the visit later that afternoon.

Neither Allan or I had visited anyone in a hospice and we sat outside for a while, building up the courage to head in, not really knowing what to expect.

The initial impression upon entering the building surprised us both, the sense of warmth and calm was overwhelming. I was expecting doom and gloom to be honest, but the staff immediately putt us both at ease.

Ada's mum and dad were also visiting which really helped to break the ice. It was lovely to see Geoff and Barbara, who have been like a second set of parents to me, giving them a third son wether they wanted one or not.

Barbara was never short of a story or two to embarrass me, but this also reinforced the bond between us. Even though Ada was clearly ill, the banter between the three of us was as good as ever and I am glad we went to see him; but I really appreciated Allan by my side.

Back in the car, Allan and I looked at each other, 'fancy a drink?' You can guess the answer, we both knew the next few weeks were going to be difficult...

Tuesday 24th May 2016 - Summer running having a blast.

I am pretty sure these are the lyrics of a classic tune or maybe it was summer loving?

Summer running makes the time in the trainers through the long winter months worthwhile. When the change in seasons deliver such a stunning morning and my fastest 4-6 mile result curtesy of Strava, even better. With the last few days I have had, I'll take that. I shouldn't be surprised really as I have been putting the training in of late and they do say what gets measured gets improved.

Sunday 29th May 2016 - heels vs wheels.

Not a great week for running, life just keeps getting in the way again, but today a chance to get on two wheels for a change.

I do occasionally take part in a sportive, which is pretty much an organised cycling event, usually timed. For some, it's a full blown race, with individual and team prizes and for others, like myself, it's a signposted route with snacks thrown in. I like following a marked route and as a rule, it avoids busy roads and takes in some stunning little villages and quiet back waters.

The event today was the Warwick sportive, although the start was at Stratford upon Avon racecourse, so not sure where the event got its name from.

A number of Zero to Hero cyclists were taking part and was good to have some company. I decided to cycle over which was fine on the way over as I found a nice quiet route. Post event, I opted for a shorter quicker route back along the main road, bad move!

On Longbridge island, I played an exciting game of Russian roulette, with every exit; another roll of the dice. I was very glad that Lady Luck was on my side and happy to be on the cycle path and on the remainder of the way back home.

Monday 30th May 2016 - Happy birthday to me.

What a perfect start to the day, a chance to get out before what would no doubt be a busy day. It was too good an opportunity to miss and this morning I was on a mission. The running tech these days overloads you with data. It does so much, I'm sure it even knows what I fancy for my breakfast! But for me the best thing it does it that it tracks the route.

The result is a record of the route you have ran and sometimes, generally by accident, you can end up with a sketch of an animal or something. Sometimes the image is planned, which as you might appreciate, is open to abuse and a far more risky rendering, but creating a phallic symbol was not my intention this morning!

I wanted to end up with '55', to mark the notching of another year on the planet. A simple concept and with the help of a couple of football pictures, the sketch was easy to execute.

Perfect timing from the postman was the delivery of a parcel. I had treated myself to a new cycling top, a really colourful specimen immortalising the iconic 1981 Genesis album, Abacab.

Putting on the top for an impromptu fashion show, my youngest commented 'very nice top dad, but did they not have your size?' She might have had a point.

June 2016

Friday 3rd June 2016 - more bad news.

It's been a pretty tough week with early starts and office politics, along with the sad loss of an old work colleague and a good friend.

Early start and office politics seem to be pretty standard in most companies these days, but the news of Keith's death really got to me.

I have worked with Keith for many years and he has suffered ill health for a while. Keith was one of life's gentleman, proper old school and we have spent many a long night in the bar of the Mercure Hotel in Krefeld, Germany.

After putting the world to rights over a glass or two of Rioja, I still managed to get out for a slightly jaded run in the morning and was always greeted by Keith, outside the hotel having a smoke with the regular greeting of 'have a good run, I went out earlier!'

I owe Keith a lot, he could see the passion I had for embracing change and helped me to achieve the job I have had ended up doing since.

Tonight, I raised a glass to an old friend, RIP.

After work, in the morning or at the weekend gives plenty of opportunities for me to fit a run in, but working in the car industry we are still lucky to keep a tradition from the past.

Fridays or POETS day, (Piss Off Early, Tomorrow's Saturday) is historically a short day and most weeks I manage to get away from the office soon after lunchtime, and long may it continue.

With no takers at the office for an after work run and the weekly conference call with my North American and European colleagues bringing the working week to an end, I headed for home and as I needed to get out for some fresh air, I called my great friend and arranged an impromptu run with Sue.

Today would be a special day in the life of our little running group.

We, well Sue to be honest, has been working on the Zero to Hero logo for a while now but with a final flourish, it is all sorted. Arriving at Sue's house to be greeted by T shirt samples a plenty and logo's too, but unfortunately not a shirt that I could actually wear NOW!

I'm not really an impatient person although many would disagree, however a quick phone call to the printers and off we trotted to get some product.

Leaving the company to do their magic, Sue and I took to the streets for a chat and a five miler, life came together and we now had merchandise. Looking forward to Sunday when we can rock up in our new tops.

Saturday 4th June 2016 - It's a good year for the roses.

Warwick looked stunning this morning but what I noticed most of all was the roses. Every turn, every house seemed to have roses, I truly felt that my late Mum 'Rose' was making sure that I was thinking about her, not difficult because I think about her all the time.

I miss her so much and feel sure that she is watching down on me and is very much part of everything I do and what I am today. My Mum was a real people person and I think that's where I get it from.

At times she would be tutting at some of my antics and escapades, but I am sure she would know that I always try to my do the best I can for those around me.

Warwick was preparing for the forthcoming annual Two Castles run and the early warning signs were up and announcing the up and coming race. Not long to go now.

But today's run was not about the Two Castles but about my Mum as I have already eluded to. It was only when I started working on editing the book that I realise that today's date was significant.

I was drawn to roses and my mind preoccupied with thoughts of her on the run this morning. The significance of the date (ok it was actual tomorrow) 5th June 1992, twenty-four years since my Mum, at the far too young age of sixty four, left this mortal planet to be at peace and pain free.

Time is a great healer they say but I am not sure, the sorrow of losing my Mum is as great today as it was half a lifetime ago.

There does not a day go by than I do not think of my parents, I would love to have some time with my Mum especially and to let her know what I have been up to and tell her all about my amazing children who she would have adored.

I know that she might have a few words to say about some of the times of my life that did not go as expected, but I hope all in all I hope she would be proud of my journey and what I have become.

I live in the hope that we will have our time together one day...

Sunday 5th June 2016 - One week and counting.

With only six sleeps to go before the annual Two Castles run and we have merchandise, looking every bit ready for the catwalk, Sue and I loved arriving at this morning run wearing our sexy new Zero to Zero running tops.

The Two Castles will be there first real event for some of the group and the excitement is obvious.

As it is the first Sunday of the month, post run we all headed for a coffee along with an variety of sample tops for folks to try on and we definitely cause a little stir in Starbucks when shirts were swopped and the correct size and style selected.

Unfortunately for the, shall we say larger, male members of the gang, who had no other option than to try my very sweaty top on, sorry gents.

Leaving the coffee shop and with orders taken, Sue and I could foresee a busy week ahead to ensure all the Heroes had nice shiny tops to run in. It does feel like we are real running group now.

Wednesday 8th June 2016

A hot and misty run today and after giving it all I had I was very hot and sweaty at the end. I was delighted too that Team IAC were out in force and today a hat trick with Mike, Ross and my good self out on the streets all competing and supporting each other with each other via social media.

'and the scores are in' and I was delighted 'Fastest 5-7 miles' – get me!

Thursday 9th June 2016 - on yer bike.

Time for some more 'Sitting down exercise 'or cycling as it's better known. I took a break from running today and I got my bike out! I am a bit of a fine weather cyclist but with my trek to Mow Cop not too far away in the diary I needed to do a bit of training on the bike.

I knew that emotion and goodwill would not help me on the forthcoming bike ride that I had planned, so with that in mind, I biked to work.

A sombre ride into the office with my buddy in the final pages of his life, deep in thought, the country miles passed by. I wasn't short on company with plenty of folks out running today too and a few cyclists as well.

It was good to see some familiar faces up and out early this morning, Steve was burning up the pavements out for a pre work sprint session. Steve does have a happy knack of turning up looking every bit the athlete when I am bulging in my Lycra but he is a one of life's good guys and little did I know the role he would play in the follow years ahead.

Also out this morning was an old friend Alison, another amazing person from my past and who would also be there for me in the future. Fanatical squash player, Alison was off for her daily session on court in Warwick before cycling home to start a busy day. This lady is one of life's doers, always in thick of the good stuff of the action.

Although I did a lot of thinking, the time in the saddle was not all doom and gloom but more as a reality check and a kick up the arse along with a wakeup call to not put plans off to another day.

I love my journal and I love a plan as my family can testify so what's next as the man?

I arrived at work to see Mike's post on Facebook, my virtual running partner is in Sweden and has already been out for a run this morning and I loved his quote on social media.

'Everything has its perks, just got to be open to them.'

I love the sentiment, business travel is what you make of it, sit in a hotel bar and you might just not be cashing in on those hidden perks.

Saturday 11th June 2016 - The night before...

I run a lot and I like an event but I don't really race, it's all about the fun, the people and just getting out there for me!

I am never going to win and I am cool with that but I do have high hopes for tomorrow, this will be the tenth time I have entered the Two Castles. Back in 2005, the first time I was pleased with finishing in a respectable 59 minutes 27 seconds, under the hour. If you want to know my finish times for the eight races in-between, just pick a number between 55 minutes and an hour and a half.

One fact about my running is that I am never consistent run to run but today I did for once, feel ready.

Race days always feels different, I know the route and have ran the distance countless times before, but come the day I have the same old issues, needing the loo and taking on fluids on the route, two things that are rarely an issue on an average run.

Every ache and pain is always worse the day before race day, the approach seems to amplify any niggle or worry, no idea why.

Tomorrow will no doubt be the same, but I want to finish under the hour – no ifs, no buts and might just have to mean that for once I run my own race and just go for it.

I am pretty good at running other people's race and with hours to go, from the posts on Facebook, folks were already getting edgy.

Sunday 12th June 2016 - Cometh the hour, cometh the man.

Today is the day, I woke up with the usual aches and pains, typical of race day, and having done my usual pre run preparation, I was ready for a cuppa having drank a few beers last night and a glass or two of wine, so I need to hydrate a little and take on a few calories.

Breakfast was a couple of slices of Cotswold Crunch, Crustums finest bread made with flour ground at Charlecote Mill, a little village some five miles from home. Perfect with some of Julie's home-made marmalade - perfect pre run fodder and tasty, food of the gods.

By 7.45am, I had a plethora of runners outside the house and a queue of folks needing the loo, just in case.

The neighbours love me at the best of times with my early morning starts and a few extra cars outside the house must have been an added bonus.

Parking in town is always in short supply at the best of times but add thousands of runners and spectators in the mix and parking at mine was a far better option for my running buddies.

To assist with crowd control at the race start, access to Warwick Castle was limited to the runners with numbers on show and just one entrance open, of course the chosen entry point was the furthest from home. The walk taking us straight past the start line and across town and it would be over an hour before we get chance to cross the start line and see the castles South Gate again.

I always tend to give the old warm up a miss, I do not need any opportunity to demonstrate to the world that I lack any signs of rhythm or coordination and it's only 10k, so I plan to take it steady for the first few miles and then ease of for the remainder until the finish.

The gathering of a race start always makes me smile as runners of all shapes and sizes in every colour of lycra descend on our home town from side streets and alleys and as it's a little moist weather wise, a few of us have donned the bin bags to fend of the rain so at least we can start dry.

Unfortunately, after the long walk, I felt like a sweaty chip but at least I was warm.

The start seemed a long time coming this year as the organisers were trialing something new and did hinder the chance for a pre-race meet up and made the traditional group photo a nightmare.

Even with the five thousand participants, I did manage to touch base with a good few of my running buddies; this is the best bit for me.

I love the start of a race and as all races; I am yet again in 'panto' mode and just love to soak up the atmosphere.

Predictably, the air heavy with the combined aroma of Deep Heat and fear – love it!

I always make time to pray to Mum and this morning I feel ready and in the groove, today I will be running with Trish, my regular running wife and at last we were off and some hour and half after leaving home we triggered the timing mat and the clock starts.

Looking like a plague of insects, we spill out through the castle arch and on to the narrow streets of medieval of Warwick.

We were on our way, the crowds cheer and the rain came down, but it was smiles all the way.

Loads of support on route and jelly babies, I love jelly babies and before we knew it, the sounds of the finish become clear with the crowds lining the streets of Kenilworth ready to cheer us home.

Sub sixty minutes was the target and to the victor the spoils 59 minutes, 40 seconds, phew that was close but I was under the hour and I was happy with that.

As always, I call my wife to let her know I have made it to the finish in one piece and under my own steam and not in the back of an ambulance.

Today of all days, running and my great group of friends I have made from all those years of pounding the streets mean the world to me.

I chatted to Trish on the run about Ada and she could tell I was upset, little did I know what was going on a few miles away as we talked and what the rest of the day would bring....

The post euphoria of the run would not last long and after arriving home to the buzz of Facebook and race photos and messages I learn the sad news that my buddy Ada had passed away, bringing me straight back to earth with a bump, talk about a reality check! Ada, today's run is for you buddy.

I am going to need my running during the weeks ahead, but with that said, running was far from my mind for the rest of the day as plans needed to be made and I knew it would be tough.

Once I had gathered my thoughts and got showered, I dropped in on Geoff and Barbara, Ada's Mum and Dad, as I knew this would be a very difficult time for them and they would appreciate a friendly face.

Ada/Adrian's parents grew up though the horrors of the Second World War and have a different outlook to later generations, death is something that was the norm, but I could see Ada's death, although expected, had come as a shock.

From a passing comment that parents should not be going to the funeral of their offspring, I knew the loss had hit it home.

An impromptu meeting was arranged later the same day with Ada's sons and his ex to make arrangements, which brought forth some great humour out of a very sad time.

At the request of Matt and Oliver, Ada's sons, Allan and I would have roles at the service. Al would help carry the coffin and I had the daunting task to read the eulogy, a job that should be very easy for me as they were under the impression that I had recently been ordained as a vicar! I have no idea where that came from, but it seemed that I would make a good vicar, nice idea as they only work one day a week, bit like binmen...

I was honoured to be asked but immediately started to panic. The humour continued as we reminisced about our newly departed friend when out of the blue, one of Ada's sons confessed that they actually thought Allan and I were an item! So funny and it seems others thought the same, not sure what to say to be honest.

Looking back to our youth, we played a bit of squash, it was all the craze, but running hadn't really become trendy, jogging came along a little later.

I guess there have always been running or athletic clubs, but that was never part of my world, so the sport passed me by.

We did cross country at school because we had to but the thought of running for pleasure, I don't think so.

Such a missed opportunity and I feel that running would have been good back then, less cars on the road with some great places to run.

I did eventually get the bug and I feel fitter now than I did when I was in my mid-twenties. I think life was easier back then, no mobile phones, internet distractions and you could actually be out!

Thursday 16th June 2016 - Under the knife.

As a result of a legacy from my early twenties, today I make a return visit to the operating theatre to have my teeth sorted out.

A car accident back in the eighties which resulted in most of my front teeth ending up in the back of my friend Roger's forearm, means I need surgery under general anesthetic for the second time in the last twenty years for some preventive treatment if I stand any chance of eating solids in the future.

I have been through the same procedure before so I know exactly what to expect and enough to say, I did not relish the thought of looking and feeling like I had a good kicking with a mouth full of stitches as post op souvenirs.

To settle my nerves, I run, hoping to take my mind off the day ahead but little chance of that, however the fresh air was a welcome distraction.

Whenever I am scared or anxious, I retreat into myself. If I go quiet, it's a pretty sure sign that I am not happy.

As I waited in the cubicle in the day surgery unit, I could not read or do anything but run through the day ahead in my mind. I wanted to be back on the ward and back in the land of the living.

The distinct smell of a hospital is enough to raise my heart rate and once in the gown I was frightened and once in the pre op room, the staff of the hospital knew that I was frightened too.

Heidi the Anesthetist, I cannot believe I still remember her name, had the task of looking after me, working quietly away at my side. She set up the cannula that would be used to pump me full of sleep inducing drugs. I openly admitted that I was scared. I know she said, you are shaking.

'What do you like to done for fun Steve', she asked, 'I like to run' ...., before I finished the sentence, I was gone.

The next I remember was waking up in the recovery room and Julie was at my side, glad to be back.

I think going under general anesthetic is as close to the experience of death you can get. No dreams, no thoughts just nothing. I am glad that I did not find out for sure today and after a chat with the surgeon, I was glad to be on my way home.

I am not good at doing nothing and rarely do I ever give myself chance to recover, but today I had taken the day off. As it was a Friday, I was happy that limited backlog of work would wait until my return on Monday.

I don't really do 'ill' but for once following some good advice from my better half, I was happy to let the painkillers do their job and post op, I took to my bed and slept when I could.

With the traditional beat up face and a mouth full of stitches, I knew I would need to take it easy for a day or two.

Saturday 18th June 2016 - Need a little patience.

The next day I felt great, the doctor told me to take it easy for twenty fours hours and I did just that and obeyed the instructions almost to the minute.

I am not good at being a patient, but I was extremely impressed with myself. Once I was the other side of the slab, I was ok and happy to take time and just recover. I chatted to the girls but I slept the clock around. I was happy to be back on it once Saturday arrived.

Apart from a sore mouth and a fat lip, I felt fine, so I had a little run around the park.

Sunday 19th June 2016 - Who's the Daddy?

As it's Father's Day, the boys have it. Having left home and leaving a mantel piece full of cards and goodies, from my daughters, stepdaughters, grandchildren and the cats of course, I felt blessed as they say in Facebook land.

Being a father is one thing in my life that I would never change, to watch my children grow up is a huge part of my life.

Parenthood is not always easy, but to see the progression from little babies into strong independent young ladies is incredible and an experience I continue to relish.

With my family extended with stepdaughters along with grandchildren the fun will no doubt continue.

Monday 20th June 2016 - The longest day - in more ways than one.

I had plans for this morning and a bit of a tradition of mine for today is to run on the longest day. When I say run, I mean run to a hill and watch the sunrise, which does involve getting up at 3.45am and also requires Mother Earth to play her part too. I have been doing this crazy stunt for a few years and generally do my best to involve others so they can also have the opportunity to get up in the middle of the night and share a magical experience.

The summer solstice run has become a regular date in the running diary and always gets plenty of likeminded crazy fools to come along, however one attendee that is a little less reliable is the weather.

This morning nature did not want to cooperate and sent rain along instead, so with regret I stayed in bed after cancelling the event via good old Facebook.

This turned out to be a good call as the dark of night turned into grey with no sign of sun for most of the day.

A real shame as this is one of those special days that I spoke about in the very first few lines of this book. One downside of the summer solstice is that from tomorrow the days get shorter and the slow march to winter starts, don't depress me.

Friday 24th June 2016 - a week is a long time in politics...

A strange week and not really sure why, but I had lost my running mojo, it happens from time to time. Life gets in the way and I don't worry too much. A week without a run is rare these days but I never mind when it does.

The country had a referendum and runners run! I don't think anyone has a clue what the fuck we are voting for but for the record, I like being European.

As my older sister would say to me, if you are not sure what to do, do nothing. Not that I ever listen to her but maybe something our trusted leaders should think about as we are being led into the unknown. I think this debacle might run on a little longer I feel, reminding me a little of Hotel California, you can check out any time you like but you can never leave ...

As I put the final touches to this book some four years later, I think we have finally left Europe. I say think because the whole 'brexit' debacle as it became known seemed to go on forever but when we stopped being officially part of Europe at midnight on 31st January 2020 and a period of transition commenced but where that will, end who knows...

Saturday 25th June 2016 - Mow Cop here we come!

Today, and still with a mouth full of stitches, is the day I will follow in my Dads footsteps or wheels to be precise and head up north to fulfill the promise I made to my Dad back in 2015 on the night he gave up his fight and joined my Mum.

I was delighted to have Nigel and Mark keeping me company on this epic journey.

Nigel my partner in crime since the early eighties, together we have had some great adventures and he has always been with me when the going has not been so easy. Mark, a work colleague and good friend who signed up to join the outing immediately as I went public.

Leaving the cars at home, we cycled to the natural start point of the journey, number one, Dormer Place. My father's childhood home where he lived with his brother William (or Uncle Bill) and their Mum and Dad, Arthur and Elsie (my Grandma and Grandad), in a deceptively large end of terraced house with a walled garden next to the cinema.

Outside the house, three became five for the start of the journey meeting up with Phil and Matt who had agreed to join us for the first section of the route.

Ironically the first part of the journey took us past Westgrove House, the nursing home where in the early hours of 2nd July 2015, my Dad left this planet to go on an adventure of his own into the great unknown.

I found passing the home extremely moving and I did shed one of the many tears of the day, it felt like we were picking him up on the way to join the gang on the journey to guide the way.

Leaving Leamington and out on the cycle path past the Saxon Mill and a steady climb up into Kenilworth, where we made a scheduled stop at Crustums, where Nick, the local Artisan Baker had promised to sponsor the ride with one of his legendary flapjacks for every rider.

A welcome treat and much appreciated, we saved our delicious treats until later in the morning as we had only put five miles or so on the clock.

Staying off road whilst we could, taking the Greenway to Burton Green, the tree lined disused railway line, providing not only easy cycling but recently cut hedges giving the one and only puncture on the day.

At Burton Green, leaving the cycle path, we joined the quiet country lanes of Warwickshire, through Berkswell and into Meriden, the centre of England marked by a stone obelisk near another stone monument in memory of all the cyclists who lost their lives in the Second World War.

The route to Maxstoke was familiar as I travelled this route when I cycle to work in Coleshill but from here on in, it was uncharted territory.

Arriving in Shustoke and a spot of map reading provided a natural break for a flapjack and time for Matt and Phil to head for home.

I have made the journey to Newcastle under Lyme many, many times in my life but always by car. To embark on the same journey and not to attempt not to follow the busy A roads was more difficult than I thought.

Leamington to Mow Cop was a straight line on the map and we soon realised that to stay away from the traffic we would have to deviate from the line more than planned, adding unwelcome bonus miles to the trip.

The route inevitably took in many familiar places from numerous trips to see Aunts and Uncles as a child, skirting Lichfield with its iconic spires of the cathedral dominating the sky line before heading off to the next landmark town of Rugley where the skyline was dominated not by steeples but the cooling towers of the power station.

I had arranged for some great friends of mine, Lynn and Paul to join us for the later part of the ride however, the best laid plans of mice and men, somehow we had got the dates mixed up and Lynn was in the supermarket doing the weekly shop, when I called her to finalise our rendezvous. 'Oh shit' was her reply when I announced that we were on route and asked where we should meet.

I was disappointed but these things happen and sometimes you just have to get on with it and that's what we did.

Rugley was coffee time and standing outside Costa the stop provided time for some great stories and anecdotes. Nigel has some good tales to tell and it was also good to get to know Mark a little more and hear of his life, his hopes and dreams.

He is definitely one of life's givers and listening him talk about his family was touching.

Leaving the industrial bad lands and power station cooling towers that dominate the towns skyline behind us, we headed across Cannock Chase exchanging the town for open countryside, trees and undulations.

The war monument and graves providing a welcome distraction along the way with some more bonus miles and fast down hills.

I don't like down hills; I don't like losing control and I inevitably hang on the brakes to slow me down so not really taking advantage of the much need effects of gravity.

Just for the record, I am not a big fan of up hills either, but generally they hunt in pairs and one comes along with its mate, not far away, but the ups feel like they are always in the majority!

The approach to Stoke on Trent was very familiar, looking up to the left I could see the imposing statue of Josiah Wedgwood amidst the wooded hills, watching over the landscape and the pottery industry that brought jobs to the area with the famous blue and white bone china that immortalised his name.

As well as a popular item in china cabinet, it was my late Mums hometown.

The potteries, as the area is popularly known, taking a nod to the main local industry. Even the towns football team, Stoke City, has the nickname the Potters, which is keeping alive the connection to its heritage to this day.

In addition to Josiah Wedgwood, Stoke has a number of other famous sons, Stanley Mathews, one of the greatest footballers of all time and everyone's favourite boy band rebel, Robbie Williams, to name a couple more.

During my childhood, seeing the statue signaled that the journeys end was close, and we would soon be arriving at my favourite Aunties and we were indeed 'up north'.

Passing Trentham Gardens, the ride become interesting as we inadvertently found ourselves on the A500, the dual carriageway skirting the merging towns of Stoke and Newcastle.

I could see Saint Giles Church on the horizon, the church where my parents married, but unfortunately thanks to a sat nav mis guiding issue, my mind was focused more on survival rather that nostalgia as we played death or glory with the speeding traffic.

We had to get off the busy road, giving yet more bonus miles, but a price well worth paying.

Back on track, I felt that we were on the home stretch and when Mow Cop Castle came into view, our spirits lifted and we knew we had nearly made it.

With over 80 miles behind us and Dormer Place feeling like a lifetime ago, we made the final push for the top.

Mow Cop seemed to rise imposingly from the Cheshire plains and we soon ran out of gears on our bikes as we tackled the torturous incline with our legs screaming to stop.

Mark and I opted to walk a section of the climb, pausing for a photograph or two, always a great excuse to stop and catch a breath.

Looking back, the route we had travelled seemed to be laid out in front of us as if we've were looking at a three-dimensional map, to say it was breathtaking was an understatement.

Rest break over and back in the saddle for the last push to the top slowly catching up to Nigel, who heroically took the king of the mountain prize.

In sight of the castle and the top, one of the funniest things of the ride and will stayed with me as one of the great memories of the trip.

Passing one of the pretty cottages lining the winding road to the top, a resident canine, didn't much care for Nigel cycling past his house and ran out to see him off.

With the dog, snapping at his heels, our fellow cyclist was telling the stroppy pooch to return home.

'Fuck off, Fuck off' came the cries and Mark and I were in tears with laughter and it definitely helped complete the last few turns of the wheels to take us to the top of Mow Cop, the castle and our journeys end.

It was so funny but maybe you just had to be there!

As we turned into the castle's car park into the clouds, I could see the welcome sight of Richard Cox, my great friend and today our driver home. What was a complete surprised to see my cousin John Nolan, son of my favourite Auntie, and his wife Yolanda. I was not expecting that and so appreciated.

The tears flowed down my face as the emotion of the fulfilled promise made to my Dad sunk in.

After taking the time for some photographs and taking up the offer of a much appreciated beer from John, we headed home having left Leamington Spa approximately nine and a half hours before and cycled just over 85 miles.

The differences between our journey and that of my fathers was touched on many times during the ride.

Our bikes, lightweight with gears a plenty, energy drinks and gels, satellite navigation and Lycra. Whereas my Dad would almost certainly been on a steel framed Raleigh, maybe three gears if he was lucky and his mother Elsie I suspect would have sent him off with a packed lunch and maybe a flask of coffee or a bottle of council pop.

I wish I knew more about his journey, but it will certainly be something we have in common and will be something to talk about when we meet again.

A lesson that I have learnt from life and one of the reason that I had the urge this write this book was that memories do not last forever in the mind and with old age and sadly death, the hard drive of life is wiped. I take a lot of photos and glad I do as these are where the words are backed up by the images, especially when these days I struggle to remember what I had for breakfast, although I can sing along with songs from the eighties, almost word perfect.

What might surprise you is that I have embarked on this bike ride because I believed that my Dad did cycle to Mow Cop, I never questioned him, but had no idea why he would.

The reason came to light later the same day, the result of some combined family history research by John and my wife, Julie.

My Dad's Grandad lived in Mow Cop, so with money tight and time and youth on his side, he had travelled to see his Grandad, as simple as that!

Wednesday 29th June 2016 - Time to say farewell.

Today was going to be a tough day, 17 days since Ada gave up the fight, it was time to officially say our goodbyes.

I have the tough job of reading the eulogy and Allan, the equally hard job of carrying the coffin. Not sure I could do the whole coffin carrying thing, so I was honored to be able to say a few words.

Not sure how I was going to cope but the words I had written I hoped would mean something.

During his life, Ada had not set the world on fire, but he was so bloody contented, a trait I always admired him for. I was always too busy chasing my dreams or the next big one, but Adrian was happy with his lot and for that I was always full of admiration.

Although happy to be by my side, Julie stayed at home better to leave Allan and I to support each other on what would be a really difficult day. Looking back at the journal, the emotion was clear, I wrote :-

"Tough day ahead and I was glad that Allan was around. A sad day, but happy that Ade had a good send off. It was tough doing the tribute, but I think I managed ok. It has got to be one of the hardest things I have ever done, but it was an honour."

The tribute :-

'I am surprised to be asked to say a few words to be honest. I do not have a good track record for being reliable. Not a great photographer, family gatherings are not one of my specialties. I didn't cut the mustard as Ade's best man either I have been told. Although I managed all my duties at the church, I just about made the speeches before being taken home in a

drunken coma. All that aside, I am honoured to stand before you on this sad day to say a few words. You will have your own memories and thoughts, whether as a father, a mother, a brother, a relative, a neighbour or friend, keep them close to you.

I have had the pleasure of knowing Ade for over 30 years, from our late teens, not long out of school and working at our chosen professions. Adrian in the tool room serving an apprenticeship when England was still Great Britain, leading the world in skills and trades. Others, like myself, took a more office based route but we always had something to talk about.

Ade's passions, motorbikes, motorsport, music and beer, together we honed our life skills and shared new experiences home and away.

Seeing Glastonbury on the television over the weekend brought back happy memories, yes we went to Glastonbury before it was trendy.

I am sure that Jeff and Barbara thought then that they had more sons than just Ade and Paul, as Rose Villa was like a second home to some of us whether they liked it or not and I still think of them as my second Mum and Dad, even today.

Although life in later years has not been kind, as an understatement, Ade always found a smile when we caught up and was so proud of his boys and so he should be.

One thought I have whenever I think of Adrian was how bloody contented, he was, I always admired him for that. Whist we were all chasing the dream, Ade was happy to enjoy his life, his family and lived in the now, a great trait to have.

Happy that he is now at peace, so pick your favourite stripy jumper and keep him close, God bless you buddy.'

The rest of the week was a blur if I am being honest, the events of the previous weeks taking their toll on my head and if it was ever needed, reinforced my immortality, now really does mean now and no guarantee that tomorrow will come.

I was glad to see the arrival of a new month.

JULY 2016

Sunday 3rd July 2016 - Coffee always brings the folks out.

What a beautiful morning, the sky was blue, the birds singing and it's just perfect. These are the days when I just love to run and the gang must have thought the same, as it was a great turn out today and good number of cyclists too to keep the athletes company.

A great route today finishing at the back of the castle and loads of folks to talk to with a real mix of runners and great to meet Dudley.

Who is Dudley I hear you ask?

Well Our Dudley was a new recruit, I bumped into him in the churchyard of Saint James in Old Milverton. He was sat enjoying the tranquility of this beautiful location, drinking a glass of cider, I liked his style and we got talking and running came up in conversation, he was local and the rest as they say is history.

A good few folks wearing the Zero to Hero tops which was brilliant to see, and I feel at last that our little group has a true identity.

Thursday 7th July 2016 - Just gotta run!

I will apologise now and warn you that the next few paragraphs will be holiday based so if you are sat in the cold or wet when you are reading this, then this will either cheer you up or piss you off.

Today was the first morning of our holiday and I have just got to run. We arrived during the previous day and drank loads last night and I did not get up as early as planned, but while the resort rolled over and had a few more zzz's, I was out and at it.

This time of the day is my time, time to think, clear my head and just be me, a little on the warm side but brilliant nevertheless.

I love my family, my friends and my life, but those holiday miles in the trainers are just the best.

We are here on holiday in Menorca, not the first time for us. I have been to this beautiful island many times before, the first time back in 1985, when in a former life as we say, I needed to spend less time in the UK to avoid paying tax and headed for Menorca for some rest and relaxation as I was in the middle of one of my first major life adventures.

It was June 1985, I was 23 and after a convoluted series of events, chance meetings and friend of friend connections, I found myself living on the over side of the pond, in Detroit, Michigan USA.

During my time in the States and then a spell in Germany that followed once my US work visa ran out, I did a lot of growing up and learnt some great life skills along with honing my culinary repartee.

My weekly menu regularly included 'tuna surprise with sweet corn' and to mix it up a bit, I might have 'sweet corn surprise with tuna' the following night. These culinary delights were pretty much the extent of my cooking ability.

I have improved over the years you will be glad to hear, and I have progressed to more adventurous recipes, good job, I guess.

Along with domestic ability that would help me through life, I made some great friends and travelled to some great places for which I am grateful. John, one such work colleague in the states with whom I am still in contact with some thirty-five years later.

When my time in the States came to an end, John wrote some haunting words in my leaving card that I will never forget, *'Good to meet, sorry to part, good to be together'*.

In my early twenties, John's words were touching and heartfelt but years on, they mean much more to me.

The price of being together is having to say goodbye which is why time with those close to us is so important.

Back in the Eighties, I hardly ever ran although I did take part in a fun run at the Michigan Country Show, a short jog around the local area with a bunch of mainly kids who if I recall correctly soon left me behind.

I have a photograph of me crossing the finish line taken by my long serving partner in crime, Nigel. I look like I am leading the field with no one behind me but in truth, I think I was at the back, but run I did in the pouring rain and got the bling and a T- shirt if my memory serves me right.

So back to Menorca, on my first visit to this beautiful island, we hired a scooter and on an evening before heading out for dinner, I would ditch the crash helmet and travel the coast path and find my thoughts.

By the time I returned in 2012, I had found the love of running, so bereft of the scooter, I retraced my steps on the coastal routes, this time on foot rather than two wheels. Returning to a familiar place, it felt like coming home. I love this island and is one place I could live and maybe one day we will.

The plan is hopefully to end our days with a bit of sun on the old bones, but the idea is still very much a work in progress.

People must think I am crazy, non-runners will do for sure, but I love to head out before it gets light and run to meet the sun. It is the best feeling ever and holiday running is my time to do this along with a chance to check out the area and to find new places that I can later take the family or sometimes I just to keep to myself.

I loved todays run, lots of people out doing the very same thing and a chance to get some local knowledge and route suggestions, I love the smile that most fellow runners give you, almost like you have a secret , a bit like the Freemasons, maybe we should have a special handshake or something.

I stayed local today, a chance to reacclimatise and check out what has changed since our last visit. The apartment that we have rented, Maghen, is brilliant, high up above the bay of Playa Arenal d'en Castell with a pool and courtesy of El Mirador, the restaurant next door, free WiFi.

Friday 8th July 2016

I was running somewhere new today, heading left rather than right along the coast path this morning towards Arenal de Son Saura, the terrain was proper ankle breaking territory and so many runners out and along with a few morning strollers as well.

These are the days that make me buzz and feel so alive. It's warm and I am a bit sweaty, but I like to get a few miles under the belt before the little beach town wakes up and the sun really turns up the heat, the route was unfamiliar, so I did not want to get to lost and I felt a bit of research was required.

On my return to the apartment, I took in the boardwalk, a new addition to Playa Arenal d'en Castell since our last visit, almost at sea level at the base of the cliffs so a little sheltered from the sea breeze which really adds to the air temperature a few degrees.

I really enjoyed running on this wooden walkway, the aroma of sun baked pinewood fills the air which was lovely and does remind me of running in Sweden on the boardwalks around Arendal, the commercial district of Gothenburg. But considerably warmer today than my last run in Sweden back in January, now that was a cold one!

Got to thinking of Ada today, I had thoughts of going to the peninsular overlooking the bay later and place a stone on the growing pile, this one's for you buddy.

I know the activity of 'rock stacking' is not widely appreciated but in its place, I like the sentiment. I think it nice to leave a stone, one on top of another as a subtle reminder that I have been.

Saturday 9th July 2016

I am on holiday and plan to run every day and today, I was up just after dawn and I was on a mission and planned to take a trip down memory lane, but with a twist.

From the balcony of our apartment, we can see a villa across the bay on the headland of Punta Grosse, the peninsula where all the 'poor' people have their villas, but one particular property stands on its own and has the air of mystery about it, windswept and isolated. My plan for today's run was to go and take me a look.

Leaving the small groups of villas, some holiday lets, others are second homes and in many of the villas, folks actually can call the place home.

The villa I wanted to investigate was very understated, away from rest and perched on the rugged cliffs alone above the crashing waves. There was something mysterious, almost magical about the place, the location in sight of the bright lights of Arenal d'en Castell but sitting alone, very much happy in its own splendid isolation, was clearly making a statement and I love it.

Getting close to the villa, I could read its identity, *'Niu de S'Aguila'*, I feel the name gave a nod to a beach in Ibiza, a local beach for the inhabitants of the fincas, or old holiday homes which are on top of the cliff, a beach to which hardly anyone else comes.

Are you on the same page as me?

I could see that the villa was in need of some love and attention or maybe the owners have done a good job of bedding the place down for the spring destined to return for the remainder of the summer staying on to winter in the sun.

All these theories racing around my head but to be honest, I will never know, but for sure I will check the place out on a future visit to the island.

As I run, I feel a plan coming together, slowly oh so slowly but a plan never the less. Julie is a different person in the summer and the warmth does her a world of good. Does us both good to be honest and the more I think, maybe a place in the sun is the answer but that's for another day and another book.

I ran alone today, must either have been earlier than normal and it is the weekend or maybe I was running just off the beaten track as I was pretty much in the middle of nowhere.

The route was rugged and a similar type of terrain as before but today I thought, 'what if I took a tumble?', although I always carry my phone mainly to take photos and of course capture those precious stats. But when I think too hard, some of these island runs are pure bone shattering especially when 15 ½ stone hits the deck, it's going to hurt, bones will break, and the blood will flow but I know the game.

I might just let Julie know my planned route in future, just in case.

However, I know that close enough to the edge, is a good place to be and always more space at the edge and that is where the good stuff is and place to breath.

The tranquility does not last for long and grateful to be still in one piece, I am soon back in the thick of life and people, and home to a lovely glass of freshly squeezed orange juice.

Same time tomorrow? You bet ya!

I have a plan for my run tomorrow – Na Macaret, one of my favourite places in the world and my planned destination for the morning.

Sunday 10th July 2016 - Maybe tomorrow.

Best laid plans of mice and men or roughly translated to 'I didn't quite make it to Na Macaret this morning.'

The bed won the battle and had a lie in so was a little bit warmer when I finally laced up my trainers and headed out of the apartment. I did run a little further than planned but the beautiful little village of Na Macaret eluded me this morning.

Today the run was all about the stunning flowers, beautiful smells and a spot of villa spotting. I learnt a new technique today, wall running having been given a crash course from a local dog, or two to be accurate and what a great way to cover distance away from the roads.

Running on a two foot wide wall was a little intensive with an element of risk and did focus the mind, but I did feel like I was heading somewhere, walls do that. Although they act a boundary marking where one place ends, a wall can also act as an artery leading to a road or lane.

I like the feeling of connecting and generally but not always walls end up at a road or track, crudely constructed and not always in the best of condition so keeps you on your toes. The added elevation gives a better perspective and feels like sticking a finger up to the man, but not quite breaking the law.

Over the years, I have been fortunate to run in some beautiful places with some wonderful people. I have run in some pretty scary places too.

One of my favourite countries to run in is Egypt, before all the troubles brought an end to our regular winter visits to this wonderful country, I was in my element.

The variety is great whether staying in the tourist areas running is a dream, great paths along the beach or out into the sea along the jetty's that seem to go for miles out into the turquoise sea. Running along a wooden boardwalk was something else, but certainly messes with your head.

But for me, the best runs are when you climb the fence marked 'keep out' and you get to run with the skeletons of old tanks in places where you know you shouldn't be.

A little less risky was heading to the back streets of Old Sharm, this was like running on an Indiana Jones film set.

It was in Egypt that I met Pippa, my new holiday running buddy from Plymouth. She was also staying at our hotel with her husband Sam.

We did ever so slightly draw attention to ourselves taking selfies with the local street cleaner under the watchful eye of a lorry load of fresh faced soldiers.

Our antics made us stick out like a sore thumb but also our appearance, running in shorts and a clearly European running top and Pippa a bare legged lady, not that anyone needed any more evidence that we were not local, it was pretty obvious.

Running in Turkey with Libby was another special place and the making of lasting memories, escaping from our all-inclusive hotel before breakfast and exploring the local villages. Nice to get away from the beaten track finding new trails and new places to see.

Cape Verde is where I really stand out but more about that later in the year when we return in the autumn, watch this space folks.

I love to run on holiday and give me time to think, to dream and I love to run with the sun on my back. But best of all I like it for the person I am afterwards.

I have ran a few times in Menorca in the past and in this area too, so I took a trip down memory lane this morning and ran around and about Noves Coves, our old hotel Marina Parc which we visited with the girls back in 2012.

As for running to Na Macaret, maybe tomorrow...

Monday 11th July 2016 - A spot of wind.

I will run in all weathers, which is part of the appeal of the sport for me, adding a bit of variety but I do make the exception. I do not like windy days, of which I have never really a big fan. The weather was showing signs of changing, but today was just a breeze so fingers crossed it stayed that way.

I had a run with a purpose today as I had to sort out the admin for a of car we had arranged to hire for later in the week. Once I had worked out the location of the car rental company, I was off exploring.

I had a place on my list that I wanted to check out - Cala Moli, I have seen the signs but never got to see what the place had to offer.

I thought it was just an extension of Na Macaret but little did I know and a surprise was just around the corner.

With no real village centre, Cala Moli was pretty much a selection of villas but the magic was all about the water.

A selection of stunning properties around a little inlet, full of boats and not much else, but to say it is stunning does even get close.

Heading down the gaps between the villas, perpendicular to the road, short tree lined steps lead to the waters edge and on to short jetties lined with small boats.

Heading down one of these little paths for the first time, paradise opened up before my eyes, I was lost for words, this isn't the place for swanky yachts, Cali Molí is all about having fun and maybe a bit of fishing.

I intended to run back down the main road to get back to the apartment but with the help of a local runner, who I ended up inevitably following a few paces behind, I found a cross country short cut across some scrub land over grown with wild oregano and rosemary dotted with pine trees adding a little shelter from the rising morning sun, I shall take advantage of this great little find in the days ahead.

One of the great thing about this holiday is after the run, trainers off, strip down to my base layers (ok my pants) and straight into the pool and life does not get much better than this.

Running in a new place is a little like flying a kite, you start with a short string or staying local and let out a little line bit by bit and before you know it you are away from the familiar and into the good stuff, the new places and the surprises and just like flying at kite, the string gets longer, the more exciting the activity becomes and so does the length of the run.

Tuesday 12th July 2016 - mission accomplished.

The day, although only just light, was showing all the signs of being a hot one so I was happy that I made an early start as I wanted to get to Na Macaret via Cali Moli returning via my new little route through the trees before the temperatures started to climb.

The morning was just beautiful and arriving in the little fishing village of Na Macaret at first light was just a perfect time of the day. The brilliant white rows of quaint fisherman's cottages leading down to the beach, the sea was like a mill pond, the colours like a painter's pallet.

There was some really interesting folks out and about this morning in this part of town off the tourist path. I greet locals with my best and only Spanish word 'hola 'and inevitably I get a 'good morning' back in return, although some of the people look Spanish, in fact many are England along with an eclectic mix of nationalities.

As I was a little off the beaten track but knew where I wanted to go, I stopped and asked for directions from a very helpful gentleman who was English and told me that he had owned the villa for 20 years overlooked the bay. A very lucky man and was happy to tell him although I feel sure he already knew that, I was hoping for an invite for a cuppa but not today.

Just beautiful and lovely to see the locals just getting on with life, a swim, a stroll to get some fresh bread or maybe a spot of fishing. A young girl, not much older than 11or 12 was preparing freshly caught fish watched by a group of hopeful seagulls hoping for a taste of the catch of the day.

Almost floating along in the morning sunlight, dressed in white, a lady of a certain age was enjoying the moment. Nicki only asked me if I had tried the local restaurant, and had my life story… I am bet she was glad she asked!

Having said good morning to Na Macaret, I left the village along the coastal path, following the red signposts along the edge of the water to Cali Moli shaded from the rising sun by pine trees, before taking the back route into town to 'downtown' Na Macaret.

If you ever visit this beautiful place, my description will make you smile, let me know.

Na Macaret, a little fishing village which is very important in our family story when, at a family dinner back in 2012, we floated the idea that Julie and I were thinking of getting married with my daughters.

A little nerve racking I can tell you, but over a lovely meal and a glass of something nice, I am happy to say that the motion was carried unanimous and the rest is history.

Wednesday 13th July 2016

Every morning, I have a decision to make - right or left, today it was right which is generally the direction of choice most days.

Once that is sorted, I then have a myriad of other options but I like going onto the peninsula that embraces the bay of Arenal d'en Castell.

I like the way the sea seems to be around every turn in one form or another, whether the calm clear turquoise waters around the pine tree lined bay or the wild swell crashing on the rocks at the foot of the unsheltered cliffs, I love the ever changing vista.

I threw caution to the wind again today and headed out along the cliff edge paths, with the sun on my skin and the smell of the sea, life does not get much better than this.

Thursday 14th July 2016 - The bed won!

A change in the weather brought wind, I will run and do run in all weathers (snow is a bit of a favourite) but I do not care for the wind. I am not talking about a bit of a breeze but when it's blowing a hoolie!

I could hear the wind whistling outside from under the sheets and my motivation was going have its work cut out if I was going to beat the battle of the bed.

I am not sure what it is about wind, but it really seems to get under my skin and makes me anxious.

So today, well this morning at least I did not run, opting for my bed instead, I will regret this later for sure but for now, what is done is done.

Weather does have an impact on the running mood and for the record, I didn't run although I had every intention to lace up the trainers later in the day after a day by the pool, but ... didn't.

Friday 15th July 2016

I put myself under pressure today and with only a few days of the holiday remaining and after a missed opportunity the day before, I had to run and try to ignore the wind and headed for Grosse Point.

The sky was blue, the sun was out but the air moist with sea mist but boy oh boy was it still blowing a bit. I don't like the wind as I have said, but love the dramatic effect it has on the sea but not getting too close to the edge as I might get blown away – fat chance of that!

I know the wind is strong but this ain't Kansas and I am certainly no Dorothy not even at the weekend.

Blown the cobwebs away, I certainly did and all set for a day in the sun, but with the end of the holiday growing ever closer and with only five runs left, I need a plan.

Saturday 16th July 2016

The weather was changing again and with just a breeze this morning, I had no excuses to stay in my bed and I wanted to test my new multi-purpose headband. Not really wanting to make a fashion statement, my purchase was made on practically rather than style and this piece of fabric is so versatile.

On the top of the small headland we can clearly see from our balcony, a french tricolour had appeared, on further investigation the reason became all to apparent...

On the evening of 14 July 2016, a 19-tonne cargo truck was deliberately driven into crowds of people celebrating Bastille Day on the Promenade des Anglais in Nice, France, resulting in the deaths of 86 people and the injury of 458 others. The driver was Mohamed Lahouaiej-Bouhlel, a Tunisian resident of France. The attack ended following an exchange of gunfire, during which Lahouaiej-Bouhlel was shot and killed by police.

Islamic State claimed responsibility for the attack, saying Lahouaiej-Bouhlel answered its 'calls to target citizens of coalition nations that fight the Islamic State'.

I have never ventured off the road at that end of the bay before so I was happy to have a bit of an explore hoping to get a good view of town looking inland but I had to but a bit of work in first.

I started the short ascent to the top heading for the flag as a focal point doing a bit of run/walking, careful of my step as this is proper ankle breaking territory and I did nearly lose my footing - phew!

Arriving at the top and with my thoughts of the tragedy in France, I took some time to reflect on this crazy world. Placing a stone on top of the ever growing pile, taking my photos (the view was actually better in my head) before taking my time to return to the road, grateful for all I have and happy to be back with the family and the promise of a cool beer in a frosty glass.

Sunday 17th July 2016 - How committed are you?

Yet another thoughtful run today taking me out to Grosse Point and a trip down memory lane. I remember doing this route many times back in 2012 and four years on, I cannot help thinking what a very lucky and I must say a slightly different person.

But before I share today's outing, I have a question to ask you, the reader...

'What do you do on holiday and how committed are you in finding the good stuff ?'

We are on holiday on the beautiful island of Menorca but you know that already, we have spent nearly two weeks in a great apartment overlooking the stunning bay of Arendal and all the lovely things that comes with it. The apartment has three bedrooms a double with a view over the bay and a twin plus a tiny room with a set of extremely rickety bunk beds, the room which we affectional call 'the bunker'.

I love running at first light so the night before, so as not to wake up my good lady, at bedtime I head for the bunker.

My alarm set for 6am just like a work day and my route all mapped out in my head. I want to run at dawn out to Port Addaia skirting Punta Grossa, Cala Moli and around around the bay back to base for 7.30am for a full English and yet another frosty beer.

What a great run, full of memories plus making plenty more along the way with the bonus of a fully loaded breakfast. Not something I do everyday, even on holiday which makes it even more special, cheers!

Monday 18th July 2016 - Hidden treasure.

I did not quite get to where I wanted yesterday and finding a way to get to Port Addaia without going down the road unfortunately eluded me but after the obligatory run to my favourite place, Na Macaret, I found some where new, a little off the beaten track and a great little bit of treasure.

A little foot back, away from the road, following the waters edge around the inlet, undulating and lined by pine trees, the smell was incredible no doubt helped by the first rays of the sun gently burning off the morning dew. This was my hidden treasure and was something else, the aroma lingered in my nostrils as I returned along the coast path back to base.

Why does the path have to go so close to the edge? I like a view but I am not great with heights, slow going today but lovely nevertheless and I did get to see the sunrise from a different location and so lovely to be running before the sun made a guest appearance, cool and fresh but once the sun was out of its bed the temperature went up like turning on the grill, lovely to be out before the world wakes up.

By the time I had taken the detour down my new little road, I was longer than expected and Julie was worried. I do kind of forget myself and along with the time to a lesser degree as the miles fly by.

Funny how your mind works, the main thoughts on the run today were randomly about my apprenticeship at IHW Engineering some forty year ago and my first bosses Phil and Colin. I dreamt that I met up with Colin, he looked the same, must have been the red wine!

I have no clue where thoughts came from although I shouldn't be surprised as I have some great memories of my early working life.

These gents have got to be in there eighties now and I ponder if they are still alive, do I want to find out?

I am not sure I really want to see them old, I want to remember them as they were and that might be something to do with my age too as I don't see anything good about the march of the years.

I could ramble on about my youth and my days at IHW and maybe I might do that, but today's thoughts were all about these two fellows. Phil was the boss, smoked a pipe and barely said to two words to me all my time I worked for him.

I hadn't been at the company very long and Phil called me over. I was absolutely thrilled, 'I have got a job for you' announced my boss. I stood in front of him, in my shirt and kipper tie, poised.

To my surprise he thrust a few quid in my sweaty hand, 'can you pop up the shop and get me some tobacco', and with that request I knew my position in the pecking order was established.

Now going off completely off at a tangent, IHW was a small family business and whole families work there, which was the norm back in the day.

I did get to know Phil and Colin's families and it was not uncommon for our little office to have visitors. Phil had a daughter Jenny, who would pop in sometimes after school to see her dad, occasionally with her mate.

To give you an idea of the time frame, this was the late seventies, the sex pistols were in the charts, James Callaghan was prime minister, the Queen was celebrating her silver jubilee and the IRA were leaving bombs around the country.

Now roll the clock forward to the noughties, you are not going to believe this, but Jenny's mate was none other than my lovely wife Julie, you could not make it up.

We didn't make the connection until recently and for the record, we both went unnoticed to each back then.

Colin was a polar opposite to Phil and it is to him that I owe so much. He taught me, guided me and did all he could to keep me on the straight and narrow, not an easy task with my good-self in my testosterone fueled prime, long hair and a partial to a beer or two.

Ex airforce, Colin was a brilliant, his draughting skills, perfection, technically a genius and a gentle gentleman and most of all, he believed in me.

I never got to tell him how much I appreciated his support and the part he played in my life.

Although as people, they were very different, on leaving IHW, first Phil then Colin, they both headed overseas to chase the big money leaving me without a boss for a while and boy did I grow up quick.

Interesting that years later I followed then into the world of contracting and the rest is history.

Music has always been a massive part of my life, it can take you back to places and events better than anything else I know.

I find it incredible that I can sing along to songs from forty years ago, pretty much word perfect but I cannot remember what I had for my breakfast.

I had a bit of music on the run today for a change and plugged my 'ears' in and listened to a bit of Marillion, the classic Misplaced Childhood, the third studio album by one of my favourite pro-rock band released in 1985, now I feel old.

This iconic album is one of many that have made up the soundtrack of my life and as I listened and reminisced, I shed a tear or two thinking of my old mucked Ada. Lavender, a track from the same album was played at his funeral, so as I looked ahead and pondered my future and what lie ahead.

In addition to tooting forward, I took a moment or two to look back not only on all the great memories of my life so far but also with thoughts of unfulfilled dreams, missed opportunities and a Misplace Childhood.

Tuesday 19th July 2016 - counting the hours.

It's our last full day on this beautiful island and we have every intention of making the most of it. I personally haven't left anything to chance and I had a plan.

This morning I ran to Punta Grosse saving the Cala Moli/Na Macaret run for tomorrow as it has definitely become my favourite route of the holiday.

I like the space running out on to the peninsula of Punta Grosse offers, a great combination of ostentatious villas with stunning bay views in contrast to the barren cliff top paths, dotted with understated properties of the beaten track and quietly enjoying the splendid isolation.

Which do I prefer, the answer depends on the day of the week and my mood.

Wednesday 20th July 2016 - The last run!

Today we go home so I was up with the sun and out the door heading to Na Macaret combining all my favourite routes from the last two weeks into one last treat and it was just stunning.

I am really sad to go home and climb back onto the wheel but unfortunately this is the price you have to pay.

This has been a top holiday and so nice to spend lots of great time together, great food, plenty of running, a beer or two and lovely to get some sun on the old bones.

Lots of runners out today but wanted to keep them all at arm's length although I generally like the company, this morning's run was all about me.

I could not go home without going back to Na Macaret and to say my goodbyes to this idyllic location, standing on the edge of the water, looking out to the horizon and the rising sun, it's just heaven.

I am not sure how long I paused with my thoughts, I was not clock watching this morning, although we had a plane to catch we had time for a leisurely start to the day. Cala Moli was one of the finds of the holiday for me and another must for today, then back across the cliff tops on my new little short cut with the heavenly smell of wild oregano and rosemary just added to the ambience.

Contented and all set for the journey home, Menorca, we will be back and maybe the place We end our days.

Saturday 23rd July 2016 - Home Sweet Home.

No it's not a spelling mistake, back from an amazing holiday to what would turn out to be a very stressful couple of weeks when we would become on first name terms with the local steak house as the ground floor of our home became a building site. With the kitchen out of action and the lounge a warehouse I needed to get out and clear my head, good to be back on home turf too.

Sunday 24th July 2016 - the corn is as high as an elephants eye...

I could not resist a quote from the timeless musical 'Oklahoma', summer running and great to catch up with the Sunday gang, off road running though the corn, hot and sticky but so much fun.

The well-trodden path through the man high corn perfectly framed one of the best views of the majestic Kenilworth Castle and a perfect end to a great trot out with the heroes.

This is always a popular route with the gang and will not be the last time you will hear about this one.

Tuesday 26th July 2016 - A bridge too far.

Having only just returned from holiday, I thought an early morning run was a perfect opportunity to show off my tan.

After a couple of weeks apart, it was good to get out with the Warwick crew and with the horse racing course on the doorstep, a couple of loops of the circuit was just what the doctor ordered.

I like running here but we always end up with getting wet feet as apart from the main access point to the caravan club and the driving range, most paths into the common ground in the centre of the course go over the grass which is never cut that short for obvious reasons and is green and lush but doesn't half hold the water.

After a few weeks away, it was good to catch up with John, Michaela and Ian but very nearly ended in tears as we had only just left the housing estate and still within sight of the road, John managed to push a trainer'ed foot through a wooden bridge over a little stream.

Not sure how he did it and even more surprised that he didn't break is leg, I will never know but he managed to unhook his leg from the hole as he fell.

With the potential disaster behind us, we headed out for a couple of circuits of the racecourse with wet feet of cause.

Saturday 30th July 2016 - 'When you get there, remember where you came from.'

Sometimes you have to take yourself away from the norm just to see what's what and that was the plan for the weekend.

The kitchen was in the final stage of completion but not quite finished, so we headed to Noss Mayo in Devon, a beautiful little fishing village on the banks of the River Yealm to just get away from it all leaving the kitchen chaos, the boxes and the dust behind.

I love it near the sea and such a beautiful part of the country once you get away from the M5 motorway.

This was the first time I have ever been to Noss Mayo and not that different to some of the beautiful little back waters of Menorca just a few weeks back but a few degrees cooler unfortunately, but this is the great British summer.

Having arrive late the night before to the Garden Flat, when it was pretty much dark. I could not wait to get my trainers on and get out and about.

Today's run was going to be a good one, I just followed my nose, along the road, well lane, actually a wide path to be accurate to find new and unexplored routes. The run started well, along the banks of the River Yealm from out little retreat leaving behind just the pub on our side of Newton Creek. There were shops and everything across the water, a proper metropolis but a visit to the other side would have to wait until later in the day.

As I headed though the woods towards the sea, every noise seemed to carry, conscious it was only seven am in this sleepy part of the world.

The tide was going out and the river was becoming more like stream and taking clues from the retreating, I headed out to find the sea, but once I was in the woods, I could have been anywhere, what happened to my sea view?

On the edge of the woods I came to a gate and intended to turn back before I completely lost track of the time and equally as important my bearings and sense of direction.

This would not be the first time I have got lost so always keep an eye on the route home. From the first gate, I could see another gate some half a mile away at what look like the opposite side of the woods, backlit by day light.

I had to go and see what was past the second gate and I am so glad I did.

Once through the gate and leaving the trees behind me, the path opened up and from was so far a woodland run, the terrain changed and transformed into to the south west coastal path and to my delight, in front of me the sea.

That's enough exploring for today and happy with my mission accomplished, I turned tail and headed for home, back in the groove and downhill all the way – always a bonus.

By the time I returned to the Garden Room, the river had become shrunk to little more than a trickle marooning the boats of all shape and sizes on the mud to wait the tides return later in the day.

Although I have never been to Noss Mayo before, I have ran in this area, back in 2014 we had a great family holiday in this cottage next of the woods, about three miles away as the crow flies in a place called Kingston but by car add another nine miles to the journey.

That holiday two years ago gave me one of my favourite runs of all time, a run with a purpose.

I had worked up to it all week and near the end of the holiday I was ready. Heading out from our cottage on the outskirts of little village of Kingston to Bigbury on Sea, some 4 miles away along the undulating coast path with Burge Island as my point of reference in the distance.

The best part of the run was knowing that Julie would be waiting for me at the end.

My focal point, just in case I got lost was Burge Island, whose claim to fame was the islands hotel which was the back drop for the Agatha Christie 1939 novel 'ten little niggers 'or 'and then there were none 'as it was renamed in 1940 for the American audience.

The island was my constant beacon to the finish line and my baby however the rugged terrain had other ideas with is harsh inclines and tough climbs with a hidden cove or two taking the island out of sight on occasion along with testing my climbing skills, at times I end up on all fours clambering like a little monkey.

I like an A to B run, no turning back, a mission and the woman I love at the end, what else would a man want?

Sunday 31st July 2016 - 'the best is yet to come.'

I had a really nice and unexpected surprise last night, as we sat watching the sun go down over the creek with a glass of wine, Julie gave me a present, a new journal and on the cover a quote, you guessed it, *'the best is yet to come.'*

Perhaps this might be the title of a future book maybe this one as I think the title of this book. I am still using a working title but by the time you read this, I hope I will have it sorted.

Today's run, the last one in Noss Mayo before heading home was a real 'follow my nose job', I had a rough idea where I wanted to end up but instinct started to kick in, out through the village and then up, up and up!

The village was just waking up, barking dogs and the smell of bacon which has got to be one of the best smells in the world which always gets the taste buds going.

As I made my way through the sleepy backstreets, I met women in their dressing gowns out walking yapping dogs and runners - bloody loads of them.

On the edge of the village at the top of the lane a group was gathering. I was hoping they were heading my way and would appreciate the company, along with the opportunity to glean some local knowledge but alas they headed off in a different direction.

Not a problem though as my instinct paid off and after a few more twists in the lane and more ups, did I mention all the ups? I could see the sea.

A quick nip over the fence and across a farmers field and I was on the coastal path and familiar landmarks. To be out on the cliff tops on such a beautiful morning was just stunning, I do love being by the seaside.

Today was a missed opportunity as my running buddy from Egypt, Pippa was close it seems, as the crow flies at least although with the rugged coast line, a little further away that I thought, maybe next time.

August 2016

Tuesday 2nd August 2016

Waking up to a very wet start to the day, I was tempted to 'bomb out' of the dawn run this morning and stay in bed, but having arranged to meet the gang, I did not want to let anyone down.

Driving across town to start the run in Chase Meadow gives the opportunity for some variety to the routes on offer and today we opted to run a bit of a favourite. Venturing out of town provided a chance to leave the hustle and bustle of the working day behind, well at least for a little while.

Heading across the busy M40, already bumper to bumper with commuters queuing to climb on to the treadmill, and I ventured out into the stunning Warwickshire countryside heading down Fulbrooke Lane towards Hampton Lucy.

The 'Monks Retreat' as we call it, or the Forest Hermitage to give it its correct title, our usual turning point before heading for home retracing our steps.

The Forest Hermitage is a branch of Wat Nong Pah Pong, the late Luang Por Chah's principal monastery in north east Thailand. A small, peaceful Buddhist retreat in the Heart of England. I always fancy paying a visit, but it's the fear of the unknown that stops me going.

The rain clouds passed over and the ran back skirting the beautiful village of Sherbourne, with the Victorian Gothic church of All Saints, built in the 1860's, silhouetted on the horizon by the hazy rising sun. Accompanied by the pungent aroma of cows made for a lasting memory and to be honest, I didn't want the run to end.

The run to the Forest Hermitage and back is very similar to that of the route from Kenilworth to Ashow, as the A46 dual carriageway and the little bridge provide the gateway between the present and the past on that run, the A429 does the same job on this route.

The area still retains an air of mystery with a myriad of 'goings on' and rumours providing the backbone of local gossip. Like all good stories, facts shouldn't get in the way of a good story.

Crossing the busy A429 and back into Chase Meadow, we soon return to the 21st century and the rat race as all good things, it seems, have to come to an end.

Saturday 6th August 2016 - variety is the spice of life.

I was mixing it up a bit today, I really miss my running of late with life just getting in the way, but today was special. I had a list of things to do as long as my arm and the look on my face in the mirror suggested that the signs of panic we starting to show.

I was desperate to run but I was on the verge of aborting the idea to get stuff done instead, but Julie had also spotted the tell-tale signs of panic and I was urged to go for a run.

The thought of a list and no run was more than she was prepared to cope with and I was just short of being pushed out the door.

I had a plan, a couple parcels had to be collected but the post office did not open to 8.30am and I also wanted to do the 'bun run'. With the timing not quite working I thought I would get the bread first, then run ended up back in time for the office to open - that would work.

I got my bread, a real treat at the weekend is a loaf from my favourite bakers and by 8 o'clock, I was back in
Warwick, parked up outside the post office.

I planned to run a route that I have not done for ages, I love the view of Warwick that the elevation offers of the run offers and it was worth the climb.

The original plan was to do run for 15 minutes then turn back and by which time it would be 8.30 and the post office would be open. But the sun was out and I lost all sense of time.

According to my plan, my time was up and I had managed to make it to the top of the hill for the view and should have turned back. But what if I go just a little further, take a left turn and I should cut the corner and I will be alright, just a little later than intended.

A break from tradition this morning as I was listening to my iPod, I am not a great fan of listening to music on a run but today I made an exception. I like to read, a pastime usually reserved for holidays when the family are actually shocked when I actually finish a book. If it's fiction then double shocked as I tend to read either motivational or autobiographical, however just occasionally I do like a story.

Sometimes I like to 'read' in the car, ok it's not really reading, that will be listening to an audiobook to be precise, but who gives a shit.

I have two books on the go moment, a real book: 'Detour de force' which I manage to read about two pages a day and in the car, an audiobook 'the ghost runner' a true story written by Bill Jones about John Tarrant, which would be my companion on today's run, a great story. Very sad but well worth a read.

Turning left, the route was not as straight forward as I had hoped and did not get me back to the Post office for opening time but what the hell, its weekend.

As I listened to the life's story of John Tarrant and how on his honeymoon, he was getting into a bit of bother with his new wife in Blackpool (not like that!) as he had packed his trainers and was off out for a run before breakfast, I could empathise with him.(you need to read the book)

I was going to get in a bit of bother too to be honest but I didn't really care – ask for forgiveness rather that permission I was told once by a chap once on his third or fourth marriage, but I knew Julie would understand and she knows what I am like.

The route was stunning, the rolling countryside of Warwickshire opened up before me and I was on the top of the world and the sun shone and I had bread, but I just needed to pick up the parcels…

Julie was ok with me being a little late and with stuff to do at home, it was some hours later that I finally took off my running gear and had a shower. Flowers bought, allotment dug, cats collected and at around 7pm, the sweaty lycra hit the washing basket and time for a glass of red.

Contented that I had successfully given my 'to do list' a run for its money and I was happy.

Sunday 7th August 2016 - home or away?

I like days like this, smack in the middle of the holiday season so I know, with a lot of folks away, the Sunday group will be few on numbers but big on fun.

To quote a line from an old classic song ' I believe that children are our future…' today was full of great examples of this musical proclamation.

One of our mum's out cycling with her children, said Hi and promised to be back to join us for coffee, another one of the gang running with her teenage lad, great to see the warmth and dynamics between the two of them. I know it's not always the case but when is works it magic. I also found it funny when another old hand at this running lark tries to drag a lad along many years his junior to join the fun as an alternative to staying in bed.

I have many techniques for getting the best out of fellow runners and this morning was about getting Sean to tell me his life's story and focus less on the fact he was tired.

I did have to keep his dad, Hamish, quiet so his lad did the talking and steadied his breathing.

I wanted to find out about the person and what he wanted to become and when he needed a break and to catch his breath, he had to listen to me. I do like a captive audience!

I have mixed feeling about the youth of today, they do get well deserved bad press but a lot of them, most of them in fact are top people and just need a chance. My experiences over the last few days convinced me even more.

I was invited to see the showcase for 'Challenge' or National Citizen Scheme (NCS), a non-profit organisation providing a life-changing programme open to all teenagers aged 15-17 at minimal cost.

My eldest daughter Libby, and now Millie have both taken part in this great scheme and it was time for her to show me what she has been up.

Whilst watching my daughter and her newly found friends explain to eager parents the activities of the previous few weeks. This included sharing their observations and activities through the re-enactment of life in an old people's home.

This could have been a real piss take but I sat in awe, as with care and thoughtfulness they approach this sensitive subject.

Clearly showing me that whist full of life and of cause knowing it all, these young adults can still be compassionate about others.

Running with Sean was also a pleasure, we touched on life and its meanings along with all the adventures that he planned to do with his own life and where he was heading.

I came to the conclusion that Hamish, his dad, might be funding his life for a little time to come as like most people of his age, he did not have a clue. I know that feeling!

He was good company and when Hamish made a detour to pick up his coffee pennies, some five miles into the run, Sean showed what he was made of and upped the pace and sprinted to the end. His reward of a visit to Starbucks, the running bug has got him, I can tell.

Tuesday 9th August 2016

It's Tuesday, so must be an early alarm call. Again, I jump in the car and drive across town to meet fellow dawn runners Ian, John and Michaela.

This morning's route was a combination of a loop of Warwick racecourse with a trot along the Grand Union canal and generally but not always, the conversation flows. The narrow toe path gave the chance to run in pairs for a change and gives the opportunity to cover a variety of subjects.

Some profound conversation today, future plans and the meaning of life and sometimes the more things change, the more they stay the same. I have learnt from my own experiences that you cannot make an omelette without breaking an egg or two.

Wednesday 10th August 2016 - A new place to run.

A family wedding provided the opportunity to run somewhere new today but before I had chance to lace up my trainers, I had the opportunity to drink copious amounts of alcohol first in the post ceremony celebrations with my nephew Gareth and his new wife Gemma at the Ashes Wedding Barns in Endon, Derbyshire.

Weddings are always a long day and staying at a little B & B called the Westfields, a couple of miles away from the venue deep in the countryside surrounding Endon, would ensure we arrived and departed by taxi. Therefore, ensuring that we drink more than just a couple of shandies whilst having a lovely day seeing the love birds tie the knot and catching up with family and friends.

With the opportunity to stay overnight I thought it would be rude not to take my trainers. A run to the neighboring hamlet of Stanley provided the destination, having spotted a lake on the drive in the day before and preferring not to just wonder aimlessly that's where I headed.

As I headed off from the hotel, the gin oozed from my pores and the dull thud in my head keeping with the beat of my trainers contacting with the ground.

Not a good combination, booze and exercise I realise, but I need to blow away the cobwebs.

I am not familiar with this neck of the woods but what I did see is well worthy of a return visit, I didn't feel the route I had chosen did the area justice but it did the trick on to kick start my over indulged body and set me up for a full English breakfast that I am sure was going to me waiting for me.

Friday 12th August 2016 - It's a berry Jerry.

A tenuous reference to Phoenix Nights for all those Peter Kay's fans out there and a link to one of the few positive sides to the pending departure of summer and the inevitable arrival of the autumn, hedgerows full of blackberries, a perfect energy boost mid run.

I love this time of year only for the chance to eat blackberries on the run, I always pick them when I can, in quantity but obviously not whist on a run. Always the spoils inevitably ending up in jam or a pie or crumble but to be honest, my money is on something alcoholic to perverse the taste of later summer to enjoy in the cold months of winter.

After a long week, the de stressing effect of my run clearly apparent and back home, I was set up for the weekend.

Sunday 14th August 2016

It was different today as I have never run around Draycote Water before, I have biked a few times and walked many times in the past putting the world to rights and sometimes having some life changing conversations, but I never ran the five mile perimeter of the reservoir.

Before the race, it started to feel different, I felt different, none of the usual aches and pains that I never have but always make a guest appearance on race day, I felt ready and I felt great.

I was fed and watered with my usual weapons of choice these days, a glass or two red wine the night before a nice slice of toast and jam on the morning washed down with couple of cups of tea. The wine helps me sleep, the rest is a good balance to keep nourished and for those longer runs, I throw a bowl of porridge into the equation.

Today I fuelled on a slice of Charlecote Crunch, toasted with generous spoonful of some home-made jam, just the job and I am sure Mo Farah has a similar nutrition plan pre-race too.

With all the liquid, I needed the loo but not problem, I found a bush and once I was a little lighter, I was ready for the off.

Six of the gang were flying the Zero to Hero flag today and as always, I took advantage of talking to strangers and to do a bit of recruiting. I like to keep adding new blood and fresh faces into the group and always prepared to strike up a conversation. I seized the moment to do a little networking for the group and invite them to come along and join the heroes.

I particularly enjoy listening to other people from the group do the talking and always nice to hear them discuss our baby, our great club with so much passion. The conversations give me a real sense of achievement, but we had a race to run and before long it was time to head to the start line.

It was like being at the seaside with the Sunday yachtsman out in force although very little wind today which makes a change for Draycote, good for us not so great if you are banking on some wind to make your boat go faster.

'Will it make the boat go faster?', what a great title for a book, but I think *Harriet Beveridge* and *Ben Hunt-Davis* have already beaten me to it, another great read if you like good inspirational reading.

I planned to run with Becky today, I like company when I run, even during events but I inevitably end up running other people's races which is not problem, I just like to get out there.

I felt strong and for once, I was making light work of the miles today, chatting away whilst others around us were fighting for air and even walking so early on in the race. I like a captive audience and the talking really does make the miles pass. The pace was good but steady and easy to chat, Becky was doing great too but kept insisting that I go ahead. But I was happy to stay together as we were both doing good and running together helped eat up the miles.

With approximately four miles under our belt, Becky was still nagging, I succumbed to the pressure to go run my own race so off I went like a bullet from a gun, very quickly putting space between my running buddy and myself. Striding out, I felt for Becky seeing me disappear into the distance and I knew she was fine with me going off and it was only two miles to go to the finish.

I was cooking, taking big strides and looking at my watch, even with my ever-increasing pace, a sub 60 minute time was going to be a big ask, but I didn't care, it was how I feeling that made the difference today, strong and focused with the time immaterial.

Soon I spotted some familiar faces cheering along the final straight and with the finish line in sight, I gave it everything I had and up the pace a little more - I should have three slices of toast.

Still passing people, I targeted a runner ahead that I wanted to pass before the finish line and gave it everything I had. The end, some 400m away, felt like a million miles. I could see the finish, but it didn't seem to get any closer and the end could not come quickly enough.

Only time will tell the results but as I crossed the finish line, I had done all I could have. I felt great and was ready for a drink. Time and the results would confirm the facts, but my phone stats showed me running the race of my life.

So the next race it is going to be all about me, I know I am my own worst enemy, but people are great aren't they?

As soon as I have my T-shirt and goody bag, I was back on the hill along the final straight to cheer Becky to the finish, only a few minutes behind me, still smiling and living the dream.

Tuesday 16th August 2016 - when work gets in the way.

Beautiful morning to run but I had to cut it short as I had to be in the office for an early meeting, I hate it when that happens. I do not like these colder mornings, this can only mean one thing - the autumn is just around the corner, but here's hoping that it's not in hurry to arrive.

Thursday 18th August 2016

One bonus of the summer months is having Libby home from uni, I needed a natter with my first born to put the world to rights after a bit of a shit week. I can always count on my eldest daughter to lift my spirits and get my head back in the zone and that's exactly what she did.

Friday 19th August 2016 - Reflections.

Nothing to do with Snow White and maybe just a little bit to do with running.

As I started to write the next chapter I am listening to an old classic Genesis track, Squonk, a little random title but some great lyrics, the significance I will explain later.

> *Mirror mirror on the wall*
> *His heart was broken long before he came to you*
> *Stop your tears from falling*
> *The trail they leave is very clear*
> *For all to see at night*

A productive and at times, emotional day, spending most of the day up a ladder doing a bit of decorating whilst listening to the last few chapters of the Ghost Runner, and I did shed a tear or two at the end. It is such an amazing story and well worth a read and the second tenuous link, whist I still had the kit out, I thought I would give the downstairs loo a lick of paint and with the boring stuff out of the way, I handed over to Julie to do the finishing touches.

The newly painted wall was adorned with a mirror, a special mirror as the new addition to the cloakroom, made by my good ladies fair hands, was not only practical but sentimental as the rustic frame was made up of pieces of drift wood, many that I had picked up when out running in numerous locations around the world.

Tears and mirrors come together...

Saturday 20th August 2016 - The missed run.

For the first time in ages I missed my Saturday run, I had all the gear on and everything ready to run but for the second time this week life got in the way. I find if I do not run first thing in the morning day then the runs away with me, pardon the pun, and I have not the time or the inclination to go for a run later in the day.

After a day of extreme painting keeping me on my feet for the majority of it, a run would just about push me over the edge.

Having showered and in some casual clothes, I put away the trainers back in the wardrobe I settled for a glass or two of red and a bit Peter Kay for a change but I think I would have preferred to have good for a run, sorry Peter.

Sunday 21st August 2016 - Who wants to go the extra mile?

Every once in a while, a post will group up on our little Facebook page from a fellow runner who wants to do a few extra miles, generally when someone is training for a half or full marathon and needs to increase the distance.

I don't mind helping if I can as sometimes I need the company on a long run and to make this happen on a Sunday, this usually means an early alarm call to ensure we meet up half an hour earlier than normal and get an extra few miles in before meeting up with the main group at 8.30am.

Today the request came from Sue, who was training for the Kenilworth Half Marathon in a few weeks' time and fancied a bit of company on her long run.

I didn't need my alarm clock this morning as my body clock is well and truly knackered so I was wide awake and after an hour of extreme ironing at home 'sleep is for wimps, plenty of time to sleep when you are dead' – quote from the James Bond film – Die another day) I was ready and out with Sue.

As we headed back to the usual meeting point we were passed by eager cyclists on route to our common destination making for a really good turn out today, a mix of runners and cyclists.

It's always better to get the extra miles in before the main group run and you do not want to have to carry on when everyone has called it a day but that is all in the mind.

As a group, We ran one of our regular routes, affectionately called 'countryside for townies' which gets its name from the fact that the route includes a well laid concrete path which takes you through the fields with no chance of getting any mud on your trainers.

I like this route, it's an out and back with a few hills and stunning views with the added bonus of adding extra miles in if required and mud too if the fancy takes and one heads off concrete.

Great conversation and support today and as I thought, Sean was back and all became a bit unclear who was pushing who, some reverse psychology going on here. I like a bit of motivation myself so to push others, I have to push myself too so a win-win situation.

The run up hill to the sports pavilion on the university campus brought out some serious mind games, the body giving everything and the head screaming to stop unfortunately the head won, always next time!

Group regulars Steve and Michela were out this morning on the run even though it was their wedding anniversary. What a great way to celebrate.

I loved the humour on the run today, passed by a cyclist who rang his bell to warn us of his pending arrival at the same time as the bells of Saint Nicholas church were calling the good people of Kenilworth to prayer. 'Good bell that buddy' came a comment from one of the runners and did make everyone smile including the cyclist – got to love a bit of banter, it's what put the Great into Great Britain!

Having starting a trend, so the bell jokes continue, 'got to go like the clappers now' 'are we going to peel off soon' – brilliant!

An interesting conversation with Steve touching on our recent outing to Draycote and his observation that I always run other people races – true I know and maybe it's time for some coaching for me, watch this space.

Tuesday 23rd August 2016 – Pillow-1, Pavements-0.

I lost the battle of the bed this morning, without a plan to meet up with anyone, I hit the snooze button and opted to stay in my bed.

It was such a lovely morning too and I knew I would kick myself for the rest of the day. Some days getting up and heading out into the cold dark morning is not so tempting although I do the early runs regardless of the time of year. But the thought of the winter does not cheer me up at all, but its only August and still the summer.

My running mojo seems to have taken a summer vacation for a day or two but, still with regrets in missing the dawn, it was good to get out with Libby and Tim after work, miles is miles!

Thursday 25th August 2016 - and the results are in.

An exciting day in the Atherton household and I would imagine the same in many others up and down the country for today is when we get to find out the exam results.

I didn't run in the morning, not sure why not but enough to say I didn't and it made a change. But I did get out in the evening and ran with Tim.

Libby was out on a driving lesson so be afraid and taking advantage of a bit of 'man time' was good to get out and stretch the legs after work. I am more the morning runner but will run whenever I get the chance as I just love to get out.

With many options available which I am grateful for, we chose to get away from the roads and run along the canal, a little warm but we did put the world to rights.

And with the results in we were all ready for a Chinese now and time to celebrate, well done Millie.

Friday 26th August 2016 - something different.

Unusual for a Friday and break from being dad's taxi, I seized the moment and took the opportunity to catch up for a run with the Friday night 'Zero to hero' ladies.

I rarely get chance to run with the Friday group, so it was lovely to meet up and gave us chance to retrace the first route we did all those years ago when the group started. A bit of nostalgia and a chance to tell the groups story to a captive audience which was lovely.

Saturday 27th August 2016 - all revved up with no place to go.

Every once in a while, a strange thing happens. Always on a none work day, when I go through all the effort to get into my running gear but never end up breaking into a sweat.

That is not strictly true, but what I mean is I never actually run with life getting in the way and I end up doing other stuff. I have spent the whole day in my runners but never tread the streets.

And what do I think? These days, not much, it's just one of them ...

Sunday 28th August 2016 - Sweating beer.

Just once in a while, the alarm goes off, a little later on a Sunday, and I really want to rollover and hit the snooze button, but I made a commitment to run a little extra today. But I did have a few beers last night catching up with old mates.

I was out with a few old mates last night, it's been thirty-three years since the last time we had a proper drink together back in 1983.

We had such a great night catching up and just picking up where we left off all those years ago. It was interesting to hear what everyone had been up to in the years between then and now.

One discussion point during the night, I was never sure how Martin fitted in to our friendship group to use a recent phrase but now I know, women!

Martin went out with Jenny, Allan was going out with her older sister Julie, hence the connection. I always thought women would feature somewhere. It was great to meet and feel sure that this will become an annual event.

It will be interesting to see what comes of this rekindled friendship, a road trip maybe or event so watch this space.

Like many people, I find running is great therapy and works both ways. I like getting people to talk whilst running, help to unload, unwind, get stuff off their chest, however you may describe it and I like to release my thoughts too.

Maybe this is something I could develop sometime in the future, life coaching on the run. I don't like the idea of a chair or an office setting, too much like an old school shrink for my liking but to run with fresh air in your lungs does help the unwinding process and together, talking about a multitude of subjects, the miles fly past, 8 miles today and as always, I feel better at the end of a run than I did at the start.

Monday 29th August 2016 - Last one of the year.

What is August Bank Holiday all this about? I can see the significance of some public holidays, Easter, Christmas Day, New Year's Day etc. but a holiday just because it's a while since we have had one and it a bit of a long wait until the next one I struggle with.

I did a bit of research and August bank holiday was introduced in 1871 by Liberal politician Sir John Lubbock as a way giving workers a last chance to enjoy the Summer. Originally the first Monday of August but this clashed with traditional two week factory shutdown so was moved to the last Monday of August instead.

August Bank Holiday always feels like the end of summer and heralds the arrival of autumn. Shortening days with tins of Roses and Quality Street in the shops, the X factor on the telly (so must be twelve weeks until Christmas and the much awaited news if the winner will be the Christmas number one.

I am kinda bored with this mass production of 'stars' to be honest. I am not doubting that these folks can sing but I am a bit of a traditionalist when it comes talent, I like the old approach of progression through the pubs and clubs, but I know it's only my opinion.

One observation, the winners and finalists rarely have any longevity in their new careers but before you shout at me, some do.

Taking advantage of a long weekend, it was good to get out this morning and get a bit of sun on my back while I still can. The weather was glorious today but signs of autumn too. Hedgerows full of fruit, leaves with the tinge of brown about them and a few more than usual on the floor. I love the seasons, but it does have its down side, but best not dwell too deeply just yet and wait until we get to 'judges houses'....

If I had my way, winter would be the last week in December and the first week of January, spring would then last until Easter and summer kicking off straight after, ending on bonfire night, perfect.

Today's run was yet another one of my many favourites, but with it being a holiday, the streets were empty, shops were closed but a lot of folks either running, biking or dog walking and the River Avon looked like the M6 motorway with so many boats plying up and down the water. Nevertheless it great to see so many people taking advantage of this beautiful morning.

With the towns narrow streets quieter with the lack of traffic, you can really get a feel the history of the old town bereft of cars and people.

I was distracted by some activity at my favourite jewellers, a plain unmarked van outside complete with rails and cones, workman a plenty and the front door wide open to the back drop of some serious drilling and grinding noises.

Was this a shop refurb in progress or did these gents have their eye on the safe. A good scam if it was the later, no one would suspect a thing.

Not wanting to be entering a witness protection programme just yet, I thought the best of my fellow human beings and headed off into the park for a bit of fresh air.

I might just keep an eye on the local news, just in case…

September 2016

Thursday 1st September 2016 - Pinch-punch.

The year is flying by and tonight, although still warm had the promise or threat of autumn.

Yet another favourite route tonight, Old Milverton village, across the fields to the Saxon Mill.

Out with Libby, my first born this evening and a good excuse to have a good old natter. The summer is but a distant memory and it will soon be time for her to head back up north to Leeds and the final year of her degree.

We plan to get a few more runs in before then and this little village with its stunning church is just beautiful on a nice balmy evening like this with its unusual pyramidical roof on the tower built in 1880.

The countryside basking in the last warm rays of the day, the village of Old Milverton could not be any more 'chocolate box' England if it tried.

I always try to make an effort to attend the annual Old Milverton horticultural show when I can, which is just brilliant. English traditions at their best; cream teas, stalls a plenty selling local produce, jams and honey, a beer tent, Punch and Judy, traction engines in full steam along with old fashioned fairground activities, bowling for a pig, splat the rat, duck the vicar, all providing the opportunity to extract a few quid and keep old traditions alive.

Whenever we visit, it feels like we have inadvertently stumbled onto the film set of 'Midsummer Murders' or 'The Vicar of Dibley', with the compare/announcer the icing on the cake. As seems to be the norm, this high-profile job is always given to a villager who really should not be ever given a microphone, but nevertheless, it all adds to the atmosphere.

The hub of the show is 'the tent' displaying all manner of goodies from a trio of perfect carrots through to a Victoria sponge to die for and I did win a prize once, not for my perfect carrot or even a bit of jam but for a photograph, 'An Englishman in Paris'. I was absolutely thrilled and delighted to go down in the archives of this little village, England my England.

Past our allotment and over the fields, but unfortunately everywhere we went we were greeted by the heavy smell of food – just torture.

Running past the Saxon Mill, with folks still outside catching up with friends over a glass of something nice. 'Chest out, chin up and look like a runner, Libs', I could have easily stopped and grabbed a beer, but miles not hops are the order of the day.

Back along the canal, then the river to home for tea, beans on toast – food of the gods!

Friday 2nd September 2016 - TGIF!

I like Fridays and always try to fit a run in before the weekend starts in anger, along with a perfect excuse to open a bottle of red. Today I was in the groove.

Braving a few laps of St Nicolas' Park and wanting to push myself and do a bit of training. That is something you will not hear me say very often.

Today was the last Friday of the school summer holidays and the park was very busy, swarms of kids, smart phones and IPads in hand looking for Pokemon.

I don't get it, what's wrong with kicking a football or something, ditch the tech kids and get a life!

The world is bigger than the two by four inch screen if you care to look up, just saying…

No Pokemon for me today, I wanted speed, the path around the perimeter of the park is flat and a measured mile, which is perfect for chasing the pace.

I haven't done this for a while and wanted to get my speed up a little, with the sub 60 minute 10 k do able even at my tender age but a sub 55 or even a PB, that is going to take a bit of doing.

I thought 'Go hard or go home' and as I have both a 10k and a half marathon in the diary to take on before year end. Maybe an increase in pace is something to aim for surely, even at my age.

It's only the second day of the month and I didn't want to peak too soon, steadily building up the effort without hurting myself, plus leaving a bit to do before month end.

I wanted to beat 27 mins for 3 miles, but today I was up against it this afternoon with stray kids, retractable dog leads and generally people getting in the way.

I gave it my best shot and managed eighteen seconds over the target and with the odds not in my favour, I was happy with that.

I feel in a good place today which always helps and Fridays are always good. Boy am I ready for a glass or two of red and a good night's sleep.

Are these two related, oh yes!

Saturday 3rd September 2016 - Cows, Corn and Cotswold Crunch.

After a red wine fueled sleep, I was ready to be up and out this morning with a bit of a chill in the air and more signs of autumn, it was still warm enough to get the legs out (I had my shorts on).

With Libby with me again, I had another favourite route planned this morning but before we ran. We stopped off first for some fresh bread from Nick at Crustum. I love dropping into this great shop and today was no exception.

No surprise with Libby having her eye on the Cotswold crunch, so I bought an extra loaf for her to take back to Uni.

With some bread bought and still warm from the oven, making the car smell divine, we headed off for our run.

Eggs and soldiers were on the menu this morning, but first we had to put a few miles in the legs. Libby did remind me that it was Saturday morning and most folks are still snuggled up in bed but not us.

Running in the stunning Warwickshire countryside is just the best and with a few cows along the route to keep us company enjoying the grass, fresh from morning dew.

I love to see the livestock out in the field although I know too well that they will someday soon end up on the dinner plate. But at least they still have the benefit of the outside living in their short life's so a little consolation.

With hedgerow laden with fruit giving yet another sign of impending winter, we took a couple of blackberries to nourish our run the hill up to the top of Chase Lane. That was a good plan, but they needed more sunshine to sweeten the taste, but scrummy nevertheless.

As the hill flattened off and the tarmac road turned to grass, the conversation got all philosophical with lots of 'what if's', all very deep and meaningful but you can do that on a run.

There is something about running that allows you to sub consciously drop your guard and open up.

So where does the corn feature in all this story I hear you ask?

Thanks for asking, the last part of the run as Libby and I turn to head for home, we take a well-trodden cross country path back to town through a field of, yes you have guessed it, ripe corn towering above our heads, out of the wind, the humidity is very high.

Upon exiting the corn maze, the temperature dropped, refreshing and out in the open, the path rising slightly to present us with what is, in my opinion, the best view of Kenilworth Castle, a vista that I would imagine has not changed for years.

By coincidence, following the destination for Libby and I's midweek run, today was the day of the annual village show I mentioned a few pages back and this year's trip later in the day was a real trip down memory lane.

After our traditional cream tea, Julie and I popped into the church and tried my hand at bell ringing and not sure how I made the connection with a random stranger but a connection I did. It turned out that it was not a random stranger after all but someone that I knew many years ago and we had a connection as we both knew someone who had had a massive influence on my life.

That influential person was Bart. Bart, was originally my brother's friend and was a family friend really, with Bart and his family part of our family's DNA to be honest.

Starting with my brother Dave, the influence of his early life clear, both my brother and I were not confident as children but time spent with another family brought us both life skills that stood us in good stead, along with the chance to see the beautiful country of Ireland on numerous trips to buy and sell furniture.

Bart was a real character, larger than life and everyone knew him. He had more sayings than days of the month, I knew him more in his later days, as the owner of Saltisford Antiques in Warwick.

A proper 'love joy' before Ian McShane brought the antique trade to life in the popular nineteen eighties TV show. I loved working in the shop and it brought me out of my shell. I look back with fond memories of my years with Bart and was great to reminisce with someone who remembered him too.

In all, a great day.

Sunday 4th September 2016 - And there off.

As the summer holidays come to an end and a new school year is poised to begin so more folks are about and ready to run or get the bike out.

A good turnout today and a few more 'sitting down' folks or cyclists than runners out to enjoy this beautiful morning, which is just what I needed after putting on a few pounds on at fat club weight in.

It was good to get out in the beautiful countryside of Warwickshire and we were on a mission as a number of the group were running in the annual Kenilworth half marathon today, so a spot of cheering was in order.

I have run this race myself back in 2012, ran and pushing would be a better description.

After promising myself that pushing Judy Wolfendun once in 2011 was enough, I succumb to the late great Judy's persuasive charm at her birthday lunch.

This was the second time that I responded to one of Judy's request for assistance, in 2011, an article in the local paper caught my eye. Judy was looking for a team of runners to push her in the Cotswold Hilly 100. I could not resist myself and made contact.

Arriving at Judy's home, dressed in shorts and a t shirt, I was surprised to be greeted by Judy in a full skiing outfit. I soon realised that with so many health issues, staying warm was important to her, but as Judy settled herself into her customized race wheelchair built for being pushed at more than a running pace, the donning of a crash helmet came as a bit of a shock and I did wonder if I had been set up and would soon appear on some prank TV show and Jeremy Beadle was going to jump out at an minute, but Judy was for real.

As I learnt more about her, the more I was in awe of this incredible lady.

Judy was born with spinal muscular atrophy, a condition that causes muscles to waste away. After being told by doctors she would not live to see 40, Judy was determined to help other people with disabilities realise their potential.

During her action packed life she has been involved in scores of fundraising events taking on several physical challenges each year to raise funds for various causes.

Judy became the first disabled person in the world to do a seven-day dog sled trek across the Arctic Circle and taken part in the Coventry Run, BUPA Great North Run, the New York Marathon and Norway Midnight Sun Marathon and in 2007, her efforts were acknowledged when a trip to Buckingham palace to receive an MBE.

Over the years Judy has helped so many charities including Coventry Friends of the Home Farm Trust, which helps people with learning difficulties; Disabled Living Foundation; Riding for the Disabled Association; RAF Benevolent Fund; the Bicycle Helmet Initiative Trust; The Young Voices of 12, a Coventry organisation which supports young carers; Warwick hospital and armed forces charity Combat Stress.

For the Cotswold outing, I roped in a few friends to join Team Judy and together I, Sue, Tracey and Bev completed the opening leg of the race and happy that we had the relatively flat section. As I lay in bed, with the rain lashing down, I thought of this amazing lady sat as the team pushed her through the night and on to the finish line setting a new record in taking part in a the Cotswold 100mile Ultra Marathon: 'First pushed wheelchair athlete' and maybe even be the first time someone has been pushed for such a distance.

The weather was absolutely awful – but Judy and her team of pushers persisted and finished 31st out of 35 – which is an amazing achievement, considering that 80 runners started – but less than half of them crossed the finishing line! Team Judy completed the event in 29 hours 5 min, that is a long time to be sat in a wheelchair chair and I am proud to have been a little part of one amazing person's life.

It was only when I attended her funeral did I realise how many people's lives Judy had touched and what an incredible lady she was. Listening to others, I some realised that I was one of many people to have fallen for her powers of persuasion.

But today, I and the rest of the Zero to Hero gang will be watching. We had plenty of friends running today so armed with a coffee from Starbucks we headed to the start. The muffled sound of a distant public address system gaining clarity as we approach the start line and in the first few metres of the route, we found our pitch and in the nick of time, the sound of the horn brought the runners to attention and the Kenilworth Half Marathon was underway. Not a massive field and mainly club runners but still a great sight nevertheless. We clapped and cheered them all as the runners ran past with 13.1 miles ahead of them.

Each there for their own reason, the racing snakes at the front in search of fame and glory and the joggers and fun runners at the back looking for personal satisfaction and the finish line. Everyone looking for the elusive personal best.

I found it quite emotional and so different standing on the side lines, I liked it!

One particular runner was in my thoughts today, one of our group who at times struggles with life was taking part and on the days leading up to the race, we had been exchanging messages. Today was more than the miles for this young lady, more than 13.1 miles of country lanes, today she was ready and going for it.

Unfortunately, I didn't get to see her at the start or as the group passed, but I was with her in spirit and delighted to hear that she was back safe and sound and worthy of a podium place for sheer determination. I was looking forward to meeting up and giving a big hug in person but for now I had to rely on social media.

This is why I love to run; not about the winners or the elite runners but real people pushing themselves to achieve what they never knew was in them. The faces in the photos, the comments, the stories say it all and time to celebrate.

Where will my next race take me, a sub 60 minute 10k, a steady half or maybe another marathon, I reckon I have one more in me but I need to be ready, but that is a problem for another day.

Today I ran in Kenilworth but tomorrow I run through the lush lowlands in the shadows of the Alps in Ebesburg just outside of Munich, Germany

Monday 5th September 2016 - To run or not to run.

I love to run before work, but on a dark Monday morning when it's peeing down I like the idea of staying in my nice warm bed is a whole lot better.

The thought of leaving the hotel to pound the dark wet streets of a Bavarian town was going to be a tough call this morning and there might always to be a chance to run later I thought, so I rolled over and hit the snooze button.

Bed 1 Trainers Nil.

I missed dinner last night due to a late flight so adding the chance of an early breakfast into the equation, running this morning never stood a chance.

Today, I made a good call, by 7.30am the rain had stopped and with a full stomach, I took the short walk to the office,

I would love to ditch the car and do this every day, but 22 miles is a good old walk to my usual place of work! But today a considerably shorter distance was an easy stroll. Ebesburg was waking up and I relished in the simple pleasures of life, the smell of fresh bread from one of the many bakers that seem to be on every corner and listening to the laughter of groups of children off to school. I love this little Bavarian town and it's my first visit this year so was nice to be back. I love this place and the pace of life here.

After a productive day at the office (I have to say that in case my boss ever gets to read the book) and an arrangement to meet up later for dinner with my colleague and great friend Thomas, I managed to find time for that run. The rain was now a distant memory and the sun had decided to make an appearance and was a perfect time to get some endorphins.

I was on a mission, on my list of places to visit whilst in Germany I wanted to go up the Aussichtsturm, a lookout tower in the woods just outside of town. The last time I was in here, the tower was closed for repair so as I headed passed the Klostersee, I had my fingers crossed that it would be open this time.

The lake was bereft of swimmers this time of year, a different story in the height of summer when the banks of the lake are awash with the locals out for an evening swim or bask in the sun at the end of the day.

The steady climb away from the lake and into the countryside along the thought provoking Heldenalle, a tree lined avenue with each tree carrying a white plaque with the name and age of a fallen soldier from the village during the Second World War.

Some of the stereotypical German names brought a shallow smile to my face, but their ages didn't, 18, 20, 22 years of age. Just kids, another son, father or brother that did return home, a lasting memorial to the young men who lost their lives on the opposite side of a common war.

A thoughtful distraction as I climbed the crude steps cut in the side of the woodland trail to the base of the Aussichtsturm to swap nature for concrete steps. I am not a big fan of heights, but I am here now and it would be like going to Blackpool and not going up the tower. With some 130 metres worth of steps to the top, it's head down and I start to climb what seemed a never-ending spiral staircase enclosed, thank goodness, slowly rising above the tree canopy heading ever higher and predictably with the top in sight and the lack of protection, the wind picked up and so did my heartbeat. The view from the top was worth every step with the lush green pastures of the Bavarian countryside laid out before me like a patch work quilt and with a quick check of the view from the four sides of the tower and a quick selfie it was time to head down to the forest floor.

The descent took an age and what did not help was the slow burning in my thigh muscles – I remember that feeling – the kind of pain at the end of a long bike ride and I did not care for this especially on these slippery steps, I did not want to fall on my arse so far out of town with not a soul in sight.

A slow run back for a shower and the promise of a cool beer with Thomas and another item off my bucket list, the sunrise or sunset from such a great elevation would be great. But that something for another day and a good one too.

Tuesday 6th September 2016 - Decisions decisions.

It was pretty dark when the alarm went off this morning, but a least it was not raining. I had planned to head out cross country to the less undulating side of town, but I love running by water and the forest path along the side of Klostersee is beautiful even on this very grey morning with no sign of the sun, making it a very monotone start to another day in Germany.

I have run this route many times before and leaving the town's natural open air swimming pool behind along with the sleepy town. Out along the forest path to the much larger Eggburger, some two kilometres away, passing typical painted houses depicting Bavarian life in glorious technicolour. It's so peaceful and I feel at one with nature.

Although quiet at this time of the day, the maps and signposts give the clues that this area is popular with the locals and with the odd carefully positioned beer gardens, I can see the area being very busy on those summer weekends, but Germany has plenty of space for everyone and out in the plains in the shadows of the distant Alps.

Dotted along the well-defined path along the edge of the big lake are some very impressive properties, obviously where the poor folks of Ebesburg live and every house worthy of a visit from the Grand Designs film crew. Each entrance carrying very clear 'Zutritt verboten' keep out signs and some very big dog kennels giving the indication that these folks like their privacy.

Leaving the locals in peace, I planned to take the path towards the slightly wider tracks servicing the lake side houses as a more direct route back to town along a fruit tree lined avenue. But I was not alone, a young Muntjac deer had joined me for our morning constitutional, but soon not wanting my company he turned tail and headed for the fields of corn and maybe an early breakfast at the pleasure of the local farmer, but these fields of corn are fuel not food I latter discovered.

The brief encounter with my new friend was a real treat and the running back to the Gasthof with a big smile on my face and a warm glow from my run.

Before long I had retraced my steps and back in town and ready to join the rat race and get back on the wheel, but first a well- earned breakfast.

Wednesday 7th September 2016 - Back home.

Back on home turf after a few days away, I have not run in Leamington for a while and when the alarm went off, I was in for a big shock. Awoken by my alarm at 5.10am and it was as black as your hat as they say, autumn has arrived.

Leaving home in darkness, a route from our selection of winter options helped keep us safe without the need for torches. But throwing caution to the wind and hoping that the progression to the impending dawn would bring better visibility, we left the lit streets and onto the canal towpath for return run home.

The sky was slowly making the transition from midnight blue to a shade of turquoise, making the return run along the canal very special and all of a sudden – it was light and another new day began in earnest.

I love being by the water and my thoughts drift back to August 1997, bloody hell that nearly twenty years ago. Arthur was a colleague and a good friend and over a beer in Tenerife we hatch an idea to do something to raise some money for a couple of local hospices, Myton in Warwick and Warren Pearl in Solihull.

I am not sure what your knowledge of English waterways is like but canals are built in rings and loop up across the country to form a navigable network, not the most direct routes but effective nevertheless.

Arthur and I chose the Warwick Ring as our challenge, a circular route which would take us from our start point at the Boat pub in Catherine de Barnes on the outskirts of Solihull, heading south or anti clockwise on the loop towards Warwick and eventually coming back on ourselves from the north some four days and hundred and two miles later.

I learnt a lot about myself during those four days, Arthur was older than I, an old hand at life and as fit as a butchers dog, we made an odd couple of pals really, polar opposites to be honest. I was half his age and weight, I ate and drank twice as much but we were pals never the less. This adventure was my first real contact with the press and we managed to get in all the local papers and was even interviewed on local radio mid walk on a mobile phone no less, hi tech back in the late nineties.

We walked approximately twenty-five miles a day, stopping at canal side pubs at night where we soothed our weary feet and I drank beer. I remember having laminated maps to help with the navigation, pretty straight forward and using the bridges to gauge progress. My mobile phone, a relatively new invention made and received phone calls and that was pretty much the end of its function, smart phone it was not, so no google maps and GPS, we had to rely on good old fashioned map reading to work out our location.

As a general observation, the canal gave minimal clues of our whereabouts especially in the countryside with only the odd pub offering help. When the route went through a village or town then confirmation of our location usually followed, with information on hand at moorings and boat chandleries, always a good place to grab a sandwich and replenish our water bottles.

To provide evidence that we actually walked the complete Warwickshire ring, we would take photographs and get our makeshift journal signed by folks offering the opportunity to discreetly ask where we were.

Canal walking comes with its constraints and minor foibles, one thing people do not realise is that canals are not flat and do have elevation at times making the walking an effort at times. Also, the paths are not geared up for walking side by side and can be narrow, not good for conversation and boring!

Canal - hedge and then sometimes hedge - canal, the miles could drag but with sheep and cows offering company, we coped and the walking in single file did give time for quiet contemplation.

The first day, a novelty, overnight at the Cuttle Inn in Long Itchington, day two all the better for a hearty breakfast and a bonus of a meet up with the family in Newbold on Avon, near Rugby for dinner. Day three... day three was like Groundhog Day, more of the same, water-hedge, hedge-water. However, the last day was the hardest, after an overnight stay in a dubious hotel in Polesworth, what followed was a day I never thought would end.

The final day of our adventure brought a change in scenery as the last twenty-five miles made the transition from countryside to city centre swaping hedge for an urban landscape, passing backs of factories and under motorways. Then passed under the iconic Gravelly Hill Interchange or 'spaghetti junction' as it is better known as.

Leaving the city centre and through the Birmingham suburbs, the end was in sight, but the miles seem to drag and the finish seemed to never get any closer.

The good old mobile phone helping keep in touch with our families, with updates on our estimated time of arriving back at the Boat at Catherine de Barnes, our start and finish point.

Regular updates prevented our families standing around based on our inaccurate estimate finish time, but we did make it to the end, greeted by a glass of fizz and soak in the bath.

A great experience and so many memories, on lasting comment from a work colleague has stuck with me.

'What was the point, why didn't you just stay at work and give your salary to charity.'

Some people don't get it do they? or maybe they do, I will let you decide. Arthur and I raised over seven hundred pounds, which was a lot of money then and appreciated by both charities.

I often think back to those four days spent with Arthur walking the ring, especially when I am near the canal.

Thursday 8th September 2016 - Rest Day – don't mind if I do.

And on the eight day he rested, ok it might have been the seventh day, but why let the facts get in the way of a good story.

I was not running today and feels a bit strange to be honest as I would quite happily run every day, but not sure that streaking as it's called in the running fraternity is that great for the old joints but for the head, works every time.

Friday 9th September 2016 - Short and sweet.

Back at it but just a short run tonight, it has been a busy day but thought a quick trot around the park before dinner would be just the job. Millie had been cooking at school so was looking forward to sampling her lasagne and has even included some veggies, the work of the devil in her eyes, but very nice it was too. Washed down with my traditional Friday treat, a nice glass or two of red and was I glad of a bit of down time at the end of a very long week.

Saturday 10th September 2016 - To run or not to run.

Which roughly translates in to 'its peeing down with rain again and I reckon I'll stay in bed.'

A run on a Saturday morning is always a favourite of mine and you will already be familiar with my weekly routine by now but today was going to be a little different. Today my ritual was going to be turned on its head.

I did stay in bed a little longer than planned but I still ran, I still had eggs on toast and still got my bread from my favourite bakers but not in the usual order and had to settle for eggs on a couple of slices of super market sliced – not the same so why the change in the routine I hear you ask?

I needed to head out to Stratford for Millie's N.C.S. graduation and time to cheer and clap another amazing achievement from my youngest and all the other great examples of the youth of today.

But before the opportunity to be a very proud parent, I had to go out and get very very wet with the weather as unpredictable as ever or maybe that's not so true. I rarely get wet on my runs, could just be about the timing or maybe it doesn't rain as much as we think, but today I had to run before the day got going or not at all, so just had to be one of those days and run in the rain I did.

Sunday 11th September 2016 - the day the world changed.

A date that we all know, 9/11 or 11th September 2001, 15 years ago today was the day the world changed forever. As those planes hit the twin towers in New York, little did we know that life would never be the same again.

I guess we can all remember that day in 2001, where we were, what we were doing and the people we were with along with the different ways we all reacted. I still find it chilling after all these years and the on-going speculation of conspiracy theories et al, but whatever your feelings, the events of that day had a massive impact on us all.

For myself along with many others I would not doubt, I just wanted to have loved ones close and this had a knock-on effect on me in the days and weeks to come.

I was due to go on a walking weekend with my buddies, but I didn't go, I didn't want to be that far from my family.

Being a child of the sixties, I grew up with the impact of the IRA and the conflict in an island called Ireland. Nail bombs, hoax calls and slaughtered horses in the Mall. I also caught the tail end of the Vietnam War and as a child, I remember lying in bed worried about the war spreading to England, too young to realise that particular conflict was being fought in the jungles some six thousand miles away from my home in Leamington Spa.

Only as part of writing this book did I realise that the Vietnam War went on so long, 1st November 1955 to the 30th April 1975 – 19 years, 5 months, 4 weeks and one day!

And even more baggage - the Cuban Missile crisis and the Cold War, when I talk to my girls about when the eighties band from Liverpool, 'Frankie goes to Hollywood' sing about Two Tribes, the memories come flooding back. I remember the booklet dropping through the door to educate the homes of Britain on how to survive a nuclear attack – bloody hell! I did my fair share of protesting in London with CND back in the Eighties with my buddy Allan, power to the people and all that.

Growing up with all this going on and there's more, the Miners 'Strike, the three-day week and Margret Thatcher aka 'Thatcher the Snatcher' stopping our free milk back in 1971, shall I go on?

I often wonder how we all ended up being so well balanced and level-headed, but 9/11 would be different.

Although some might disagree, when both sides of an argument live with the fear of being killed, the conflict is equal and is fought on a relatively level playing field, but when your enemy thinks death equals utopia then your screwed.

On today's run, a lot of the talk was around 9/11 and the pretty predictable 'where were you?' Question. The inevitable conversations followed and became oh so clear was the fact that as a planet, we seem to have made very little progress. If as much effort went into good, the world would be a much better place, but alas I think that this could be a little outside of my brief for this life. So you just have to do what you can for those around us and 'love on the run' or love of life to be more precise in something in our control and we need to just make it happen.

Today's run was not all doom and gloom, far from it and whilst the heroes ran in and around Kenilworth, 220 miles away, 54000 runners were on the start line for the Great North

Run in Newcastle. 13.1 miles of fun in Geordie land. I made the trek to what felt like the other side of the world back in 2012 having won a place in the ballot to run in this iconic event and it's on my 'to do' list to do again.

But todays run was not just about the past, it was about being in the here and now.

We grabbed a coffee after the run this morning, always a treat to grab a cup of java after a great run and the fun of beasting the youth and that photo by the castle - that took a bit of taking I can tell you.

So arriving home in time see the Great North run on TV brought back all the memories and I might have shed a tear or two.

I have only ran the Great North Run once, back in 2012. I remember driving up to Newcastle some 200 miles from home on the Friday night. Julie could not believe how far it was, I guess Newcastle is not that far from Scotland. With the traffic busy with rush hour in full swing, the journey felt like forever.

My cousin John had recommended an accommodation option, Castle Leazes, university hall of residence within easy walk of the start. A group of us were taking part and all staying at the same place. I did not have a problem with the place, basic I grant you and not so spacious for the fuller figure, but perfectly adequate and cheap as chips.

Unfortunately, the choice was not to everyone's liking and will be relinquished from any future accommodation booking by certain members of the gang. The cosiness of the rooms and the compact nature of the bathroom coined the immortal phrase 'too fat for uni'.

The late nature of our arrival meant that we didn't meet up with Michaela, John and Kieron until the following day. Julie had entered the 5k fun run, a great route taking in both sides of the river in the shadow of the iconic Tyne Bridge. Although we had to get up early and head into the city centre, the riverside area was buzzing and finding a great viewpoint on Gateshead memorial bridge, I was delighted to cheer Julie over the finish line. After a shower and a much welcome breakfast, Julie and I joined the rest of the gang for a day in the 'toon' and a few beers of course.

After a day soaking in the atmosphere with Newcastle embracing GNR fever, the evening was all about carb loading not that seems to make much difference to me if I am honest.

A good breakfast is always a better option for me and after taking advantage of a brilliant spread provided by the halls and saying goodbye to Julie, we made the short walk to the start line. The only way the organisers can get over fifty five thousand participants over the start line is to close the A167 and turn the four lanes of the main route through the city into a running track.

From the elite runners at the front to the fun runners approximately a kilometre away at the back, the spectacle is an incredible site.

By the time I made the start area, I had successfully met up with Steve, co-founder of our running group, to take our place in the same start pen.

Micheala, John and Kieron were nearer the front, we would meet up later in the day in South Shields, some 13 miles away at the coast.

Whist, I waited to start, Julie had her work cut out having to make her way on public transport to the finish along with thousands of others with the same idea.

As Steve and I patiently watched the huge screens as wave after wave headed to the coast, the distant mass of heads gentle bobbing as the start line drew closer, gradually increasing on passing the timing mats and their race underway.

Looking ahead unaware of the dramatic arrival of RAF's crack aerobatic team, the Red Arrows from behind us complete with red, white and blue smoke. Steve and I beamed and this was one of the lasting memories of the day.

As the nine BAE Hawks followed the route to the sea, our wait was over and time for our wave to gently come alive and the line was crossed, watch started and our race was underway, next stop, South Shields and my wife, just the minor detail of 13.1 miles in between.

With such a massive field, I was never more than a few feet away from my fellow competitors, staying in our lanes for a few miles added to the banter with friendly heckling from the other carriageway and any under pass or tunnel brought on the chanting - aggy aggy aggy! as the fun continued. Soon it was my turn to cross the iconic Tyne Bridge, the crowds pretty much continuous for the 13 miles, three or four people deep in places.

The boast zone at around 10 miles did exactly was it says on the tin, talk about sensory over load, it's like Ibiza meets Parkrun, banging tunes, sweets and support that is off the scale.

With three miles to go, the Red Arrows are back and at round 12 miles, heading ever closer towards the finish, another moment.

As you run up a short straight incline, ahead you can hear the shouts, 'I can see the sea' and before long, we are shouting the same, over the brow and down hill with a sharp left and along the coast to the finish line which goes without saying is the focal point of any race along with the chaos and crowds that go with it as spectators keen to get a glimpse of the moment their loved ones cross the finish line.

Julie and I are old hands at this mass participation lark and much prefer to enjoy are far more leisurely reunion at either the charity stands or a point a little away from the bottle necks at the finish.

Although I had ran the miles, Julie shows the tell tale signs of an emotional wait, the big screens dotted around the event village told the stories of many of today's runners draining at times.

Tales of lost love ones, fights against the odds to recovery, along with the many charities and the amazing work they do.

I love the reunion, time to stop and reflect plus that all important sweaty hug. I always give a thought to my mum who had looked over me again and got me to the finish line safely, thanks mum.

With so many people, the phone signal is a bit hit and miss but we managed to rendezvous eventually with my fellow runners before head back to the toon. I am sure it would have been easier to run back but the organisation was brilliant and soon we were on the metro back to the city and a beer.

After a shower and fresh clothes, it was time to eat before the long drive home. We couldn't face it so stayed another night on the house, thank you Newcastle University.

So many great memories of the Great North Run, funny stories and great friends.

Tuesday 13th September 2016 - early start day #1.

The alarm going off at 5.00am was a bit of a shock to the system and opening my eyes to a very dark morning giving no clues to the beautiful day to come.

A lovely route today and yet another favourite, this one always amazes me how quickly after leaving the urbanisation of Chase Meadow and crossing the manic M40 motorway humming with the early morning commuters transfers into the tranquillity of the country lanes around and about Sherborne.

From the darkness, an orange glow in the autumn sky gave signs of the sunrise that would stop us in our tracks.

Great dynamics and banter on the run today with Libby and Ian, a spot of house hunting on the hoof with some absolute beauties on the route towards Hampton Lucy, from the cosy cottage on the corner to the impressive 'doctors house' (my favourite) or maybe the house on the hill.

To stand any chance of fulfilling this particular dream, I had best start saving my pennies or maybe write a best seller. (The later is in your hands, as the reader - like the book, tell a friend to buy a copy!).

On this particular route, the turnaround point as always is the forest hermitage and always a source of speculation and intrigue.

The secluded setting, CCTV and high fences might lead the investigation to something sinister but a Buddha or two at the entrance gives a clue to what really lies within the gates.

I know I have mentioned this place before, but I love the sense of mystery about the place and I want to find out more, I am really into all this type of stuff, so something else for the list.

This route is an out and back, so the return run retraces the outward journey, but as always, the run back is always quicker and have no idea why. Libby did not believe me, but was convinced at the end, doubt your dad? Trust me I'm your father.

The highlight of the run was the sunrise, absolutely breath taking and with some good farmyard smells to add to the ambiance, a perfect way to start the day, but all too soon its back over the M40 and back on the hamster wheel.

Wednesday 14th September 2016 - early start day #2.

I am not sure I can take two early starts on the trot but struggle to miss out on the chance to run in the morning.

Running with my first born again today, but this time heading in the opposite direction this morning. Leamington today and so warm after last night's storm, it was like running in a tropical rain forest as the spa town was still rubbing its eyes and coming alive.

All the places from my life on today's run, through Victoria Park, cloaked in ground fog, a legacy of the previous night's rain, across the Mill Bridge or 'the bridge of love' as we affectionately call it these days, stopping for a "runfie" as these mid-run self-portraits taken on smart phone are now officially called these days.

Leamington is a real town of contrasts with some a proper regency spa town and the bottom of town like Camden in London, but I do love this town.

Along the canal and talk of friends and Christmas – perfect.

Steve Atherton

16th-19th September 2016 - Off to the dark side.

It's that time of the year when running takes a back seat for a few days as I head over to the dark side or cycling to be more accurate and a chance to use some different muscles for a change.

To mis quote Lance Armstrong, from the title of his 2000 autobiography 'It's Not About the Bike' (well worth a read, whatever your opinion of the disgraced athlete). We were heading to mainland Europe for our annual lads cycling trip which as previous years are anything to go by, are definitely not about the bike. The trips to the continent with Rob, Paul and Nigel started back in 2014 when we rode the 406km Avenue Verte, one of the iconic cycling routes from London to Paris and from then on, the yearly outings have become a regular slot in our diaries.

Nigel and I started the bike ride routine a few years before in 2010 when we marked Nigel's 'fiftieth birthday year by doing the 'bucket list favourite' journey coast to coast ride from one side of England starting in Whitehaven on the west coast, having dipped our back wheels in the Irish sea before finishing some 140 miles later in Sunderland doing a similar tradition with the front wheel in the North Sea.

The years that followed took Nigel and I on some great adventures, before Rob and Paul joined the gang and the rest, as they say, is history.

Friday 16th September 2016 - Day one.

The first day of the trip is always an early start and it's all about trains, trains and more trains. I didn't sleep that great, always happens when I need to get up early. The fear of over sleeping and setting off late, and missing the train is always the underlying fear, although in all the years it has never happened.

To assist with the logistics especially on the journey home, I decided to leave my car in Coventry, negating the need to get up even earlier on day one. Meeting Nigel on route, together we cycle the empty city streets on the short ride to the station to meet Paul and Rob.

The anticipation and excitement already building on this chilly, dark September morning as two become four and ready for the off.

With the bikes in the guard's van, we settled in with a coffee on route to Euston.

We always give ourselves enough time to make the connections, trains rarely run on time these days and arriving in a very wet London we made the short ride across to St Pancras station. This connection is always the tight one, Eurostar do not make it easy or cheap to take a bike with you. Bikes are treated as freight, so much palaver and is unbelievably time consuming.

Once the bikes are checked in it's a dash across the station to get the boys aboard. Dressed in our gear, we do stand out just a little and seem to need four hands to carry everything but as always, we coped.

A very different station experience today from when my wife and I travelled to Bruges for our honeymoon back in 2015. That was champagne and smoked salmon as opposed to Lycra and energy drinks.

Once on the train, we relaxed, chatted, snoozed and had a bit of breakfast. Soon we were in Lille and time to be reunited with the bikes, this end is a lot easier.

Going out of the city is no mean feets but is all about maps, maps, maps and more maps along with a sprinkling or two of Mr google. We seem to quickly adjust to riding on the wrong side of the road, we left the rain in London and although a little windy, the first few kilometres on foreign shores were dry. But with the feeling the rain might be following, we anticipated more wet stuff on the way.

Heading south out of Lille with the aim of visiting the 'Memorial to the Missing of the Somme' at Thiepval, but a late start and a strong wind in our faces we opted to take the short cut to Arras realising that we would have been trying to find our hotel in the dark and wet if we not changed the plan and had we not took this shorter option.

Arras was to be our first overnight stop and keen to get to the hotel before the rain came, we opted for a late lunch in a supermarket car park, which was not fine dining but filled a gap as we headed to the French market town.

Whenever we cycle on the continent, the one topic of conversation that without fail crops up as we ride is where are all the people? Once you leave the hustle and bustle of the cities, the streets of the villages and towns are generally empty, regardless of the time of day. Ok we tend to travel during the day, but you would think that we would see the odd person out and about. Where do they all go? Asking for a friend...

With Arras in sight, the predicted rain came and before we got a real soaking, we were installed in our hotel. Home for the night was a lovely hotel, situated in a quiet fifteenth century building. 'Les Trois Luppars 'or 'The Three Leopards' full of character and a perfect location next to a bar.

Although each year our annual trip is different, the days do have a bit of a tried and tested routine. On arrival at the hotel, we divide and conquer. A couple get checked in whilst the bikes are looked after outside the hotel and once the bikes are safely garaged, it was time to call home and a quick beer.

After a few miles in the saddle, a beer is most welcome, seventy-five kilometres today. I am not a big lager drinker but after a bit of exercise, a cold one always hits the spot. There is nothing better that a chance to sit in the sun, usually on a soft seat and blow the froth off a large beer.

The French are not great at making beer to be honest, but with Belgium not too far away, the bar had Leffe on draft. So, four large blonds it is then. 'Could I have a drop of lime in mine please, gents?'

You would have thought I would have murdered someone asking for lime!

Beer drunk and phone calls made, we check out our rooms. We always go for twin rooms, which all adds to the fun. With a stint in the saddle, a nice shower is always a treat before heading off into town for a few more beers and some food.

The hotel's location was perfect and by now the rain was lashing down and obviously in for the night. We travel light so we were not really dressed for the weather in our traditional t shirts, shorts and flip flops. Fashion icons we certainly are not but when it comes to food, no corners are cut. Rob is the master of finding the best places to eat and over the years that lad has excelled but tonight due to an issue with the original choice of restaurant, La Bulle'd O, the number one place to eat in Arras, according to trip advisor, We headed to Bistrot du Boucher, the second best restaurant in Arras.

The food was excellent and a great atmosphere, Nigel and I sampled the kidney casserole, which was superb, so good we still talk about years later. Our well-deserved culinary delights washed down with a few of glasses of red.

The rain continued to lash it down, so we chose to stay local once we were fed and watered. It had been a long day so given the choice of an early night or one for the road, we did best thing and headed to a local bar to drink loads, the bar was packed and just happened to have karaoke. Needless to say, a great night was had by all and soon we were in with the locals. Nigel belted out some karaoke classics and before long he had the bar eating out of his hands.

The combination of exercise, good food and alcohol, a good night's sleep albeit short and sweet was most welcome.

Saturday 17th September 2016 - Day two.

The first morning on foreign shores started with disappointment, what no tea! Tea and coffee making facilities in hotel rooms is pretty much standard back at home but less so on the continent. Having had a lifetime of early morning alarm calls, a lie in does not come easy for neither Nigel nor I, so with both of us wide awake at six o'clock, a nice cup of Rosie would have been just what the doctor ordered.

By contrast the breakfast at 'Les Trois Luppars 'did not disappoint, the breakfast room located in the cellar was a sight to behold with a fair feast of goodies to delight the taste buds, great coffee and tea too. The four of us made a good job of taking on calories that we would need for the miles ahead. Rainy Friday turned into bright and sunny Saturday and a chance to see Arras, historic centre of the Artois region in all is glory.

Our hotel was on the edge of the stunning baroque square, 'Grand Place' and with the arrival of the weekend, came the hustle and bustle of the market. Cycling is big in France and a couple of members of a local cycling club offered to escort us out of town. From my own experience, one cobbled street looks pretty much the same as another, so the offer of help was very much appreciated and a chance to connect with genuine people, we were soon on our way to Vimy Ridge and the spectacular Canadian monument and memorial park.

Visiting the reconstructed trenches brought home the horrors of the first world war. The place has a connection with Nigel and Paul as we visited the grave of Lieutenant Colonel Mike Watkins a Bomb Disposal expert buried alive in 1998 carrying out that work.

Lens provided the location for lunch as we headed north towards the Belgium border and Ypres.

Stopping in the border town of Armentieres provided the opportunity to keep hydrated with less than twenty miles left on the bike. The coffee shop gave the opportunity to people watch as well a chance to 'drop in' on a local wedding at the town hall opposite, the bride and groom travelling in style in a classic Ford Mustang flanked by a cavalcade of hogs. We would see more of these American iconic motorcycles later in the day.

The route to Arras was well sign posted with towns and roads turning into country lanes and tiny villages. Signs offering fresh strawberries for sale on every corner with farm shops a plenty selling a plethora of local produce. The sun continued to shine with blue skies replacing the grey rain clouds of the previous day. So much nicer to cycle in the dry weather as we stayed where possible on quite county lanes, although enviably adding a mile or two to the trip.

The occasional need for running repairs on route are few and far between which is a bonus with any issues generally sorted with a bit of duct tape (aka duck tape) or a cable tie or two.

Hedgerow trench cemetery was unexpectedly stunning, understated and peaceful with a woodland backdrop. It was nice to stop reflect. Finding a grave with my surname on was a little off putting, not sure if we were related, that might be worth some future research.

The ride continued, stopping at the odd roadside cemetery just to contemplate the futility of war with so many names of the youth of the nation's forever immortalised on a granite column. Chester Farm Cemetery five kilometres south of Ypres or Lepers in the pretty hamlet of West Vlaanderen was lovely. I did wonder off a little to take a couple of photos of rusty farm machinery much to the delight of the boys, attracting a bit of banter if any evidence was needed to confirm that I maybe I am just little special.

Today's convoluted meandering route would take us to Ypres, just under sixty miles in the saddle and to The Albion Hotel which would be our home for the next couple of nights.

You know the plan now so following the regular routine of a call home and a couple of beers followed by a quick shower then out. Our first stop on arriving in Ypres became our bar of choice for the rest of the weekend (and in future years too), just off the square and seemed popular with fellow cyclists. Allan, landlord of the Times could not have been more helpful.

The bar's location, to quote the website ...*within a stone's throw from the Cloth Hall...at a bow shoot from the Menin Gate.*

On the edge of the market square, which was full of Harley Davidson's, the significance we would find out later in the night.

I couldn't resist a chat with a couple of the bikers, a friendly bunch even if they were just ever so slightly intimidating.

This book was never intended to be a travel guide however the last post at the Menin Gate should be on everyone's bucket list. The large hall of memory has the names of over fifty thousand soldiers whose bodies have never been found or identified and every night at 8pm, the last post is played. Bands and choirs from around the world can apply to take part in the ceremony and on our first night, a moving performance from a bagpipe band and escorted by a cavalcade of Harley Davidsons who we had seen earlier. I am not sure that I have witnessed such a poignant tribute to the fallen of the First World War. Farmers continue to this day to find remains of soldiers and if they identification can be made, then a conventional grave is prepared, usually near where the poor soul was found, and the name removed from the Menin Gate.

After a day in the saddle visiting numerous memories, the magnitude of the numbers who died from all sides of the conflict was becoming ever clearer. Described as the war to end all wars and with conflict continuing around the world to this day, I am not sure if mankind has learnt a thing. When you hear astronauts, who have been into space and looked back on the earth all say the same thing, it's one planet, one world. When will we ever learn!

Best laid plans of mice and men continued in our search for culinary excellence when the recommended eating house of choice could not fit us in on Saturday night. An issue that had already been addressed for the following evening courtesy of the host at our now local. So we opted to eat in the square, with so many restaurants to choose from, it was a case of picking one at random, pulling up a chair and going for it.

Sunday 18th September 2016 - Day three.

The Albion Hotel provided tea making facilities, what a result! Sunday started with a cup of tea and courtesy of our body clocks, Nigel and I had the opportunity to take a walk around town including another visit to the Menin Gate. It looked so different with streets bereft of crowds and very peaceful and the scale of this memorial clear to see.

The marktplatz, deserted with only street cleaners cleaning away the signs of a busy Saturday night.

We are staying in Ypres a second night which means we can travel light with no panniers, always a treat, so after another hearty breakfast we headed out of town. So many cyclists out this morning, many in huge groups but no one speaks, not even a nod of the head. I can appreciate that those taking part in a race might be focused on the prize, but solo cyclists out for a bit of exercise, would not hurt to show a modicum of acknowledgment, miserable bastards.

Taking advantage of being 'bagless' for the day along with having no real time constraints, we took a round trip to the coast. You've got to love a trip to the seaside, Ypres to Diksmuide to Nieuwpoort and back to Ypres - ninety five kilometres.

Leaving Ypres along the excellent paths that follow the waterways, Belgium and France for that matter take cycling seriously and really are geared up for it. Mid-morning, we took a coffee break at Knokkebrug, a lovely little cafe called 'De Knoke' situated on the side of a canal. Sitting in the sun we could hear the thunder of the approaching peloton, best let these boys pass. I was amazed by the noise forty plus bikes can make.

Leaving the cycle path and joining the road we headed to Diksmuide. On the side of road and canal stool the stark peace monument called the Yser Tower, the original was built after the First World War in the 1920, but was subsequently demolished in 1946 because during the Second World War it had been the scene of Nazi ceremonies and collaboration. A new tower was built in the 1950s towering 84 metres (276 ft) tall and is one of the highest peace monuments in Europe and stands as a symbol of Flemish nationalism. Continuing on our way, it was getting time for some food and lunch was something special, well it was Sunday!

We dropped on a lovely little brassiere on the picturesque market square in Nieuwpoort which was a real find. The food at the *'Brasserie Nieuwpoort'* was top drawer, the place was busy but we managed to find a table outside in the sun, overlooking the square. Saving ourselves for the evening meal, lunch generally is on the lighter side usually with no beer as a rule, but the menu was amazing and every plate of food leaving the kitchen a work of art. Nigel and I both opted for the fish soup which served with bread, rouille and parmesan cheese was amazing. A place I would love to go back to for dinner. I still have the business card, just in case.

Nieuwpoort was only a mile from the coast but this was as close as we actual got to the seeing the sea, the beaches of Belgium and Holland would have to wait for a future trip maybe.

Heading south, Nigel's carefully planned itinerary continued as we headed back to Ypres via Vladslo German Military Cemetery. German cemeteries have a completely different atmosphere to other countries tributes to the fallen. The headstones are generally ground level black granite tiles inscribed with the names of the dead, sometimes multiple bodies in the same place, the location often lined with Oak trees, the symbol of strength and endurance in many countries including Germany.

From the numerous Germany cemeteries dotted around France and Belgium, Nigel had carefully selected Vladslo, famous for the sculpture of the grieving parents, 'Die Eltern ' (The Parents) by Kathe Kollwitz whose work under the Nazis was considered 'degenerate 'and was banned. She made the statues in the 1930s as a tribute to her youngest son, Peter, who was killed in October 1914 and is buried in the cemetery. The eyes on the father-figure gaze on the stone directly in front of him, on which Kollwitz's son's name is written, so simple but unbelievably thought inspiring. This one particular tribute provided one of the most lasting memory of any of our trips in my opinion.

In addition to 'Die Eltern', the cemetery contains the remains of 25,644 soldiers with each stone bearing the name of twenty soldiers, with just their name, rank, and date of death specified.

From Vladslo, on the outskirts of Diksmuide, we zig zagged across the country back to Ypres.

Sunday is 'the day' it seems, the day when people appear from where they have been hiding, appear in their masses. The streets of towns and villages become pop up markets with stalls a plenty selling an eclectic selection of shite, most of which, in my opinion should have been loaded in the car and been taken straight to the tip. With the streets full of people, we had no choice than to get off our bikes, have a stroll and take in the atmosphere. So this is where people go on a Sunday and I like it!

As sure as night follows day, after a day in the saddle, a couple of beers at the Times bar was a given this time with a plate of cheese, cold meats and a bit of mustard, what's not to like.

Our final dinner on the continent was at the restaurant recommended by Allan, 'mein host' from 'The Times' and after a quick aperitif in the said bar, we made our way to the restaurant, only a couple of streets from the main square, but a little off the tourist trail.

Dressed in our evening attire, we made our way into the swanky restaurant, t shirts, shorts and flip flops not really in keeping with the obeisance of a fine dining establishment but to be honest, the maitre'd did not bat an eye, showing the four of us to our table and we were treated like royalty.

The food was delicious and fitting of our last night. Finishing the evening with a nightcap or two back at our local, I was introduced to Jura, a malt whiskey from the island of the same name by a fellow cyclist from as it would happen from the Scottish island of Jura. It has been a favourite ever since.

Steve Atherton

Monday 19th September 2016 - Day four.

Time to head home, always my least favourite day of the trip, not because I am going home, but today comes the constraint and pressure of the clock. We have trains to catch and these will not wait for us. I find that I always am mindful of time on the last day. The schedule always factors in a bit of fat as they say, or a little extra time as a contingency in case of any problems on route ensuring that we inevitably arrive at the final destination in good time, allowing a chance to grab a beer once we have checked the bikes in at Eurostar. But that is some eighty kilometres away and first we have places to go and sights to see.

From Ypres we headed out to the 'Tyne Cot Memorial to the Missing', a massive immaculate Commonwealth Cemetery. The cycle path out of town was flat and wide allowing good progress to be made before fate played its card. A piece of tin managed to cut the wall of my tyre and slash my inner tube bringing the group to a stop. Spare inner tubes we carry but unfortunately a tyre we don't. With the inner tube replaced, the extent of the problem became clear. 85 pounds per square inch of air does not help a thin tube of rubber stay within the confines of the tyre and soon the inner tube started to bulge out of the slit. Duct tape to the rescue and with a few loops of the black stuff holding the inner tube in place we were back on our way.

Just for information, that temporary repair was good for at least another fifty miles until I could get into my local bike shop for a new tyre.

Tyne Cot is the largest cemetery for Commonwealth forces in the world, for any war with the remains of 11,965 soldiers of which 8,369 are unnamed. The name 'Tyne Cot' is said to come from the *Northumberland Fusiliers*, seeing a resemblance between the many German concrete *pill boxes* on this site and typical Tyneside workers' cottages (Tyne cots). A peaceful place and so glad we paid a visit, when we visit a place like this, we all seem to find our own space and take on the atmosphere and emotions in our own way, a lasting memory.

We were making good progress, so we stopped for a coffee in Passendale, a lovely little cafe called Cafe Sint Joris, these little places do the best coffee, proper cafe culture. The sun continued to shine as we headed through rolling Belgian countryside on route to the coast with the fields littered with graveyards and memorials. The poor souls were buried where they fell it seems, grouped together as a symbolic reminder of a fatal skirmish with many graves marked with the inscription 'A soldier of the great war', others carry a different wording, 'Known to be buried in this cemetery'; this one I find more hard hitting. Both poignant reminders of a family grieving with the final resting place unknown, heart-breaking and must be extremely hard on those left behind.

Our ride continued in the direction of Lille for the train home and with one eye on the clock, we took in the 'Island of Ireland Peace Park 'and the 'Ploegsteert Memorial to the Missing'. You could easily take all day to cover a few miles if you stopped at every cemetery or monument, but Nigel had done his research and had the significant places baked into the itinerary. Retracing some of the route from the first day which was enviable as we headed back to the border town of Armentieres and back into France to follow the path alongside the ship canal towards Lille.

Lille is the fourth largest urban area in France, so navigation in and around the city can be a little tricky especially on bikes. So we were delighted to delivered to the Eurostar Terminal by a friendly local out for a leisurely afternoon ride. Some good people around.

After the shaky start to the day, we arrived in good time and once the bikes were safely booked in for the journey back to London, it was time for a beer. Eurostar like to have the bikes with them two hours before the train goes, which always provides more than enough time to head to La Grand Place, a stunning vibrant square a short walk from the station, for a couple of beers.

Only just over an hour on Eurostar to London St Pancras, a short bike ride to Euston, another train to Coventry, back on the bike then a short drive and we will be home!

A great trip lads and some amazing memories.

To go completely off at a tangent, this book has been in the making for some time as the events of Friday 2nd December which you will read about later kind of took over the months and years proceeding so this book, originally book one has become book two. The spring of 2020 turned the world upside down with covid-19 or the corona virus turning life on its head. Sat in our garden, with a glass of wine talking to Rob desperately trying to remember where and what we ate reinforcing the fact that at the end of the day and beer is drunk, food becomes a bit of an afterthought. I love these guys, an enclitic mix of people that over the years has grown into something that I never thought would be possible, the warm and friendship is special. As the years progress, four become five as Paul L. joins the family but you might have to wait for book three to find out more about him.

Wednesday 21st September 2016 - Houston we have a problem!

Ok, may be a little dramatic and hardly life threatening, but to a runner, wanting the loo mid run can be as bad as being lost in space. Fortunately, I have a tried and tested routine that has worked for me for many a year, but just occasionally life or my body to be more accurate, has other ideas. Unpredictable and never a pattern or early warning signs, occasionally my routine does not work and without putting you off your dinner, I need a poo. Today was the day, at the point in the run furthest from home of cause. The first feelings of a rumble in the jungle start to make their presence know. A little flutter in the tummy, followed by three miles of clenched buttocks to focus the mind, Oh yes, give me the wall any day of the week.

Just for the record, I did make it back home in time – just and what else did we talk about on the run – not a clue!

The day continues and certainly went running off at a tangent ....

Got to love social media and a master of the book of face is my running buddy – Pippa. We met back in 2014 in Egypt when we had some great if not scary runs in Sharma el shake. Pip lives with her husband, Sam in Plymouth and I kept in touch with her since our holiday via Facebook. She is a really full on lady, never stops, but this weekend she was on one, inviting me to some bazaar event. 'Will I be eaten by the 30th September ?' some whacky facebook event tracking the fortune of a packet of Cadbury Mini Rolls bought for her mate, absolutely barking but very funny never the less. I really want to try and meet up with the two of them soon.

We have been in our happy home for three years today and we fell in love with the house on the first visit. Love at first sight as they say but I very soon realised the running potential of the location. On the banks of the river, near a park half-way between two fabulous towns, the house picked us.

After a day at work, it's time to celebrate, fish, chips and champagne in the garden – tradition....tradition! Forgive the Fiddler on the Roof quote, but the day we moved in and with everything in boxes and no sofas, a chippy tea outside sitting on old garden chairs was the order of the day and we have continued the tradition ever since.

Friday 23rd September 2016 – end of the week run.

A quick run around the park and back was just what I needed to end the week and get me ready for the weekend. It is really handy having such a lovely place to run right on my door step. Now is the bar open, I am ready for a drink.

Saturday 24th September 2016 - MT.

To run or not to run or 'Where the f**k did my energy go? excuse my French.'

Busy old day today but I still wanted to run and managed 0.8 of a mile! I don't normal give you the stats, but today you needed to know. So tough to drag myself around today, absolutely no energy what so ever. I ran to Kingfisher Lake and back and that was enough, but the run was about getting some fresh air, I need to do better than this for sure.

Sunday 25th September 2016 - Back in the groove.

Having had a break from the running last weekend taking a chance to sit down for a few days, but it was good to get back in the groove. I needed to run but wanted to check out the horse fair on route, got to be done really.

The route was good today with a few hills and some great therapy with a number of stress heads about today, including me! A bit of fun on the run is always good for the soul.

Almost feels like running and being out in the countryside absorbs all our cares and worries, a bit new agey I know, but to run and chat does the trick every time.

Sometimes it's good to run alone and let your head do the crunching and stress busting too. But today was all about the company, the people and I need to be back on it now with a couple of key events coming fast on the horizon.

A 10k run with a half marathon on consecutive weekends and scores to be settled, but I have lost my running buddy Trish for the Birmingham Half so best get a plan B.

Wednesday 28th September 2016 - boys will be boys.

Talk was all about childhood memories on the run today, conkers, marbles, British bulldog (I don't think so, I still have nightmares) and all those great traditions that we grew up with.

With the ever shrinking planet we seem to have lost the seasons, strawberries in December, hot cross buns any time of the year and don't get me started on Easter Eggs! The calendar is all to cock but the catalyst for todays run, the spark, was conkers or the seeds of the horse chestnut tree to be precise.

As young boys, this time of year was all about conkers, the tree lined avenues of our beautiful towns were a magnet for every lad in the neighbourhood. They would be endeavouring to tempt the fruit from the wise old trees, leaving the floor littered with sticks and broken branches as evidence of the mission to persuade the conkers prematurely from the branches, ready to be prepared for battle in the playground the following day.

The routine was repeated across the country with every school yard up becoming a stadium for battle, I might be accused of being sexist but conkers was a lad thing, right?

We all had our little secrets to win the day and end up with a 'forty niner' or what ever the victorious score was.

Whether it be to soak the beast in vinegar or baked it in the oven to prolong the life of our stringed warrior, the ideas were the talk of the playgrounds.

Today the floor was littered with potential winners that we would have sold our soul for back in the day, but time has moved on. Today they lay waiting for a school boy to take them into battle, but alas on the floor they would stay. The trees free from the annual attack and the streets bereft of young boys, we have gone health and safety mad and conker season is now a thing of the past.

Yet another lost tradition, such a shame, did anyone die from playing conkers when we were kids? I doubt it, a few bruised knuckles and the occasional black eye maybe, but instead today we have pale kids who do not know how to socialise – not sure I would call it progress.

Return home from work, a surprise waiting for me, my race number for Birmingham Half marathon, just over two weeks to go, exciting.

Steve Atherton

Friday 30th September 2016 - Just one more maybe?

Its only 26.2 miles and I have done it a couple of times before so maybe for my final marathon I should do something a little special. On the day entries open for the 2017 Birmingham marathon opens, I am in a real dilemma. I really want to run one more marathon to make it a hat trick and to run pretty much on my door step would cut out all the travel issues or is that part of the attraction.

Do I make it really special and go international, I would love to take part in the iconic New York marathon and would also like to go to New York so it's a win win situation and there is always the London Marathon ballot although the odd are better for me becoming pope and winning the lottery.

The time when the letter arrives is days away, either a 'woop woop' you're in letter, give us your money or the far more common it seems, a 'quack quack oops' reply, which according to social media in October, the more regular post.

I have entered the ballot for who knows how many times so like myself, you will have to wait and see as I take my chances along with the other five million in the pot...)

But tonight my thoughts are a little more imminent and closer to home as I plan to take part in the local park run in the morning, and a change from my usual Saturday routine which by now you know all too well and I am under a bit of pressure to be honest, my buddy Steve is going to push me round the undulating Leamington Spa Park run course, it's home turf and I want to do the 5k circuit in less than twenty eight minutes.

October 2016

Saturday 1st October 2016 - time to make the changes.

It's quarter four, so already three quarters of the way through the year. Best get a wiggle on if I want to achieve some of my goals for 2016.

After a really crap night's sleep due to a combination of excitement and nerves for the pending assault on the Newbold Common park run course, Saturday morning was upon us.

Not sure why I am nervous, Park run is five kilometres, half the distance I generally run on Saturday mornings. Half the distance I generally run when I put my trainers on actually, but today was different, I was on a mission. I had work to do, I had a target, but as I left the house the heavens opened. Just what I needed! If it ain't raining, it ain't training as they say. But I would have liked a dry start to the day on the first day of a new month.

By the time I parked up and hooked up with my running buddy and newly appointed coach, Steve and the rain had stopped – a good omen.

Park run is such a great concept and this is only my fifth appearance according to the database and after a break for a month or two, it was good to be back.

Loads of familiar faces on Newbold Common this morning and a great turn out as always and with all the pre-amble before the start, it felt like race day. I needed the loo and my heart pounded.

I love Newbold Common, a place I know and love and not a million miles from our old flat. So I have ran this route many times before and although in the opposite direction from Park run, the route around Newbold Common is half the route of the annual Regency run (my first race back in 2005 where it all started in my first race since leaving school).

I know the route and I know the hill and today, I was going to smash it and get a good start. I thought that with the dreaded hill out of the way and about a third of the run out of the way, it was time to get in my stride and enjoy the view.

Phil, a great friend and fellow Sunday runner had already showed me a clear pair of heels, but today was about me. I love to see my home town from the top of the hill in whatever direction you take around the municipal golf course.

Today I ran with Vince as well, an old school friend and, after thirty years, he is now a work colleague. Strange how life works!

We were cruising and I might just have finished ahead of him, but the final results would tell. The race was not yet over, we still had about a kilometre to go; Steve suggested that we push it a little more and maybe a little less talking would help.

With the finish in site, we were cruising, and I gave it all I had.

Did I manage to run sub twenty-eight minutes, and did I beat Vince? Both questions would be answered later the same morning.

The results are in :-

Me, finish position 225, time 27 minutes 51 seconds,

and

Vince, finish position 240 time 28 minutes 16 seconds.

Get in, really happy with that, thanks Coach Steve!

Sunday 2nd October 2016 - Early doors and new blood.

With the Birmingham Half Marathon only a couple of weeks away now, I thought it was about time I got a long run in so an early start to squeeze a few extra miles in before the main group head out.

I always feel it is better to get the extra miles in first and today gave me a chance to meet up with a fellow member of a great Facebook group, 'Running the World' and also a local runner, Ali who wanted to join the group for a while, but a little nervous about the thought of running with new people.

Running clubs or new groups in general can be a little intimidating regardless how much the sales pitch promotes the friendly and welcoming of its organisers and members to new people.

The first visit to a running club can be daunting, especially if you are new to the sport and I know what it feels like to be always at the back of a more experienced group of runners.

By their very nature, running clubs want good runners, stands to reason, but does pee me off a little as the strive for the best can exclude some great people. Real people with potential, but their loss is my gain and our little group is the perfect place to build confidence and help people achieve.

I don't normally do this as a rule, but this morning an hour ahead of the group I met up with Ali. The Greenway and Hollis Lane provided a perfect back drop for our maiden run together and four miles in the bag on this wonderful morning, back to the car for a quick gel and a glug of water then off to Ashow for a spot of 'house hunting' (I wish, the houses down there are mega!). If ever in doubt, my faith in human nature restored and confidence of the members of our group to make Ali welcome, a given, but it was lovely to see her chatting with everyone, doing the rounds and oozing new found confidence.

Looks like the group win again and the planning starts for an outing to the panto and maybe the rugby.

Thursday 6th October 2016 - The future.

'The best thing about the future is that it comes only one day at a time'
– Abraham Lincoln

I love this quote and was quite apt on my run today as I missed out last night due to a conference call at the time I was planning on heading out. I am in Dusseldorf at the moment, and I was hoping to catch the last weak rays of the sun at the end of a workday, but alas was not to be.

But that was yesterday, so with a new day ahead, I was hitting those German streets this morning. It was a little chilly, the shape of things to come and my face had a bit of a cherry on.

The hotel, although lovely is in the middle of an industrial estate and in the dark, my choices of places to run are limited. Today it was a pretty dull route to be honest, very grey such a shame as in daylight, it's a different story with some stunning routes around lakes and woods but not today.

With nothing else to do, I picked up the pace and had a good old chat with myself. I have said many times before, but life is all about people for me, unless you live as a hermit in a cave you need people in your life. We are by nature, pack animals when all is said and done.

I do love to run with others, and I do most of the time, but on occasions I do run alone and it's then when I feel the inner me comes out for a run too. Some proper deep thinking sometimes, a little on the heavy side I cannot deny and other times I am all over the place, but always make progress.

Just because I could and as the hotel happens to have a great gym, I finished my exercise session with some fit ball sit ups – ouch!

I did enjoy the view from the tenth floor and the sun was rising on yet another busy day.

Friday 7th October 2016 - good to be back.

Running on a Friday afternoon with my friend Sue used to be a regular entry in my diary, but we haven't managed to get out of late, but today taking advantage of a short workday, we did.

For reasons I cannot recall, it's been a while since we managed to run on Friday afternoons, work I guess. So after a long break, it was good to get them back in the calendar.

Sue lives in north Leamington, we used to live around the corner from each other, so it was also nice for me to be back on familiar territory.

The location gives endless route opportunities, either town based or out in some stunning rural locations, but as it's a favourite place for both of us, we head to Newbold Common.

Autumnal colours and some sunshine providing a breathtaking back drop to the end of the week with a lovely afternoon run. A phone call on the run from my Zero to Hero buddy Steve with good news about a new job, congratulations buddy!

The phone back in the pocket we head around the edge of the common, paths flanks with golden leaved hedgerows and rays of sun like lasers penetrating the tree canopy. Running does not get better than this, and heading back into civilisation, Sue increases the pace, hold on Sue, slow down!

Saturday 8th October 2016 - run fat boy run.

I think I have cracked it, red wine is the future, but combined with an early start, I am not sure it will catch on. But definitely worked for me this morning.

Another run today with my new training buddy Steve and less than 24 hours since the last time, I am back on Newbold Common to take part in Leamington Park run.

A lovely morning, very autumnal and such a beautiful place to run as I told you yesterday. But this morning was not about the view but was all about speed. I was ready, Rioja fueled, a good turn out and a good to see an old buddy and great supporter from the past Clive.

Starting steady we soon got in the groove, Steve was watching the clock and I could tell that he was happy, then the hill, it's always about the hill. I am not a big fan of hills and its pure physics as far as I am concerned.

I would love to quote the formula, but it's been a year or two since I was a school so will have to settle for the effects of angle of the dangle. But I am sure mass and elevation have something to do with energy somewhere along the way.

I was blowing like an old steam engine by the top but recovered quickly and time in settle into a rhythm and enjoy the view from the top.

It did not help with my phone going off constantly in my pocket, my car was in for a service, but I was in the zone and for the next few kilometres, the garage would have to wait.

I was in the groove and felt good, then Steve had to go and spoil it didn't he. With four hundred metres from the finish, came the challenge. Which of my fellow runners we were going to pass and leave behind on the final up at the finish line?

I was not convinced but turning the corner, seeing the end and boom, I was off, dropped a gear and the result twenty-seven minutes, two seconds. I was so pleased and felt great and hoping this result would stand me in good stead for tomorrow.

Sunday 9th October 2016 - As good as it gets.

A break from tradition last night and although it was Saturday night, I decided to not hit the bottle and behave like a real athlete, the impact, good or bad, I night never know.

A new event for me today and the other 300 or so runners as it's the first ever GreenLeek, a 10k race from Burton Green to Leek Wootton hence the name and a real mixture of terrain.

It was a bit chilly at the start and was questioning my kit choice, shorts or leggings? I went for shorts as I do not like being hot but wondered if I had made the right call.

Registration was a cracking social event in itself with the great and the good of the area out to give this new event a try.

Lovely to see so many familiar faces, some I actually remembered their names and a nice hot cup of coffee too, just what you need pre-race.

I wanted to try and get a team photo with our local sporting celebrity David Moorcroft, but he was being a little elusive at the moment so would have to be patient, not a problem as by nature I am patience personified. I can hear those close to me laughing already!

The atmosphere at the warm-up was great but why did I need the loo, here we go, usual race day malarkey. An apprehensive walk down to the start and time for some Zero to Hero recruiting on the hoof, has to be done and never miss the change to swell our numbers.

As we crossed the field to the start on the greenway, David appeared but too late for that photo. With the safety briefing done including a mention of the wobbly bridge for good measure it was time to edge a closure to the start, we needed to be a little closer to the front today.

Today was the day, the day Coach Steve and I were working up too and we were on a mission. The route included a stretch down the greenway, a disused railway and a good surface to run on, plus the greenway was an old friend and I knew that she would do me proud today.

The wait was over, boom and we were on our way, a bit of banter in the early few strides and time to overtake a few people to find some space and soon we were in the groove. The first few kilometres, straight and flat - just how I like it and gives me chance to talk to Steve a little to calm the nerves and a bit more recruitment on the run.

I knew change was ahead but for now it felt good (how good? I would find out later) no technology on the run for me today, we agreed that I would not wear my Garmin. Coach Steve was in the driving seat, which meet no distractions for me this morning, today was all about me and today I was going to run my race.

Steve Atherton

A few roads to cross as we ran into Kenilworth, today the cars had to wait for us, still on familiar territory and a route I have done before which helped the confidence. The familiar territory was about to come to an end as, after being directed by some very friendly race marshals it was time to head away from home turf and try a new place to run. Off the tarmac paths and back to nature and a bit of trail running.

The second half of the route came with a little undulation, but not a problem as halfway in we were still passing people. The fast runners of the group had already showed Steve and I a clean pair of heels when we arrived at the drinks station and more friendly marshals.

I was ready for a bit of water and with my body temperature a little warmer than I started, a cooling head bath was lovely.

From now on, the route was all off road and I was not sure what lies ahead but I could see Rouncil Lane ahead. Surely not, I had lost my bearings and sense of direction. We were further into the race than I thought, which has got to be a good sign.

A short section of road then I could sense the end wasn't too far away and just what I needed.. some of the zero to hero cyclists who had come along to cheer us on – 'Stevo' I heard the cry and what a pick up, cheers folks!

I could see Phil ahead and I knew I now had another challenge, I was in my stride now and off into the woods, surely the finish cannot be much further but then a hill, just what I needed.

I had a bit of a wobble, short lived to be honest, I could hear the finish and I have this. With Steve still at my side, we pulled out the stops and I'm back, around the corner catching glimpse of a stunning view – England my England, but this morning was not for sight-seeing, that could wait for another day.

Head up, chest out and sprint to the finish line and what a feeling, crossing the finish line the strongest I have ever done and I was buzzing.

Collecting my medal and a goody bag – banana, drink and a Mars bar, which did not touch the sides.

A very happy bunny and time to watch the rest of the heroes return home. Kathys first 10 k and the biggest cheer of the day and well deserved. Special times and with everyone home and the arrival of David Moorcroft, time for that photo – result!

Today, for once, I ran my own race and it felt amazing, thanks Steve!

Monday 10th October 2016 - When is a good time to taper?

You will have gathered by now that I like to run but I never know when to stop. I have another race coming up on Sunday, a half marathon this time, so I really should ease off a bit or tapering to get all technical. But I will be away for a few days for work and want to catch up on the goss with my dawn runners, so out at the crack of dawn this morning around the streets of Warwick.

I am off on my travels again, flying to Sweden later today and I will want to run there too but need to take it easy – bloody hell!

I might just give my Saturday run a miss, maybe Thursday too – watch this space….

Tuesday 11th October 2016 - Gothenburg, Sweden.

Ok so I ran again! I love the air in Sweden and take any excuse to get some good lung fuels into me and I am not going to miss out on the opportunity. A tough busy day ahead of me today so needed to get the blood pumping and for me, there is no finer way.

The run along the river is beautiful and did bring a tear to my eyes, but not from emotion but the howling wind. Just amazing and feel very lucky to have the chance to get out and about in such a lovely city. I have two more days here and I have a plan, run the river and cross the bridge.

Wednesday 12th October 2016 - change.

'The ability to change and adapt is what separates humans from the animal kingdom' or the bed won!

I try not to deviate from my plans if I can help it, but today I had little choice but to do just that.

I am not sure what happened yesterday, what was different or out of the ordinary, I had nothing strange to eat or drink, but all through the travel day and again this morning my heart was racing, talk about hyper.

No more coffee for me today and I avoided anything that could potentially raise my heart rate. I thought I would listen to my body and boy oh boy it seemed to have plenty to say these last few days.

I really missed my usual kick start to the day today, but opted for an early start and with an early start comes the chance of an early finish and the offer of free bikes from the hotel, the answer had got to be a yes from me.

Swopping wheels for trainers, the bikes gave Thomas and I the chance to check out a little further along the river to the beautiful little village of Nya Varvet.

Although in sight of the city of Gothenburg, the houses in this stunning little place could have been very much in place in New England. Brightly painted wooden houses on every corner and so peaceful, but if you lived here, you would have to have a boat.

The water was a magnet and I would love to see more of this place. The bike was interesting too, like an old butchers bike, no gears and backward peddle brakes. It took a bit of getting used too but helped to blow the cobwebs away and a little easier on the old ticker. So nice to spend some time with Thomas away from the office and did tick off one of my routes for this trip, even though it was not quite to plan. But adaptable I can be and sometimes spontaneity is a bonus.

Thursday 13th October 2016 - Take me to the bridge!

The bridge has been on my list for a while, Mike from the office has tempted me with selfies from the elevated vantage point overlooking the city for a while, but I thought the route up from the hotel seemed to be a little tricky on foot but actually was a piece of cake.

It was dark and cold and ever so slightly windy (ok it was blowing a gale) and after I made it to the top and on to the path some forty five metres above the water, construction on the city side of the bridge denied me the view I was after and it was still very dark and windy.

I think I mentioned it was windy, so I did not run all the way across, that will be for next time and my heart was still going faster than I wanted it too. I was craving the wow of the view and not the rush of the wind, call me a wuss, but still have memories of Normandy, the nightmares of cycling over the Pont de Normadie last year – deep breaths.

Saturday 15th October 2016 - Tradition – a different Saturday.

Tapering, what's this tapering of which you speak?

With an event tomorrow I wanted to do just a short one today and it was a beautiful morning with a busy day ahead, so good to get out. I always love running in our hometown and I love the square in Warwick on a Saturday morning, the sounds and smells of the towns regular market. But today my usual stalls of fruit and veg and great things to eat have taken a break for a couple of weeks to make way for the annual Mop Fair, a tradition going back... I have no idea so did a bit of research.

Warwick Mop Fair began when King Edward III granted a legal charter that it be held in the town centre, at a time when the stone version of the castle was being built and before Lord Leycester was even born let alone building hospitals. Many significant towns in the area also have similar charters including Stratford upon Avon, Southam, Banbury, Tewksbury,

Alcester, Evesham, Abingdon and so on. Each year these towns have fairground attractions in their town centres and surrounding streets.

Warwick Mop is held every year on the Friday and Saturday following the 12th day of October, with the 'Runaway Mop' held the following Friday and Saturday. Other local towns in the area also have a fair, usually midweek as the rides do the rounds, the timing is believed to be linked to when the harvesting was expected to be completed.

When the Mop first started nearly seven hundred years ago the event was a hiring fair for local labourers and employers to meet in a social setting. Workers would be hired for a trial period of a week; hence the Runaway Mop the following weekend allowing either party to back out if they were unhappy with the arrangement. Once the formalities were over, the labourers could spend their token wage (given by the new employers) at the stalls gathered for the occasion or the local pubs!

The title 'Mop' has been a subject of debate by historians for a number of years and the most likely theory is that labourers wore a symbol (a badge almost) to identify their trade. This meant employers would instantly recognise those wanting work in their industry. These symbols were believed to have been known as mops.

The pig roast, or ox roast as it used to be, provided food for the visiting crowds and a nice fire to warm by on a cold winter's evening. Today the pig roast remains and is one of a number of ways the Mop fairs raise money for the Mayor's charity. The first slice of meat is auctioned, Councillors, Showmen and residents of Warwick bid on the meat, which is often re-auctioned a number of times to increase the charity donation made. Then the rest is sold in batches with apple sauce and crackling, great!

The streets close in the afternoon of the Thursday preceding each fair to allow the rides and attractions to be set up safely. The main rides are brought into the market square and parked at 4pm to minimise disruption to rush hour traffic. The build up of the rides then takes place from 6pm to minimise disruption to shop keepers.

The Town Mayor officially opens the Mop at 12 noon on the first Saturday supported by the Town Crier and representatives of the council in their traditional attire. The Mop Charter is read aloud and then the mayor takes a tour of the fair granting free rides to anyone present at the time. Why don't you come along and see the opening this year? The showmen *work through the night to remove all the rides and attractions from the town centre by about 2am on Sunday morning.*

Warwick Mop is arguably the towns oldest tradition pre-dating even the Saturday market and centuries before the Victorian Evening and Warwick Folk Festival. Over the years it has brought joy and amusement to thousands of Warwick residents and many from further afield. Local shops used to stay open into the evening and hold special Mop promotions to cash in on the extra customers the event attracted but now generally shut up shop and head to the pub to avoid any undesirables which unfortunately follow the fair it seems.

So there you go, seven hundred years and pretty much the format has stayed the same although these days, an afternoon at the mop can soon empty the wallet in next to no time.

Today the regular market stalls with their inviting rows of apples, oranges and fresh vegetables have been replaced by dodgems and candy floss, burger vans and hook a duck stalls and all felt so so different. It was still early and the streets were very quiet, but the jeweller's window was lacking the sparkle of expensive items, not sure why...

The town did not smell the same either, the aroma of local produce and freshly cut flowers replaced with diesel and fried onions – not the best for building an appetite, but you have got to love tradition.

I know the Mop is not to everyone's taste, but I think we should cling on to some of England's quirky traditions. With the market taking a week off, I must not forget the bread and I still need to do the bun run.

Sunday 16th October 2016 - To run or not to run?

Race day arrives and I get all those predictable race day feelings, I have the runs, my legs ache, I feel sick and to add to the fun it is peeing down with rain – brilliant but the number is on the shirt and today is the day. Time to head to Birmingham for the annual half marathon.

The weather is always a bit of a lottery and I have run in rain loads of times, but on race day I prefer not to start wet. The rain was hammering down on the conservatory roof as I put my trainers on and saying my goodbyes.

My wife Julie always worries when I head off and does not like to fill the emergency contact info on the back of my race number, so I always do it on the QT but I do understand.

Today I could have quite easily stayed at home snuggled up in a nice warm bed with a nice hot cuppa but that would have to wait until later.

The drive to the station was very sombre; none of us relished the thought of getting a soaking, but the weather forecast was promising for around about the start of the race so the only option was to bring in the old favourite, the good old bin bag.

Not the most flattering fashion statement but does successfully keep the rain out and the body warmth in and at least we can start dry, but to our delight and just as the met office said the rain stopped and a few glimpses of blue in dark sky and the promise of a better day ahead.

Today's run was special for me, a chance to run with Libby on her first really big event. Twenty thousand fellow runners is a good turn out in the second city and nerves were starting to show.

How many trips to the loo are too many, asking for a friend?

The start was amazing, the smell of deep heat almost intoxicating and it was time to head off to our pink pen, the last wave to go, the real people heading out to take on the 13.1 miles of the Birmingham streets for the first time.

The bin bags off and last photos with Libby and Ali, my friend from Zero to Hero and Running the World and we were ready for the off and with my usual ritual done and a last minute hug with Libby. 'We are about to run 13 miles dad!'

The Brummies 'had come out in force and the support was a great lift as the timing mats screamed and as technology did its magic and all our individual stop watches had started, we were on our way.

And so it began, the miles passed, we chatted, we smiled, we laughed and we joked. This was going to be a good one and we all felt in the groove, you could just tell, and we played off each other for support.

Like all cities, Birmingham has a mix of good and bad, those first few miles as we left the buzz of the start, the support in the back streets was a little light. But as we hit the Pershore Road, the crowds increased and the diversity of culture was a great distraction.

Such an eclectic mix of people all offering support in so many ways. Jelly babies, smiling faces, cheers and banging tunes. As we headed out of town, from around the two mile mark, for two to three miles, the route out and back run on with side of the dual carriageway with the racing snakes already heading back into town with only low single number of miles to go.

It would not be too long before we would be doing the same, crossing the half way point in Stirchley was a great lift but at 9 miles and the Edgbaston Cricket Ground I did not feel great. The concerns of my minor heart fluttering in Sweden racing around my head, but I am not going to stop and played my poker face not wanting to alarm the other two. It was a short wobble and with the help of my trusted running buddies I pulled it back and with four miles to go and I was not for quitting.

Time to dig in and look within but Libby and Ali were great company and we started talking about future runs and food, with the hills out of the way the finish was in sight and the effort all worth it – boom, a PB for Libby and Ali and for me I was back and loads better than last year, so happy with that. Today showed me that the world is full of great people, far outnumbered by the tossers of life, unfortunately they do get around a bit.

No boundaries of ability, sex, race or colour on the run today, just runners giving their best. Some for a good cause in memories of loved ones or close friends, some proving a point to either themselves or others and them some just doing it for the love of the run and a T shirt.

The end is always the best prize and with a call home it was back on the train and home to a lovely roast and a glass of red – such a good day.

Tuesday 18th October 2016 - running jargon.

On the wind down or negative tapering, ok I just made that up!

I had every intention of running today, but at 5.10am when the alarm went off I just could not face the cold damp darkness of this October morning, and my legs were still a little tired from the weekend, so not for the first time in recent weeks, the bed won.

I did the usual wrestle with myself, but thought in light of my recent heart fluttering, I think it was not a bad idea to give my body a breather.

By the end of the day and listening to an omen or two and with my heart still racing a little faster than normal, I though a chat with the old doc could be a good idea.

The visit to the surgery went well, repeatedly being asked about my potential use of artificial stimulates or have you been taking drugs Mr Atherton? And being told I was obese and that maybe running a half marathon was not one of my best ideas, the conversation continued. And the outcome from my trip to medics, the doctor didn't know and with that response the journey begins.

Hospital tests and a bit of bloodletting to establish possible route cause of the racing pulse together we yet more questions, 'are you sure you are not taking anything Mr Atherton?'

More news on the outcome later in the book I hope, but for now I can keep on running, as I could do with the exercise!

The medic did remark that he didn't think it was anything to serious or I would have curled my toes in Birmingham, cheers doc.

Thursday 20th October 2016 - Farewell to Leeds 2017.

With both Libby and I still buzzing from the Birmingham Half, we have signed up to run Leeds Half marathon next May.

I have always wanted to do this run, I read Jane and Mike Tomlinson's book – *'How Good is That?: The Story of a Reluctant Heroine'* a few years ago which followed her seven year battle with cancer. Jane died at the age of 43 in September 2007, the book described her last few months and I do not mind admitting I cried at the end, such an amazing lady and to run this event in her honour would be great.

To add to the sense of occasion and very symbolic, the event will come at the end of the final year at Leeds Uni for Libby and time to say farewell to her home for the last three years.

She wanted to run with me and give me the tour and I am thrilled to be part of this and plan to smash our Birmingham time – bring it on.

We would have to wait until May 2017 before Libby and I hit the undulating streets of Leeds along with the final year and graduation, something to look forward to.

Friday 21st October 2016 - A first!

Not a single run this week, five days without putting on my trainers as it has been one of those weeks. I will be back on it tomorrow, Saturday means Park run and I have a target to beat and it could be interesting.

I want to get back in under twenty seven minutes so I have subconsciously been saving my energy, will the rest do me good?

I also plan to stay off the bottle with no red wine for me tonight, along with an early night, but I have broken the basic experiment group rules by having more than one variable at the same time.

If I achieve the plan, what will be the reason, rest, sleep or no red wine and if I don't make it back in under twenty seven minutes, what will be the reason , lack of running or no wine, who knows, might just have to wait and see.

To give me something to think about on the run, I have a return visit to the doctors this evening for my test results. I plan to go straight after my run still in my running gear just to prove a point. I wonder if he will ask me if I take drugs again?

With many visits to the doctors these days, this time it looks like I will live to fight another day with the diagnosis, the progression of life to old age it seems.

Saturday 22nd October 2016 - first I was afraid...

In the words of Gloria Gaynor – I will survive, which is just as well as I had a very busy day ahead.

Park Run was popular today and a few issues with timing but for me it was all about dogs and buggies with both getting in the way.

I am all for exercise and sport for all, but some routes do not lend themselves to loads of runners and dogs and buggies.

Buggies, what is that all about, enjoy your kids folks but don't shake the life out of them please, it might be ok on the boardwalk in Miami but on a country trail, I think not but that's only my opinion.

Apart from the dogs and buggies as I might have mentioned, I enjoyed Park run today. My great friend and running buddy, Sue aka Sarah was doing her 50th Park-run today and one of her many claims to fame was doing the very first Leamington Park-run and was first lady back to boot, so I had to dob her in and get her a mention at the race welcome, even though they got her name wrong hence the Sarah reference.

The weather was perfect for running and with Leamington cloaked in mist, my hometown looked stunning from the top of the common. The hill got me again but I blame the dogs holding me back. I felt good and the heading down the path on the long straight decent I was cookin', felt great and living the dream only for it to be spoilt by some cheeky mare who basically wanted me to move aside so she could pass me. I was cruising!!! 'move to the right please' but un be known to me, Steve my coach, had clocked it and four hundred metres from home I knew a challenge was coming. 'You know that bitch who passed us, she's just ahead, go on buddy, go get!'. I didn't need telling twice, I'm on it, I drop a gear and left her in my dust – result!

As for the research, crossing the line thirty seconds slower than last time, was it the rest, was it the lack of red wine, I cannot risk this happening again so ditch the rest days and where's the Rioja – back on plan.

Just in case you wondered how I got on at the doctors, nothing to report to be honest, results didn't show any issues of note so a plan to repeat tests later in the year, but the good news, I am not having a baby.

'Are you sure you haven't taken anything?' Yes - he asked me again.

Sunday 23rd October 2016 - Down South.

Today's run had hills, something I need to work on and today felt a bit like training. I'm not sure I liked it, but did have some moments of goodness and after putting the effort in, I feel I am making progress.

Great to come back from my run with the heroes to see the Grout South Run on the TV.

I really loved doing this run back in 2013, on that occasion it was a tad windy, but at least it was flat and we were by the sea side, you can't have it all.

I loved taking part in the GSR, a gang of us took part in the event so we made a weekend of it, heading down to Portsmouth on the Friday afternoon, carb loading on the evening with pasta and a few pints of Peroni got us all in good spirits.

The running circus had come to town and just like in Newcastle when the Great North is on, Saturday had loads of events to get everyone involved plus a bit of sightseeing too.

Something for everyone! All the hotels in the area were full of runners and supporters, run fever had definitely taken over.

For some reason Michaela took control of booking the accommodation after the alleged 'appalling job' I did in Newcastle, I might have mentioned this already. I still have no idea what the issue was, but never fails to take any opportunity to remind me.

Sunday was the main event and after a nice pre exercise friendly breakfast surrounded by Lycra clad runners of all shapes and sizes, we headed off to the beach side start. The route was great and took in the city centre, in the shadow of the one of its many landmarks, the iconic Spinnaker Tower. *United Kingdom's tallest structures* at 170 metres (560 ft), along the water front passing HMS Victory, best known for her role as *Lord Nelson*'s *flagship* at the *Battle of Trafalgar* on 21st October 1805, and into the naval dockyard.

It was hard to focus on my running with so much to see. Skirting the suburbs of the city and Eastnor back along the esplanade for a two-mile dash for the finish at Southsea and just what you need at the end of a ten-mile run, a nice juicy head wind!

A great weekend, oh I do like to beside the seaside! Maybe this is one event I should do again before I hang up my trainers.

Wednesday 26th October 2016 - Lost.

Anyone seen my mojo again? I know this happens to most runners, not sure why but I have lost the plot. I do know it will be back, life just getting in the way again. For the second week running (pardon the pun) the bed has got the better of me and the pillow has won the battle.

No dawn runs for me this week and when the alarm went off at 5.10am it was so cold and dark and I had already sowed the seed of a no show, it was back to bed – did I regret it, always and my days this week have been the worst for not having got those trainers on, but all is not lost.

One of the strangest of traditions on this crazy planet of ours is moving the clocks around, not sure if it is a world-wide thing, but I know most of the western world does it and never ceases to amaze me.

Why piddle about with the clocks? I am going to research the reason and let you know. I never have understood the logic and always knocks me for six regardless which direction the clocks go. But, frantically looking for a positive, today the benefit of Sundays time manipulation means the mornings will get lighter for a couple of weeks and at a time when my mojo has left the building, I am glad of any help life can give me.

I will set off for a run in the dark for sure, but will finish in the light and get to see the sun rise, sometimes at least, a real treat! But the downside is I will need some lights on my bike for the gym the next day as the nights get darker earlier.

What the Lord giveth, the Lord takes away.

Friday 28th October 2016 - *It's a real runner.*

Back in the groove after a week off, a little run down to the gym but technology let me down, but who need data.

A nice night to run, but autumn is here with a vengeance. The sky was stunning and with leaf covered paths, running is a pleasure.

The yanks make a big deal of the autumn, or '*the colors*' as they call it and in Michigan, back in 1985, I had the pleasure of seeing the northern part of this mid west state in all its glory. Spectacular for sure but we have autumn too and the field maple tree outside our house is a thing of beauty and at this time of year is a thing of wonder.

I took the river path to the gym today, the scenic route and passing a somewhat older gentleman out for a run too announce 'look a real runner' much to my delight. Although my newfound running buddy was trying to beat a new path across the flood plan so not sure what he was up too to be honest. Something about getting ready before the area is turned in to the somme, nowt as funny as folks they say, but I relished in the 'Real Runner' comment and headed off on my way.

Loads of memories on the run tonight though, running through the fallen chestnuts on Warwick New Road brought back childhood memories of waiting for my dad to return home from work. I will definitely put this on my memory lane run later in the year.

Saturday 29th October 2016 - England my England.

The different seasons give the area we live in the chance to demonstrate the beauty of nature, spring, summer, autumn and winter each having its own traits to show.

From the stunning flowers of spring with snowdrops and crocuses the first to push their heads above the ground and not far behind them come the daffodils, one of my favourites and give signs of hope of the warmer weather to come.

Hot on the heels of the daffodils who's stay is short lived, but stunning and they always come on mass, come the varied and spectacular blossom bringing the wide regency streets to life with subtle petals and delicate scents.

The summer is when the town centre borders, local parks and shop fronts come alive in well-orchestrated display of colour thanks in the main to our local council.

Alone with the arrival of the sun, comes the people and any open space becomes a gathering point, where young and old alike catch up on the gossip with some folks actual take their rubbish home!

The autumn in contrast to the spring, heralds the threat of winter and today gave a glimpse of what was to come.

The morning was a little cold but on a nice crisp day like this, I love to run. I gave Parkrun a miss today as I fancied a little 'me time', to run with others is always my first choice generally but on occasion I opted to go solo. I combined my Saturday run with a trip to the bakers so as I have got the car out, I ran somewhere a little further a field. Not that far from home but different never the less, I posted some pictures of my run. Warwickshire looked stunning this morning, autumn leaves and rolling countryside, hence England my England.

I liked my new little route today, a combination of the 'two castles' and 'green leek' routes and back through the village and my car.

So what did I buy at the bakers?

Times were tough when I was a child, money was tight, but it was the same for everyone in the neighbourhood I grew up in, keeping up with the Joneses was never an issue as they had bugger all as well.

Life was simple and as kids we made our own amusement, don't get me wrong, we didn't live in a shack or anything and we did not walk around in rags, but as kids were not surrounded by technology.

I remember getting a colour tv, rented of course, Radio Rentals if I recall; no one bought a telly when I was a kid. We had a telephone and central heating, so we were doing ok. My dad was very much a traditional eater which did surprise me considering how well travelled he was in his younger days but a meal without meat was not well received.

I remember him being introduced to cheese and onion pie and my mum had to conjure up a couple of rashers of bacon to provide the meat element. Simple food it might have been and tasty, I should say.

My mum was a great cook, but she was all about comfort food, stews, roast dinners, pies, toad in the hole, all the favourites, proper comfort food.

A favourite Saturday dinner was a dish called simply 'onions, cheese and bacon' and was just that. I loved it as did my dad, but not as popular with my brother and sister. Reminiscing recently, they both pointed out that it was only me that actually liked it, they did not know what they were missing.

Layers of sliced onion, cheese and bacon, slow cooked in the oven on a low heat with a bit of salt and pepper and a dash of water for a couple of hours served piping hot with chucks of crusty bread and butter. Food of the gods. On an autumn or winters night, coming home to the sweet smell of all those flavours as I open the front door takes me back to my youth and always sure to bring a tear to my eye as I almost feel my mum with me in spirit, give it a try.

One word of warning, don't plan anything to social the following day as unfortunately you might just smell of onions, but it's well worth it.

So at the bakers, I bought a fresh white loaf to have with my dinner, God bless you mum x.

Sunday 30th October 2016 - All Souls Day.

So today is the day, an extra hour in bed and the promise of lighter mornings if only for a few short weeks. I changed all the clocks in the house before bed but somehow the time movement passed our cats by and at 4.30am Norris thought it was time for a snackeral and brought the day to an earlier than planned start. But great to wake up with the light and the day kicked into action with a nice cuppa.

Following my bit of research yesterday, I shared my new route with the gang. I loved our run this morning and a great turn out, a new route too – the 'castle leek' as one of the group christened it as it was a combination of the Greenleek and the Two Castles and was brilliant. I love Leek Wooton with all its little nooks and crannies. I had checked out part of the route yesterday, but I did still wing part of it to be honest, but I think I got away with it.

The banter on the run today was top drawer, we had a new runner as well as some folks I hadn't seen for a while, so I was doing a bit of lurking around at the back so we could all have a bit of a natter. I missed my front running buddies so was allowed to take it easy a little. I do get emotional on a run occasionally and today was the day as we approached point in the new route which was the finish of the GreenLeek, the view was amazing – England my England, that phrase again.

The beautiful Warwickshire countryside opening up before us and more banter as we exchanged tales of the event earlier in the month and Steve took the chance to remind me that I nearly stopped in the same place as I did on the actual run, cheers mate. From here on in the route back was evolving or I was not sure of the best way back, but it turned out to be a great route as we joined the return leg of the Two Castles, we all knew this one! Its' good to see the poor folks of this lovely little village roughing it as we cut along the back of picture postcard houses!! Then the talk turned to items of sportswear and it was all about the bra, why do women always want to talk about bloody sports bras?

Some good humour though and all the old favourite jokes – sheepdog bras, they round em up and point them in the right direction, American bras, one Yank and they're off, reckon we could have kept the gags coming for ages… I was intrigued about front loaders – come on girls.

On a more serious note, today is All Souls' Day, also known as the Commemoration of All the Faithful Departed and the Day of the Dead, in the Christian calendar a day of prayer and remembrance for the souls of those who have died.

I have attended church, an All Souls service in the past but found the experience a little hard going. Listening to names of our loved ones being read out, then walking to the alter to light a candle was tough for me, so now I sit with my memories and the scent of a rose.

Steve Atherton

NOVEMBER 2016

Tuesday 1st November 2016 - Thanks a lot William Willet.

Not quite what the doctor ordered as was a dull grey morning and really not worth all the hassle of playing around with the clocks, but it was great to get out and I enjoyed running at the front for a change leaving the fat boys behind.

Whose idea was it to change the clocks? Well I am glad you asked...

An American politician and inventor called Benjamin Franklin first came up with the idea while in Paris in 1784, He suggested that if people got up earlier, when it was lighter, then it would save on candles.

Later, the concept arrived in the UK after Coldplay singer Chris Martin's great-great-grandfather, a builder called William Willett, thought it was a good idea too and in 1907, he published a leaflet called 'The Waste of Daylight', which encouraging people to get out of bed earlier.

Willett was a keen golfer and he got cross when his games would be cut short because the Sun went down and there wasn't enough light to carry on playing. The idea of moving the clocks forwards and backwards was discussed by the government in 1908, but many people didn't like this idea, so it wasn't made a law.

Our William spent his life trying to convince people that it was a good idea, but it was only introduced in the UK in 1916 - the year after he died.

It was actually first introduced by the Germans in World War One. During World War Two, the UK actually used what was called British Double Summer Time (BDST), when the clocks were ahead by an extra hour during the summer, but this didn't last for very long

Now, the UK's clocks always go back by one hour on the last Sunday in October and forward by one hour on the last Sunday in March and moving the clocks like this is now done in some countries across the world, but many still don't do this.

I always think of myself as a smart person, but I could live to a hundred and never seem to be able to work out what will happen once the clocks change, is it going to be light in the morning or not? I am not alone am I?

One thing I am sure of is that playing around with the clocks always knocks me about and after a few days, the change doesn't seem to make a jot of difference.

Wednesday 2nd November 2016 - taking a moment.

Now that's what I call a dawn!

I always seem to spend my life chasing my tail, balancing work and life and my diary is never far from my side as I try to make the most of the time I have on this planet. My work day starts pretty much as I open my eyes as I try to makes some semblance of order out of the day ahead.

When I got in my car this morning, the outside temperature was -1°C, a bit of a chilly one today.

I set out to work with the sun yet to make its appearance. However, the sky gave a clue of the sunrise to come so and when I got to Leek Wootton I had to park up and watch the sun make its appearance to start a new day.

Fifteen minutes out of my day will not make a blind bit of difference in the grand scheme of things, but to see natures spectacular display in all its glory, I need to get a little higher.

Leaving my car at the side of the road, I walked up the hill towards the church, although I wasn't really dressed for a country stroll, the increase in elevation made all the difference and the view was just stunning.

It was lovely to take time out of the day and just 'be' for once and nobody died...

Thursday 3rd November 2016 - Days like this are rare.

I have never been a great fan of the dentist but seem to be one of these professions that do not work in conjunction with the real world, start at 9am finish at 5pm, don't work a full week, evenings or weekends i.e. when most folks are at work, what is that all about.

My appointment today is as always, inconvenient, pretty much half-way through the work day, so a change from my usual routine and start time today.

I took advantage of the late start and ran at a more sensible time for a change and was shocked to see people and cars on the streets. This gave it a really different vibe, making for a very enjoyable run and it did help that the sky was clear and the sun was out in all its radiant glory – Warwick was very photogenic today.

Friday 4th November 2016 - Show time.

Not directly running related but it hasn't stopped me so far in this book but today, straight after work, I went to the Wellness Show at the NEC.

The show was recommended to me by an old mate and work colleague who is into all this yoga, spiritual and self-help stuff and he thought it would be right up my street.

I didn't know what to expect, I thought it would be all crocheted jumpers and dreadlocks. Before anyone kicks off, there is nothing wrong with either, but never really been my thing. However, I am I touch with my spiritual side and I am very open to trying something new.

Once I got over my self-consciousness and realised that people were not looking at me in my shirt and work trousers, I really enjoyed myself and picked up some great ideas and a contact for yoga which is something I really want to try, thanks Darren.

Saturday 5th November 2016 - Inspired.

Inspired by the Wellness Show at the NEC yesterday, I was ready for the challenge of a sub 27 min park run this morning.

Up early and ready for the task ahead, but why did I feel so nervous?

'I can do this' I kept telling myself. OK, I had a bottle of wine last night, but it was Friday and I have already established that missing out on a beverage has a negative impact on my performance, so why not.

The banter started early with Steve, Phil and Vince but on the start line, I was on the edge and after a few steps I was nearly hyperventilating. I had really got myself wound up, what a silly sod.

Even before the hill I could have called it a day and jumped at any excuse to walk up the hill and walk I did. The rest of the run was a blur. I was in the groove but still fighting for air. My positive head came to the party way too late and I was giving it my all and push, push, push – I felt sick, what a wimp.

Young kids were running past me, but this boy was not for stopping. No sprint finish this week but finish I did. Had the sub twenty-seven-minute park run eluded me for another week, the results were in 27.08 minutes, close but no cigar, but I did beat Vince.

Vince was my nemesis, we went to school together, the same year but different class. Thirty years on and we work at the same company which I find amazing considering the company is on the outskirts of Birmingham, so not even in the same county, let alone town.

Vince is a good runner, he is built like a runner and guess he weighs half as much as me and always finishes ahead of me. But with my new found focus, I am managing to keep ahead of him, only just.

Vince is my benchmark these days and once I have checked my own time, next I check out how Vince did. Nothing like a bit of friendly rivalry.

As for my own training, it's all about the hill now, hill training is going to be the focus for the last few weeks of 2016 and I have given myself a good talking too, 'It's a hill, get over it!' I want to do the Mow Cop killer now.

Sunday 6th November 2016 - What a difference a day makes.

Love a spot of porridge in the winter and off for a weigh in before the run this morning, so eased off on the brekkie. I need not have bothered as I had a little gain as they say in fat club land. I was not alone but have I been on plan? Eh No, so reaped what I owed.

It was bloody freezing, but great to see everyone and I had my running buddy Trish back, haven't see her for a while.

We have done some great runs together in the past, Coventry, Regency, Birmingham, Regency and the Two Castles. Trish is such good company, but today with my new front running status, I had to keep shifting from the head of the pack to the back as the peer pressure built.

The banter was lovely again today and everyone looked out for each other.

Running can be a bit cyclonic and that's the best bit, when you're down and need some support, there is always someone around to lift you up and today was no exception.

I loved the way Steve waited for me at the bottom of each and every hill ready to push me to the top, all part of the master plan.

A beautiful blue sky and such a great way to start the Sunday. Happy that the running plan up to Christmas is all sorted and the sub 27 minute part run in sight and talk of sub 26 minutes in Stratford as it is flat – easy tiger!

Tuesday 8th November 2016 - Mammals (MAMILs) .

Men in Tights or Middle Aged Men In Lycra or it's -4'C and I am a little chilly.

Today was proper cold and for once I was up before the cat at 5.10am when the alarm went off. I could have just hit the snooze button and rolled over, but the chilly streets of Warwick beckoned, and I am glad they did.

I love Warwick at this time of day, every dark alley and timbered building holds years of history and mystery. Quaint hotels and small B and B's offer a warm cosy sanctuary through lace curtains, with the tempting offer of a hot cuppa and a full English breakfast. But alas today we stayed on the cold side of the leaded windows to pound the frosty paths of this medieval town whist putting the world to rights.

Yoga, meditation and a street cat called bob were the main topics of conversation, sure beats the shit out of the car industry and the pending election of a looney to move into the White House.

Friday 11th November 2016 - Lest we forget.

I always think about my grandad on Remembrance Day or 'poppy day', so many different names and pretty much every country has a day to remember the fallen from conflict around the world.

My grandad, my dad's dad fought in the First World War or the Great War at the start of the century. Described as 'the war to end all wars', shame that it seems not to have been the case.

I know my late grandad, Arthur Atherton lost his leg, but never did know the full story, best find out then. I was only young when he died and even younger when my granny, Elsie passed.

My mum's parents died way before my arrival so I didn't really have the whole grandparents thing especially in my teenage years and I do feel I missed out.

Traditionally our running group have not ran on Remembrance Sunday, mainly out of respect, but also because our meeting point in the war memorial and on the day, preparation is usually well underway for the service later in the morning.

This year I will be a little out of the loop with the Sunday gang as will be on route for some 'hot climate training' in Cape Verde, but more about that later.

Two minutes silence on an airplane travelling at 35000 feet above the earth was a first and so glad the airline did, *lest we forget*.

During the six hour flight, I did a multitude of things to keep myself occupied, a bit of writing, spot of reading and some music too. With my iPod loaded with thousands of songs to choose from, a classic from George Michael got under my skin and made me think.

Change is a stranger you have yet to know – a great line from the track - *Older*.

The title track from the third studio album, released in 1996. I love these words and love the sentiment and very apt as we head off for a week in the sun and a chance to run somewhere different and warm.

This is my dream place for me to run, a deserted beach, the roar of the waves and a chance to just be. This is a return trip for us to the island of Sal in Cape Verde. Such a beautiful place so be prepared to be bored by stories of stunning dawn runs on sun drenched beaches...

Saturday 12th November 2016 - Out of our comfort zone.

On this holiday, we were taking a break from the cocoon of an all-inclusive holiday bubble and gone native (well a little bit). We rented a beach front apartment which means we had to look after ourselves and buy stuff, hardly Bear Grylls I know but a very different experience.

Finding a local source of wine was the first worry to be honest as the local shops sell what they have with no sign of a supermarket. But with the first shopping expedition in the bag and wine bought we were off to a good start. Our first wine purchase was not the best, the picture of a cat on the label should have given us a clue as it did taste like it had some feline connection. Ok it tasted like cat pee if my description was a little subtle.

The beach view apartment is not that far away from the Melia Tortuga, the hotel we stayed in last time. The island of Sal is only thirty kilometres long and twelve kilometres at its widest point, so nothing is far from anything. So many places are familiar, but not all.

And with a change of location comes some different places to run. Once I was away from the cosy promenades and board walks of the hotels, this morning's run took me through the back streets of Santa Maria and a glimpse of the real Sal.

Leaving the beach fronted villas and apartments, I found real people in real homes, real life and it was only my first run of the holiday. Some of the route I had run before but some of the miles were very new for me and boy oh boy did I stick out from the locals mainly for three reasons.

Firstly, the sun was out, it was hot so why is this person running? Number two, I was slightly paler than the locals if you know what I mean and last but not least, I had the BMI that must be twice that of the Cape Verdians I have seen. I nearly crossed the street a few times to prevent anyone comparing me with any local lads.

One guy was out for a run, clearly a local braving the early warmth of the day and that fact is where the similarities ended.

He was six foot something, slim, ripped with muscles on his muscles and about as much body fat on him as I have in my toenails. He smiled and gave me 'the nod', the international symbol of acknowledgement us runners give each other as we pass, before he sprinted off out of sight heading out of town towards Kite Beach. The footsteps I shall follow later in the week.

He looked every bit an athlete and I was jealous, but the sun was out, and I was on holiday. With the parting of our ways, I headed into the back streets, it's Saturday morning and locals were out.

Old men sat on the doorsteps of the brightly painted shacks putting the world to rights, the women cleaning dressed in the most colourful outfits I've ever seen. The younger ladies paraded about in pairs looked like catwalk models, naturally stunning, trying to catch the eye of a young lad hanging around as lads do. Most smiled and bid me good morning. I wondered what was going through their minds.

The locals are very inventive, money was clearly tight, and they seemed to have many ways to make a buck or two. Every other doorway seems to be selling something, wood carvings, bags and postcards with 'no stress', the local catch phrase featuring on many of the hand made products.

As I ran, I passed ladies with baskets of souvenirs confidently balanced upon their heads and the more successfully salesmen, with fruit and veg in a wheelbarrow. We learnt on our last visit that the sign of success around these parts a wheelbarrow. If you had a wheelbarrow, you were somebody and you had a friend for life. You had ways of generating an income, you had a seat, a pram to transport the family around. It seemed the uses are as endless and only limited by imagination.

This main use of a wheelbarrow this morning seemed to be as a mobile fruit stall with young ladies wheeling around colourful cargos of mouth-watering fresh fruit and vegetables to local restaurants, homes and camera toting tourists and so photogenic. I'm always a little wary of taking photos away from the tourist routes especially of people, so generally store the images in my head.

As the morning progresses and the fruit produce dwindles, after successful beach side sales, the cargo of the wheelbarrows change from fruit to fish as the men folk take control of the wheel and return to the pier to fill the versatile vehicle with the catch of the day, and off to local restaurants to feature on the menu hours from leaving the sea.

A sight I will never tire of is the short quay which comes alive with the freshest fish you will ever see, caught just offshore in the stunning turquoise water. The hustle and bustle of the daily fish market is not for the faint hearted as the sun drench wooden boards turn crimson red with fish blood and guts. But to the locals it's just another day in the office, as local housewives and restaurants barter for the succulent tuna and wahoo for the night's dinner.

The morning fish market is a photographer's dream, but also a place to just take time out and people watch. Fisherman's wives filleting fish whist putting the world to rights, children young and old have their place in the process and the fisherman looking on as the game of life unfolds. Some in random European football tops, which never ceases to amaze me the world over.

I do take time to think. The pier and all the hustle and bustle makes a fabulous back drop for holiday memories, but this is life, these people bust a gut to make a living, they work their arse off seven days a week.

The end of the pier is wheelbarrow central and as the boats arrive according to the tide, the one wheeled chariot becomes a mobile fish market or special delivery to a local restaurant for a note or two. However, anything touched by nature is not an exact science so patience plays its part too and when a wait is required, viola – your barrow become the perfect sun lounge and time to grab a few rays and a chill whilst the boats come in. No stress!

As the boats arrive and the fish change hands, the wheelbarrows become transport to take the work weary toddlers home for a nap and the cleaned wheel barrow rest up ready for the next day when the process starts again.

As I take the stroll back to the pool for a dip, I think about my childhood and my dad's wheelbarrow. I recall great memories of my dad taking me for a ride and then as I grew a little older, wheelbarrow races with my mates around the garden, but I do not recall any fish. I have wheelbarrow at home at the allotment but in England that means jack shit.

In the top ten list of the best things us runners love amongst getting a PB, finishing, good bags and new trainers, is a trip to a chiropodist or beauty salon for a pedicure to get your feet sorted.

Black toenails, the true medal of honour for a runner and crusty soles or 'you have feet like camel' as I once had my peds 'described in Egypt. They always benefit from a bit of TLC.

I have pretty horrible feet mainly from years of pounding the streets and wearing uncomfortable business shoes. Now my trotters would not look out of place in the Sahara at the corners of one of our humped ships of the dessert, so on holiday I always take the chance to pay a stranger to sort out the old claws.

As I wondered into the hotel spa, I did not see the staff fighting over who was going to have the delight of rejuvenating the battered feet of a middle aged runner and the look of relief on the rest of the staff as Patricia drew the short straw and was nominated to take on the tootsies.

I chatted to take her mind off the task in hand and then we had to decide on the choice a colour of nail polish. With the assistance of a slightly older Germany lady who was going through the same but less stressful treatment on her feet, we did eventually settle of this shocking pink war paint for hers and I opted for the slightly more conservative clear anti fungus coating for mine. But the luminous green was a pretty close second.

My newly refurbished feet did shimmer a little in the morning sun, so all in all money well spent. The mound of dry skin on the floor was testament to the miles in those sweaty trainers and pondered that my DNA would be imbedded in the soul of the spa for many years to come.

On leaving the spa, I paid and of course leaving a generous tip for Patricia. I was given a fridge magnet with a toothy camel embossed on it along with the obligatory 'no stress' slogan.

Yet another nod to my ungulate connection, but who cares, money well spent I thought but I might not leave it so long before I get my feet sorted next time.

Sunday 13th November 2016 - Fancy a cuppa?

I couldn't sleep. We had an early night after a day's travelling so by the early hours I had slept enough and with no sign of the nights end, the early signs of our first dawn in paradise were starting to show. The idea of a nice cup of tea regardless of the time was not to be sniffed at.

Fortunately, Julie was awake as well so sitting on the patio with my baby and a cuppa, listening to the sound of the ocean was magical and when the sky showed the promise of the pending dawn, my trainers were on and off I went.

I had a plan for today, along the beach to greet the dawn as it rose over the sea.

Even though the sun had yet to make its dramatic appearance, it was still very warm and the cloud flecked sky was just stunning. Again, I had the biggest smile on my face – I am a very lucky bugger and I know it.

I had swapped running stories with a larger than life character we had met in a bar the night before. He was a rugby referee and from Wales, so the odds were stack against him, but he did run so I gave him the benefit of the doubt.

I had already established from his tales that he was a pretty quick runner but regardless of that I threw caution to the wind and invited him to join me for a dawn run.

I had to smile at his response, so funny 'oh no boyo, I don't run early – I like my bed'.

Running on my own, I did think about my new welsh friend, he did miss something special this morning. Today was all about seizing the day or Carpe Diem, as a phrase that continues to feature in my life can to mind and living in the moment.

Pausing to see the local lads working out on a homemade beach gym did focus the mind. No fancy kit or video screens, but just the sun, sea and a bit of graft, go hard or go home.

I would have loved to stopped and pumped some fat with the skinny boys, but I had an appointment with the sun and the quest to find Kite Beach. This Beach had alluded me on my previous visit to the island, but I did take a picture of the gym to share with Al and Tim back home who I knew would get it. (and they did!).

My timing was a little out and the sun made its appearance before I made the water's edge, but the sight was stunning nevertheless. A new day. The dawn and the sunrise is my favourite time of the day and every single ray of the new sun helping to recharge my batteries. This was not the easiest of running terrain but good enough to run on and breath in lung full of salty air, great to be alive. Kite Beach took me by surprise, too early for kites but one of the most beautiful places I have ever seen.

The wild turquoise sea, brilliant white waves and golden sands, so with my photographs taken, thanks said, I head back to the brightly painted houses of Santa Maria and an early breakfast. I like this shift in the days timing, early up but we will be ready for our baskets as the sunsets, but who cares. This is the life and I am loving it, now I could live here!

Monday 14th November 2016 - Paul Allen and the Octopus.

A real morning of contrast, running on a deserted beach with the shanty town of Santa Maria in the distance, then just off shore is the Octopus, the multi-million dollar yacht owned by Jody Allen, sister of Paul Allen, the co-founder of Microsoft.

Now when I say yacht, it is actual a ship with more tech than you can shake a stick at. That only comes with serious wealth, way out of the league of overpaid footballers and talentless pop stars – this is proper wonga.

I am not sure what the Allen's were doing in town, but the Octopus has been around for a day or two so they must like it here, and why wouldn't you?

I did a bit of research, our Paul has got a few bob in the bank, estimated net worth of $18.6 billion, born January 21, 1953, American obviously, the Yacht, Octopus, 126 m (414 ft) long, sleeps 26 guests in 13 bed cabin looked after by a crew of 57 in 28 cabins. The yacht worth 250 million dollars.

Shall I continue?

The Octopus has a large helicopter hangar on the main deck, giving shelter to two helicopters, the first one is a MD900 and the second a Sikorsky S-76C.

The yacht has a large glass bottom pool and a 10-person submarine. The submarine and the main tender (named Man of War) float into the yacht through a large hatch.

If that wasn't enough, there is a recording studio on the bridge deck, an observation lounge, a cinema, a juice bar, a gym, a salon and a medical centre.

If I want one of these bad boys, I best start saving my pennies.

A lot of runners out this morning, most speak, some don't but I do like the subtle roll up of the thumb, just enough to acknowledge the moment.

Today I was on a mission, the plan was to hire a bike and tour the island with a local bike group, but best laid plans as they say, maybe next time.

With all the tooing and frowing I managed to clock up a few extra bonus miles. My other half was planning to do a bit of provision shopping so was heading to Delta, our regular little shop which managed to cater for all our wine requirements and also sold food too.

It was only about fifteen foot square and nothing like the shops or choice that we are used too, but we managed and who really needs all this crap anyway.

We bought all we needed with the exception of bread, that came from 'the' bakers and our fresh fruit would have to wait until we saw a passing wheelbarrow.

Mondays, who likes Mondays? Monday is the day of the week that successfully brings the weekend to an abrupt end and heralds the time to get back on the wheel. But Mondays on holiday are the best, no alarm clock to wake us from our slumber, no watches and we get up when we want to, no stress!

Oh you're the runner!

I bumped into the welsh chap from the other night, clearly the cheap booze and his pagan ancestry had puddled his brain, but he did call me a runner which is ok in my books.

That's twice this year I have been given that accolade, I am getting to like it.

Tuesday 15th November 2016 - For Carlos.

It's six o'clock in the morning and you would think that the beach at this time of the day would be empty but no. This is the best part of the day, the sea is warm and inviting and the locals know it so this is when they head down to swim before they head to work or start on the chores of the day.

I love to see the folks from the town on the beach enjoying the beautiful turquoise sea and they have such a good time. They laugh, chat and are full of vitality. Most have a strong Christian faith along with an obvious respect for nature and the strength of the sea, and this is apparent in their morning rituals.

Observing from a discreet distance, it was humbling to watch, stopping in the shallows of the breaking waves, before entering the water. They scoop a handful of water and almost anoint their bodies followed by making the sign of the cross...

'In the name of the Father, and of the Son, and of the Holy Spirit. Amen.'

... and with respect paid, into the water, very moving.

We have slipped into a routine which works for us, early to bed most nights then up at the crack of dawn wide awake to take full advantage of all the daylight hours.

A very special morning, up again before the dawn and a nice cup of tea (you cannot take the English out of the Englishman).

We have only been back on the island a few days and already we have attracted the local cat population and we are now greeted in the morning by a row of kitties, sleek and noble and very very cute.

Today was all about beach life; we were out on fishermen's beach by 6.30am and was already very busy with the locals taking time out to welcome the new day.

Swimming is not really my thing, not a great fan of the water or heights, the extremes I guess. I can swim but Phelps I am not. I should be a good swimmer as lessons were compulsory at Junior School, but I never quite made it and was one of the very few who left school not being able to do even the basic of strokes not sure why – confidence I guess.

However I did 'learn' later in life early, I didn't have lessons or anything, but resorted to a combination of a private pool, peer pressure and alcohol, on reflection, I probably would not recommend it. But it worked and so I'm glad I did learn as 6.30am on the beach in Santa Maria was amazing.

The water was warm, the sea calm and out with the locals doing the routine was great. The feel of a gym, busy of a morning and even more smiles from the locals – magical and I can see the attraction.

The light at this time of the day is stunning and the colours so beautiful and this is the time of day to swim with warm golden sand under foot and the ocean calm enough to actually swim. To see my wife's face going loco was a picture with a smile from ear to ear and radiating life – very special.

Drying off after the short walk back to our home, off for a run now baby, Julie knew it would not satisfy my craving to run...

We had realised that maybe I should let her know where I plan to run, it is pretty wild and remote in places so this is a good idea just in case I do not return, at least Julie can direct the search party to roughly the right location.

Kite Beach today becoming a favourite, so bleak but magical. I ran a different route through town and across the dunes today, just the odd runner and stray dogs to keep me company.

I feel sure that I am not alone and in every little clump of grass or rock, I was sure creatures are watching. Snakes? never thought of snakes but from looking at the spiders, there has got to be some creepy creatures out there.

Kite Beach again was lacking kites, but such a special place, I kept getting drawn back.

The lack of kites became obvious in the years to come when Julie and I made many return visits to the island. The beach I thought was kite beach actually wasn't, in fact the beach I loved was actually Igrejinha beach or little church and not Kite beach after all.

On arriving at the beach, I could see something out the corner of my eye, a very unnatural protrusion at the water edge and as I approached, I could see a simple rectangle column of marble set in a concrete base. On one side of the monument was a small plaque with the following inscription :-

*« Homenagem ao grande amigo
de todos os salenses e familiars
Carlos Silva Andrade
Conhecido por
Carlos Paula
Falecido no dia
16 de Novembro de 2003"*

My Portuguese is not great but with a bit of help, the words roughly translates to :-

*"Tribute to great friend
of all salenses and family members
Carlos Silva Andrade
Known for
Carlos Paula
Deceased on the day
November 16, 2003"*

Today's run was dedicated to Carlos, returning home along the coast path past my favourite gym, already full of ripped bodies working out in paradise.

No gym for me though as just like at home, I had to do the bun run and collected bread on my way back.

A great start to the day, fresh bread and jam and a nice glass orange juice.

Wednesday 16th November 2016 - Choices.

Each day I am faced with a choice, a similar decision whenever I am holiday. Shall I turn right, or shall I turn left? Generally, by the very nature of a seaside location, rarely am I tempted to head away from the sea.

Today I went right but not just a random decision, I was on a mission. I wanted to do a bit of a loop and I knew exactly where I wanted to end up and that was Turtle Beach, not its real name I will quickly clarify.

We spent a magical and emotional evening on the said beach the night before when we had the opportunity to see first-hand the amazing work that Project Biodiversity, an environmental conservation organisation are doing on Sal and I had to return for no other reason than I could.

The beach on the edge of town is a regular breeding ground for sea turtles and to give the eggs a fighting chance of hatching, the team from Project Biodiversity, stand guard until they are ready.

I make it sound so simple but there is a whole load of science and expertise around looking after these Loggerhead turtles, one of the eleven most threatened population of sea turtles in the world and are the reason the charity was founded in 2015.

The odds are heavily stacked against the turtle, for every ten thousand baby turtles released, only one will make it back to Sal in the years to come.

Conservationists and volunteers from Project Biodiversity painstakingly collect the eggs, meticulously recording when they are laid and reburying in labelled hatcheries then patiently waiting until the time to hatch.

The clever folks know almost to the minute when each batch will hatch, such an incredible sight from the gentle movement of the ground as the eggs crack and the baby turtles take their first glimpse at our planet before making their way to the sea to take their chances of survival.

Nature is given a helping hand and the tiny turtles are carried to the water's edge by charity helpers and a plastic bucket. But once at the water's edge, the turtles are pretty much solo heading for the setting sun and only minutes old we can only wish them well and with teary eyes hope that at least some of the newborns make it to swim another day.

The impromptu evening gave Julie and I one of our lasting memories of our lives and certainly one that neither of us will ever forget.

That was last night, and this morning Turtle beach was bereft of people except for the dedicated team from the project on round the clock duty watching over the incubating eggs.

Today I made another choice in addition to my destination and that was the choice of footwear in fact more radicle than that and went without trainers. I have never done this before but was very different, tough on the old plates of meat but very, very liberating.

Giving the run a completely different feel and not without a little pain, but bloody hell I will definitely do this again, who needs trainers?

Ok, it helps having a sun kissed beach, stunning golden sand and nothing to hurt me making it a lot easier than back at home without a doubt. As the holiday draws to an end and only two runs left, the choice can only be Kite Beach and barefoot running, unfortunately the two do not go together.

Thursday 17th November 2016 - Real.

Ok, for every rule, there is an exception, after telling you of my limited run choices, I added another choice. Neither left or right today but another alternative route to one of my favourite places.

The location of Sal and our location gives options to get to places, so instead of following the coast path, I went out through the back streets to the edge of town away from the tourist area, this is where Santa Maria is very real, no swanky villas or hotel complexes but tough living, old cars and not the nicest of street dogs, some of which would love to rip a chunk out of my arse.

Along with numerous little bars and tiny shops and restaurants, mainly for local people and amongst the dust and obvious poverty, was the cleanest of washing, the prettiest and happiest children I have ever seen and always a smile.

This area is not on the tourist trail, but glad I have the opportunity to see it and I did not feel in the slightest bit intimidated; people acknowledged me and I smiled back.

Heading out of town across the dunes for a look at the sea and the views were very clear today with the neighbouring island of Boa Vista in sight for the first time since out arrival. I took a final visit to the beach and Carlos, then back along shell beach past the best gym in the world and a quick swim before coffee at our favourite café – Del Mar and free WiFi too, always a bonus.

Friday 18th November 2016 - Ponta Preta and freedom fighters.

My final dawn run of the holiday and still leaves some time for relaxation before we head to the airport. Last night you could sense the changing of the weather and Blinky, a fountain of knowledge who runs the local One Stop Shop, had already started to batten down the hatches with hot chocolate and a box of milk tray. But she was right, in the night it absolutely hammered it down.

Julie and I were all cosy in our waterproof apartment, but I could not help thinking about the locals in their makeshift shacks affording no protection to the elements.

Rain, an infrequent visitor to the island must run riot though these folks lives when it does, because when it does rain boy oh boy does it rain.

By the morning, the rain was gone and as Julie had already taken her last dawn stroll to the beach for one last swim on fisherman's beach, I wanted to run barefoot today, mainly because I could.

The change in the weather brought cloudy skies with no real clear definition between the sea and the sky, the horizon blended seamlessly from one to another. Today was still very warm however no spectacular sunrise, instead just a gradual increase in the light.

The beach was pretty quiet this morning, mainly just locals taking time out before the challenges of a new day.

Will today be good for business? Will the lack of sun mean a lack of tourists wondering aimless in search of whatever, reducing the chance to sell a carving or two? Or maybe the opposite, as it's a little cooler the folks might head out for a stroll...

I ran with my thoughts looking back on a great holiday, amazing memories, and some pretty cool running.

I love to run barefoot; it is such an amazing feeling, although you do have to carefully select the terrain to save the feet. The lack of support from a pair of trainers did render me a little stiff the following day, but I soon recovered.

Today I wanted to run to Ponta Preta and the big sand dune, another favourite place, so idyllic with so many memories - dawn runs, spectacular sunrises and sunsets, good food at the beach shack, plus it's a special place for other reasons, but that's between me and the fish.

Heading for home, my thoughts turned to freedom fighters and those who dare to be different, why I can hear you ask.

On the cobbled road leading to the pier in Santa Maria, stands a bronze bust of Gaspard Vynckier who is a bit of a local hero. He is responsible for the first desalination plant and sewage system on the island and built the first hotel bringing tourism to Sal.

Mr. Gaspard Vynckier and his wife got involved in the village life with the help and support of Mr. João Maximiano. They lived in Sal during the winter months and the couple had studied the problem of seawater distillation with Dutch specialists.

After having succeeded in convincing the governor, Mr. Gaspard, Vynckier devised (using Belgian and Dutch materials) a heavy fuel distiller with a 90m^3 daily production capacity.

From 1970-71 he had the Santa Maria water castle built. A special barge that was constructed in order to empty the 40-ton boiler. Mr Gaspard Vynckier presented the administration with a plan for the implantation of a sewage and potable water distribution system.

A small anecdote:

An expedition had left Belgium for the Antarctic to bring back penguins for Anvers 'zoo. A 'refrigerated' stop-over was to be organized on the way back, so that the animals would have an opportunity to recuperate prior to continuing their voyage. Having been contacted, Gaspard Vynckier ordered a 16m^3 cold chamber from Belgium. During the excursion's stop-over at Sal, some of the penguins were installed in it and survived.

The same cold chamber was used by the hotel for many years.
Mr. Gaspard Vynckier passed away on January 30th, 1972.

Running along the beach, I spotted a fish caught out by a sly wave floundering on the beach, his mouth gasping for the last breaths of life. Easy pickings for a local seagull, but today it was the fish's lucky day and I thought he or she, (not good with telling the sex of fish), deserved another chance at life so I gave nature a hand and helped the brightly coloured fish on its way back to the sea.

With the support of a well-timed wave, the fish bid me farewell with a flick of his tail and off to fight another day, a bid for freedom against the odds. The last couple of km's were less eventful and became a competition between a local runners and I both heading back to the pier as our newly assigned finish line.

Reducing the gap between us with every stride, I was running my own early morning race, oblivious to my opponent I think, but drawing close he must have heard my muffled steps hard on his heels and turned to look. I passed him and sprinted to put some distance between us. Today I was the victor and as I crossed the impromptu finish line, I turned to claim my prize and my opponent had gone. Did I imagine my dawn running partner?

A great end to a lovely holiday and quality time for both myself and together with Julie. Tomorrow back to the cold and familiar running but that's tomorrow....

Sunday 20th November 2016 - Angus, Angus!!!

Unfortunately not the promise of a rock legend joining us for a run this morning, but hurricane Angus threatening to reap chaos across the country with warnings of ninety seven mph winds and lashing rain was enough to put off the cyclists this morning, but us runners are hard core.

Storm Angus, the first named storm of the season caused flooding and damage across the country but by the time we planned to run, Angus decided to head north and out to sea. Luckily, we had no rain, a little more than a breeze than normal and it was a little chilly, with a lot of leaf-less trees.

So with our spirts lifted, with lots of positivity on the run today, comments like 'we can do this' 'I always feel better after a run' 'I didn't know I could run this far, I think I am better than I thought.'

What would happen when you are faced with opposite comments, 'you will never be able to do this' etc. Different comments bring different results, it's not rocket science, generally things aren't . I spent the best part of 9km convincing one of the group members who has recently successfully completed a 10k event, that a half marathon is do able ' —but its twice as far as I have run before' and so was the 10k some weeks before, it's all relative.

We also learnt today that a good run is maybe not the best cure for a hangover, as I know from personal experience.

Running post alcohol is like having your head squeezed in a vice whilst riding on the waltzers, with every step a pulse through the grey matter, get the picture?

This morning it wasn't me that was suffering though, but another member of the gang who was feeling a little worse for wear, and in the words of the late great Elvis Presley, ' all shock up' – poor Anne, I do feel for you.

Tuesday 22nd November 2016 - South of the river.

As predicted, running in the light or finishing in the light was a short-lived experience. A weekday dawn run from home, made a nice change and a chance to enjoy Leamington before the town wakes up. I like being in places at a different time, closed shops, empty streets and clear pavements, still people around but far from busy.

The overnight rain had subsided and now just a few spots to wake us up, not at all cold for the time of year and so overdressed. What's a little sweat between friends?

Talk today was of sunnier climates, birthdays and bloody Christmas. I like Christmas but does it have to start so early? We have only just packed up the BBQ and folks have got the tree up. It's November FFS!

With the Christmas and Diwali lights ups in Leamington and the big switch on in the past tense, I feel like I am fighting a losing battle. I know that but I will try and grump it out for a couple more weeks before I concede and succumb to the inevitable and take it on the chin.

We did get 'aligned' when we passed a poor soul curled up in a sleeping bag in a doorway of an overpriced gallery. Talk about a contrast, people should not be sleeping on the streets in this day and age – so sad. I know that for some it's a lifestyle choice if you can call it that, but for many shit just happens. They say we are all just three pay checks away from poverty, not really sure what that actually means to be honest, but I do get the sentiment and yet more food for thought.

To lift our spirits we had to trot over the 'bridge of love', rude not to really but that would take us over the river to the bad side of town.

Unofficially the 'royal borough' is a town divided by the river that gives the town its name, north of the Leam, the affluent stylish Spa town, with its parks, elegant Regency crescents and wide imposing streets with tree lined avenues. This contrasts the working, industrious badlands as you cross over the handful of bridges to be greeted by narrow streets, terrace houses et el of south of the river.

I pride myself that I was born in north Leamington, but only just. So in the words of Dire Straits in the timeless classic tune, Sultans of Swing, we head 'south of the river', passing my old senior school, Myton, and back across the river to home and a nice cup of tea ready for the day begin and it's still dark.

Friday 25th November 2016 - Black Friday?

What is all that about? Oh it's a sale, I like the idea of a sale before Christmas and long may it continue, but don't make such a fuss about it and does every retail outlet in the country have to fill my inbox up with so much crap?

I might put a filter on my email account ready for next year – any mention of 'Black Friday', straight in the old trash folder, sorted.

Short run tonight, not because I was shopping or on the search for a bargain or two, but I have parkrun in the morning and I was saving my energy.

Saturday 26th November 2016 - Park-run.

I am still chasing that sub twenty seven minute parkrun and with my old school and work buddy Vince in the Far East I have less pressure to go for it today, other than beating the clock. I need this one in the bag before the end of the year and maybe today is the day.

I had a pretty good night's sleep curtesy of a bottle of red and a whisky laden milky drink, so I'm all set. It's going to be all about the hill today, get that sorted and the rest should be ok. The weather is fine, a little chilly and might be a tad muddy but here goes....

I won't bore you with a full run report, but enough to say twenty- seven minutes, twenty-nine seconds was not the result I wanted. But on this occasion, it was the head that was on form, just the body let me down. My hamstring was giving me a lot of gyp after the shock of running bare foot on the beach in Cape Verde, so I eased off a little. But with the help of my buddy Steve, we pulled the time back and still in the right ball park.

Will a sub twenty seven 5k be in the bag by year end? Watch this space, maybe the Christmas eve park run will be the one.

Lots of memories on today's run, oranges with the leaves on reminds me of Bruges and Christmas Eve - that was such an amazing run.

By accident, I stumbled on the local market which was not for the tourists, but for the real Belgians and laden with goodies for the festivities ahead. Such a very special run and Christmas Eve will never be the same in England.

Once or twice in this book I have mentioned that I like a drink? I find especially before a big run or an event, a glass or two of something does help me relax and sleep better, so the tradeoff is worth every penny if that makes sense.

Steve Atherton

I am never going to win anything, but to stand a chance of finishing anything these days I need to relax and not wind myself up. I find alcohol is the answer and the aroma of sweating wine on the day is a bonus.

Sometimes it's all about location, location location. One of my favourite places to run or cycle and also to drink beer is Belgium. I have had a long relationship with this unassuming northern European country from work trips back in the happy days working on the on the Jaguar X type launch, numerous supplier visits to Leuven. A great university town and home of Stella Artois, making this place the party centre of the universe but never a good idea on a school night.

Roll the clock forward a few years and more great memories of Belgium and beer when back in 2014, we spent Our honeymoon in Bruges was just magical. Every time I taste a Belgian beer the memory lingers on. One of my pleasures or shall I say our pleasures in life is to enjoy a glass or two of something nice in our garden backing onto the river.

The garden and the house location were some of the selling points of the house to be honest when we were house hunting, and when you bought the ease of running into the equation, signing on the dotted line was a unanimous decision.

Post run, I planned to spend a bit of time in the garden and have a little tidy up, put the garden to bed as they say. I love spending time in our garden, catch me outside maybe mowing the lawn and you will see a man with a smile from ear to ear.

As a treat, I might light the chiminea and have a glass of gluhwein or maybe a Belgium beer.

Sunday 27th November 2016 - Ouch that brought tears to my eyes.

What would you do you do when faced with the dreaded running injury?

There are several trains of thought on this particular subject. One idea is to stop and listen to your body, letting nature work it's magic and follow the steady road to recovery.

Option two maybe, you could opt for the opposite approach, la,la,la - working on the principle that if you ignore it, it will go away. A concept usually assisted with some useless cream or gel smeared in handfuls, or maybe some over-the-counter pain relief.

What about option three, the alcohol approach, drink a glass of two of wine the night before and the calming effect of wine rushing through the veins helps numb the pain.

I don't want to take the moral high ground, but do I always go for option one? I don't think so, usually a combination of two and plenty of three.

I needed to seek professional help, and as one of the Sunday's group is a doctor and another a nurse so I never need to worry if I need the kiss of life mid run.

I love the dialogue between the fellow experts, the non-medics I hasten to suggest Ice, elevation, rest and many more alternatives. The doctor listens intently and on occasion, I could see her shaking her head all whilst still enjoying the beautiful Warwickshire countryside.

My approach today, in the absence of a bottle of wine or muscle rub, was keep running, keep talking and ignore everything else. However, as a bloke multitasking is not second nature and I was pleased to say on the whole it worked, I ran the 10k run with a troublesome hamstring. However, I may never walk again! But watch this space as only time will tell. The doctor's advice for the record was to take it easy, yep...

I really enjoyed our run today and this was a nice route fast, becoming one of my favourites, I love how the route delivers fantastic views over the Warwickshire countryside, England my

England. This route was a new one for fellow runners and delivered a nice surprise.

I love how running helps people relax, let the old guard down and open up. There's something about the fresh air and exercise that helps folks talk and unload. Great therapy which is good for both the talker and listener generally in even measure.

I often wonder if I have a potential business venture, 'life coaching on the run'. I am sure being outside without the whole face to face, eye to eye contact does take away the feeling of therapy and definitely promotes honest conversations, food for thought.

The diversity of the conversation also never ceases to amaze me as does hearing what interesting lives people lead. Nothing mundane here, but scary that everybody is busy busy busy, phrase 'fully loaded' springs to mind. I can see that in this day and age people's lives including mine are so full on and complicated, and sometimes the cracks start to show.

Looking at my own life, I need to find a way of decluttering, sometimes you need to clear out stuff to make space, some headspace and an area to think.

For me and after listening to a lot of other people, headspace comes once you put on those trainers, and start the run. When you are fighting to get some air in to your lungs, life can take a back seat for a while and in that freed up space, we all find a place to be just be.

DECEMBER 2016

Thursday 1st December 2016.

White Rabbits, White Rabbits, White Rabbits or pinch punch! Either way, the first day of the final month of the year means only thirty one days to the end of the year, and so much to do in and so little time.

I don't like the idea of not running and having not been out for a few days and it is getting to me a bit so tomorrow I run, wish me luck.

Friday 2nd December 2016 - Back in the groove!

After four days off, the trainers are on and it's great to be back on the streets again.

It's been a few weeks since I have being running on a Friday with Sue, so a double bonus today. As most of my running these days is done in the morning or on the odd occasion after dark, to run on a Friday afternoon in proper daylight is different and dependent on the chosen route, can be interesting.

Away from town and into the countryside, the run is influenced by nature rather than people, whereas heading into town is a different kettle of fish. Friday afternoon, three weeks before Chrimbo was always going to be busy.

Most folks go about their business, but I can always count on a bit of banter, and occasionally some abuse, generally from groups of lads. As a rule, we are past them and away too quickly to take note of the content, but one day I would like to stop and take them on. But alas common sense prevails, and I leave the fate of these tossers to karma, hoping that revenge will be sweet.

Art on the run was the plan for today. I wanted to check out a new gallery in town where one favourite photographer James Callaghan was exhibiting. Many of his amazing works adorn my home, but alas today the gallery was closed for an install, there's always next time…

Our route took us away from the hustle and bustle of town and into the Jephson Gardens. I love this place, so many memories from a young child feeding the ducks with my nan right up to now.

Every time I come through those wrought iron gates, the memories come flooding back and whatever the time of year, the park always looks stunning. I love to see people taking advantage of this wonderful place.

Popular with dog walkers, mums and toddlers, dads and pushchairs, lovers, thinkers and of course, the odd runner.

The park has not changed that much since my childhood, the aviary has swapped its caged birds for overpriced coffee (although the café did smell lovely today) and the addition of 'the glasshouse' in 1999 is a fabulous addition to the park, and was also the venue for our wedding reception back in 2014.

It seems appropriate that we should celebrate here, the gardens run through my veins and felt the connection with them many times and with many people in my life. It was perfect, although it did make Christmas that year interesting.

Long gone is the floral clock, but I always live-in hope that the soul still hides beneath the flower borders and in my lifetime will be brought back to life to enjoy being the centre of attention again under the watchful eye of the statue of Dr Henry Jephson. The clock was put in the gardens in 1951, in memory of the mayor at the time Mr George Purcell. It was made by the same clock makers as the Westminster Clock or Big Ben as we all know it. The clock was never the most reliable bit of kit as I recall, but I always ponder its fate when I run past it. So with one loop of the park it was back to the faster pace of the parade.

So many homeless people on the streets of the royal borough these days, going almost unnoticed as our materialistic world spins franticly around them, many oblivious to the plight of these poor souls. In this day and age people should not be living on the streets.

By contrast, running past Binswood Hall, a luxury retirement village where the not so old can end their days in almost regal surroundings. With a one-bedroom apartment starting at around £300,000 but you do have to be over 55 to live here, so that will be me then! With its own health club, library and restaurant providing an independent lifestyle in a secure environment. And going by the signs it was already pretty much sold out! A far cry from a cold damp shop doorway and a scabby couple of blankets. Very sad and certainly made me think....

On a positive side, my hamstring held up and it was good to be back in the groove.

Today's run would be very significant to myself and those around me.

This is the day when '56 not out challenge' went from being a passing thought from a seed sown by my buddy Nigel, to a concept growing legs and above all, having a purpose. No surprise that the purpose is to help the homeless, as I felt I could not just sit back and let this happen.

The plan, 56 challenges in my 56th year on the planet. Starting on my birthday 30th May 2017 ending one year on in 2018 or maybe on the 29th May, so I can stand down from the challenge on my birthday.

'56 not out' will be all about raising awareness and hopefully a bit of money along the way. I will need to work with local charities who know their stuff, as I need to know what to do for these people on the streets. I am buzzing, I will not be able to sleep tonight! Thanks, Sue, for the ear, I am going to make this happen.

The rest is history, check out '*56notout- the book - One year - fifty-six challenges'!*

Saturday 3rd December 2016 - A proper Saturday.

I feel a little jaded this morning having had very little sleep, but great to be back in the trainers and is does feel like a proper Saturday today, although my head is still buzzing from last night. I had factored in a run and a trip to the bakers.

I loved my run today, a little chilly, but I was dressed right, and life is good. It's still early for a Saturday morning and in these shorter days of winter, it's not quite light yet, but light enough to give me chance to see the hidden view of Kenilworth castle one of my favourite routes in Kenilworth.

Not the view most people are familiar with, approaching from the west across the fields. The sky was so dramatic, so pace was traded for photo opportunities which seems to becoming the norm for me these days. But with stunning views like this, there is always another day to run a little quicker.

Considering that my head has gone into overdrive overnight in the hours since yesterday's run, surprisingly enough, this morning, my head was clear. I just enjoyed just being out in the countryside with thoughts only of bread and what I planned to have for my breakfast.

Run complete and with those thoughts in mind a detour for fresh bread from my favourite bakers and home to boiled eggs and soldiers, the prize for today's run.

Sunday 4th December 2016 - If Carlsberg did runs…

Today's outing with the heroes was just the best, such a beautiful morning, I absolutely love days like this, freezing cold – minus something, cobalt blue skies, crisp frosty ground and heatless winter sun, perfect to run and great for those photos.

Gloves and hats the order of the day, but a few crazy ones amongst us still braved bare legs. I for one love the feeling of having a warm body and a bit of a zing to the legs. It really does take me back to my school days and the hated weekly games lesson.

Today was the first outing of the winter of my *'Frulander'* ice hockey beanie from Sweden. I want a romper suit made in the same material and I would not take it off for the whole of the winter, so toasty.

A big turn out today and some new faces, I love telling the 'zero to hero' story to new folks and not to long after I have done my sales pitch, it's great to see the subtle rotation and everchanging groups of chatting people running along a little bit like speed dating on the move.

On a typically sixty minute run, most runners do the rounds and get to have a natter with everyone and this happens as if by magic.

The sky was the most amazing colour of blue and for the second day running, I found myself approaching the castle from my favourite angle.

Today's running reward was a nice hot beverage (hot chocolate to be precise) and the most delicious cakes I have ever tasted. White chocolate lemon blondies – food of the gods!

Unfortunately, with these particular home baked treats come sadness as we say farewell to some great friends and fellow runners, Annie and Herluf as they head for a new life in the sun, a good excuse for a holiday I guess.

Tuesday 6th December 2016 - Man flu and the circle of trust.

I am certain that I am skating on thin ice now, and going to divide the sexes as I approach the delicate subject of influenza or man flu in the male of the species.

Without a shadow of a doubt, men and women are different. We all know that 'men are from mars, women from venus' to quote the title by the very astute author John Gray who tells it how it is.

Men and women without question are not wired the same or plumbed the same, sorry ladies. To keep our little group of runners entertained for many a mile today on this foggy and grey dawn run, the larger male contingent were showing caring support for our recently ailing brother who bravely had fought off the dreaded man flu and was back out with the gang.

The poor lad clearly had not received any sympathy from his wife, who mentioned childbirth and the fact that she along with their two daughters had also been ailing. But to be honest I was struggling to see any relevance of the pains of having a baby compared to our buddies man flu.

She was dismissed while we supported our friend on the slow road to recovery with a man hug, relegating Michaela to outside of the circle to stand and watch in longing admiration of the power and strength of the brotherhood.

A cold indeed, women just do not get it and if proof was needed, they are not of this world.

As a run itself, very grey, very damp and nondescript but the banter – top drawer.

The perfect end was seeing my buddy with his gloves on a string so he didn't lose them- bless!!!

Made me smile all the way home.

Friday 9th December 2016 - Christmas and the lights of shite.

Checking the diary, it is time and from here on in, it's now all about Christmas and time to decorate the outside of your house with the finest tat from the local cheap shit shop.

What is all that about? Why would you do that?

I love a few white lights in the trees, classy that but this is the time of year when good taste seems to go out of the window.

Inflatable Santa's, Santa's climbing ladders, Santa's stuck in chimneys, Sparkling reindeers and the combination of illuminations that would make a blind man proud.

I would not want that light show outside my bedroom window thank you very much, but on a cold winters night treading the streets it does make for a welcome distraction.

It would be unfair to single people out, but I do have friends who do excel in the house lighting department and never fail to deliver the goodies. It does make our little offering by the front door a little unstated in comparison, but you can't buy class…

Maybe we should get some snowflakes next year….

Saturday 10th December 2016 - Momma said there be days like this!

A very damp December morning, barely getting light and busy, busy, busy. It's one of those days when I spend what seems to be an age in my running kit, but never get out the front door to actually go for a run.

I have a list of stuff to do this morning, including the obligatory bun run and I know it's a little early but I manage to get the Christmas and New Years bread order in whist I was picking up my goodies. It was all about the timing and another bonus this morning and a real treat for my youngest.

Lucky for Millie the cinnamon buns had just come out of the oven when I arrived at the Bakers, so had to be done and I just love seeing her reaction! She loves the brown food, especially when they are still warm.

Back in Warwick for fruit from my favourite market stall – and then at last a chance to run and with my hamstring holding its own I managed to pick up the pace a little. The sub 27 park run was still in sight, I reckoned the Christmas event was the one and my tenth park run and I really wanted to make it special.

Short and sweet run today, but I love the little nooks and crannies in the back streets of Warwick. A bit of memory lane too, past 'the vine' - one of the first pubs I drank in as a youth, barely out of school but I was working so that's ok.

Then past IHW Engineering or at least where the factory used to be. The buildings long gone, no longer echoing with the ring of hammers or the thud of the presses. Silenced are the drilling machines and the millers, now a little housing estate called Charter Approach. Sad really with not even the name gives a nod to the past or it's place in Warwick industrial history.

Fondly known as 'the hinges', IHW, or Improved Hinges Warwick, the factory had many names over the years, but soul of the workplace remained the same.

I have already mentioned that this little back street engineering company before, it's was where I did my apprenticeship and from 1978 until 1982 I was the youth of the drawing office, and as seemed to be the way of the day, once the company had to pay me a real wage, I was made redundant.

I have some good memories of those years where I made the well overdue passage from boy to man. Occasionally, the old place crops up on those 'memories of' pages on social media, so at least a few folks remember, I have some photos somewhere, I must dig them out.

During the early days of my apprenticeship, I didn't have a car or a driving licence, so I used to bike to work. Only a couple of miles door to door, not a great distance but a hill between home and work, so regardless of the direction, the end of the journey was always downhill.

Continuing the memory lane theme this morning, I ran past the sight of the old Warwick Printing Company, where my dad worked when I was boy.

On the outside of the building, the signs remain, but they have moved to new premises on the edge of town. I can still remember going into the premises in Theatre Street with my dad and him typing my name on the monotype keyboard and as if by magic, the machine produce the little lead souvenir of my visit.

I used to love the smell of the building, although the product was in essence printed goods, there was a great sense of industry. I never felt the need to follow my dad into the print business, the options were pretty much predetermined by the education process really. Such a difference compared to today where, for the youth of today, the world is their oyster limited only by imagination.

Today's run gave me an idea, memories are always the best when shared.

Sunday 11th December 2017

I could have done with a lie in today, it's been a busy weekend already, but the chance to grab an extra few hour in bed might have to wait for another day.

After the appalling weather yesterday, today was the polar opposite and was just stunning. Not super cold but chilly enough to produce a bit of 'breathage', I think I have just invented a new word, you know the frozen breath on a cold day.

I was going to pop into Sue's this morning for the fat club weigh in before the usual Zero to Hero run, and as it was such a great morning I ran over. I don't run this way that often these days, so it was a chance for more nostalgia and another trip down memory lane. I passed the 'old offie' as we called it back in the day.

The Off Licence on the Rugby Road, Milverton was the closest place to my childhood home to get sweets, crisps and fizzy pop once the shops had closed. Twenty four hour shopping was unheard of back in the sixties and a really treat was to take back the empties, the glass beer and pop bottles back for the deposit and hopefully enough pennies for some sweets.

The building is still there, but no longer is a shop. It is now a chartered surveyors office, but the outside looks very similar.

I did pause on route to take a couple of photographs of St Marks church which also has played a part in the Atherton family history. My big sister Linda was married there back in 1971 and for many years was my parents church, the closest to home but a change of vicar and worship style saw them move to join another congregation.

In the words of my dad, it went all 'happy clappy' if my memory serves me correct, and he always preferred the high church with all the bells and whistles and most of all the organ. As for my mum, she just loved people, not sure where I get it from!

Years on, my girls frequent the church hall for Zumba, funny old life.

Sunday 11th December 2016 - Have you seen Santa?

A change from the regular group run, with most of the crew taking part in the annual Myton Hospice Santa Dash through the streets of Leamington Spa.

I joined in the fun and along with thirteen hundred other runners and walkers dressed in the festive garb. We were all set to make an amazing spectacle.

The group had planned to meet up before the start, right - over a thousand people all dressed the same, that might be a tad tricky, but foresight from one of the group and we cleverly agreed a specific meeting place so we managed the obligatory photo although you couldn't really spot who was who.

A lovely route, a great atmosphere and a good cause, what's not to like. I am always in awe of the amazing work hospices do and when you need help, you got it.

A charity close to my heart, helping my close friend Ada, in his final days on this mortal earth.

Monday 12 December 2016 - Putting the world to rights.

This morning's run was all about the countdown to Christmas and with the fact that the more I talk to people the more I realise how busy everyone is with no letup in sight. Christmas does seem to be one huge logistical nightmare for most people.

A juggling act of work and play with the amount of extra pressure is so apparent, added to by the influence of health with so many bugs around its worse than the millennium.

The weather does not help either. It's warm now which is very unseasonal and my poor body doesn't know what is going on.

It's party time and life is full speed ahead, but I know that once I stop then my immune system will go on strike and end up joining in with the rest of the of the nation and going down with something. Although I find the secret is not to stop and keep drinking the famous Grouse. There are antioxidants in whiskey I hear and who might doubt this gem of knowledge and I do like a drop of whiskey in my cuppa.

In my personal opinion, Christmas, the whole thing has lost its way and it seems for some folks, the festive season starts about October with restaurants being the main offenders, closely followed by the shops, and then the endless countdowns on social media.

I don't want to know how many bloody days it is until Christmas. I think this early start does make the period running up to Christmas very long and I am not sure I have the legs for it these days.

The target is to try to get everything done by Christmas, it seems like a mythical milestone. Whether it be getting new sofa or decorating the lounge, the list is endless. I am also aware of presence of another minefield, gifts. How much shall we spend and the looking for that present that people don't really want really want or need, resulting in spend too much money and the point is missed.

I am fifty five years old and I don't really need anything, however I have a bit of a bad habit of buying stuff before Christmas although I am under the threat this year so best keep away from Amazon and drop hints instead.

I am on a roll now, food is another seasonal bugbear of my mine. Why does Christmas food have to be so brown and do we really need to eat your body weight in crap?

With our fridges and freezers bulging with food and drink we don't need with so much waste ending up in the bin. Then there is food shopping... be careful folks the shops shut for a day.

I am going to shut up now...

Tuesday 13th December 2016 - Busy.

Consecutive dawn runs, different people, common theme, I will leave it there.

Friday 16th December 2016 - Where does your dad work?

One thing I like on my runs around Leamington and Warwick is seeing the changing face of employment, what used to be familiar household names replaced by new.

I have touched on this before, when I was at school, meeting new classmates, the inevitable question always tended to come up, 'where does you dad work?'

Back in the sixties, women rarely went to work and with the choices limited, most married women with kids, stayed at home, housewife's and looked after the family. How times have changed!

The answer to the question at my school was pretty predictable, the number one response was AP or Automotive Products, by far the largest employer in the area. Closely followed by Fords, Pottertons and Flavels in no particular order and in the majority of these companies many generations of the same family made a living. Grandads, Fathers, Sons, with Aunties in the canteen, Sisters in the office.

Employment was very stereotypical in those days with these large companies not only offering wages, putting food on the table and a roof over heads, plus sustaining the local economy. In addition to the obvious financial rewards, industry provided the fun stuff too, the social side of life.

Brass bands with darts, cricket and football teams making up most of the local leagues. The pavilion, the hub of AP sports and social club was a big part of my school days for myself and many of my classmates with many a birthday party attended. I met my first real girlfriend at a class mates and lifelong friends', Julie's sixteenth birthday party, maybe more about her another day.

I find it really sad to see these local companies that were once the heart of the community gone, just wasteland or an empty shell, but more often these days it seems, another supermarket.

It's not just the companies along with the jobs that are gone, the soul of our community is lost too.

Progress is progress I guess, but not all change is good. Sometimes the memory of many of these companies still lives on though. The odd band or sports club, Leamington's local football club called Brakes has its roots in the works team of Automotive Products whose main product was, you have guessed it, brakes.

I would like to ask the question 'Where does your dad or mum for that matter, work?' in schools today and see what the answer is.

You know, one day, I might just do that.

The run up to Christmas is going okay at the moment and my hamstring niggle seems to be behaving itself, so far so good. Although my food intake seems to be hindered by continuing to eat brown shit that goes with the season.

Saturday 17th December 2016 - just go!

The conversation with my wife started something like this, 'I might not go for a run today...', I had a busy morning ahead and I thought about giving my usual Saturday morning run a miss. But as soon as I showed a hint of my thoughts to my other half, came the reply, 'pardon, you are going for a run today aren't you?' and when I hesitated replied ' –please go for a run, you will be a bloody nightmare otherwise.' Sad but true.

So after the bun run and a bit of fruit from the market I manage a lovely run around town. I felt strong today and always good to get out on the streets of my hometown, my car smelt amazing on my return. Fresh bread and the zing of satsumas – proper nice to get my taste buds fired up and I am glad I took my others half's 'advice'.

This weekend is the closest weekend to my wife and I's wedding anniversary and traditionally we head down to London for a bit time together before the chaos of Christmas rampens up to a frenzy.

We both love London and we always find something new to see and the buzz is something else. We do have a favourite place to stay when we head to the big smoke. Hazlitts Hotel in the heart of the West End is lovely, dating back to 1718 which the guide books describe to a tee.

'Civilised, charming and Oh ! So curious.' 'One of England's best kept secrets'.

I love getting off the train at Marylebone station, jumping in a cab and saying 'Hazlitts please'.

The hotel in Firth Street is a proper home from home, proper old-fashioned hospitality and they have a cat. Sir Godfrey is a legend, a ginger tom who has a taste for the good things in life and certainly likes his comfort. He is never far from the open fire or a comfy chair, he is certainly part of the charm of the hotel. The nature and layout of the hotel makes it a great place to lose yourself and is popular with the celebrities, the hotel is a particular favourite of J.K. Rowling to name but one.

The building does show its age in places, the distance bed to floor can vary as much a 8 inches side to side due to the slope of the floor and after a beverage or two, the camber can mess with your head a little.

Sunday 18th December 2016 - ' let me take you by the hand and lead you through the streets of London…. '

Of all the places I like to run, London is up there near the top, every corner a different landmark. It's like running around a monopoly board, just brilliant but thought provoking too.

After a lovely meal and visit to a west end show, I always try to head out in the early light of Sunday morning, on occasion, a little worse for wear. Some of the streets around the hotel echo my own feelings and take on the guise of a war zone showing the signs of a good time, but always the hints of the darker side of the capital at this time the day.

The contrast, the opposite ends of life's spectrum are very apparent, just a few feet away from the hotel, rows of shiny luxury cars in neat rows outside swanky city townhouses but your eye is drawn to a tent pitched on the pavement – the haves and the have nots. I could not resist the photo opportunity of a tent in the shadows of an apartment block bearing the words 'house of charity' kinda ironic.

Whenever I run anywhere new, I always worry about getting lost, even though I have technology in my pocket it has never stopped me before, although I do make a note of the hotel name and street just in case.

No one would be that stupid to head out in a strange city not knowing either surely? Yes, I have done just that – I remember Bruges, December 2014. The route on my Garmin download post run was that of a dying fly – frantic or what.

But today I was prepared and I do know my way around London a little better and I always head to the river, the life blood of the city. With Big Ben making its presence felt, rising out of the foggy morning sky I was reassured I was heading the right way. And right on cue, as I headed across Westminster Bridge the mighty bell tolled 9am and once again I was running with a big smile on my face. Even though it was quite early, the bridge was bustling with tourists eager for that selfie with that icon bag drop of Big Ben and the houses of parliament.

I have never seen so many selfie-sticks in one place. What are these things all about? I realise that they are practical and help take great photos, but you cannot fail to look a knob. I must confess I have one myself, bought as a joke rather than a useful addition to a keen photographer's gadget bag.

On the odd occasion that I get it out in public – the shame and embarrassment on my face is apparent, mainly because I look so clumsy using it rather like a novice angler.

Joining the masses, I stopped to take my obligatory selfie without the aid of a stick I hasten to add, and as always I managed to capture the less than flattering escaped loony image which I seem to have perfected.

The London skyline looked very grey today, but still gives me a buzz and leaving the Thames, I headed to see if any one famous was in town. Passing number ten Downing Street hoping to say hi to the prime minister, but a friendly smile from the on duty coppers was the best I could ask for then a detour down the Mall to see if her majesty was in town. The police presence in London and all our cities for that matter is very apparent, but I do admire the fact that they seem to do this difficult job with dignity and always pass the time of day.

And with no offer of a cuppa from either the PM or HRH, I headed out to check out Oxford Street before the shops open and the hordes descend on this retail metropolis. The evidence of temporary sleeping places of the city's homeless still apparent, buts it's now time for city to put on its show face ready for the masses to overindulge in the Christmas excess.

I love London and its many faces, and I also love running in London. I always find the place thought provoking, happy that I didn't get lost today and successfully made my way back to Hazlitts for a cuppa.

Tuesday 20th December 2016 - Santa Hats!

The last dawn run before Christmas, so best get the Santa hats on, I do like a Santa hat, but does make your head sweat. We did get a funny look or two as we ran around Warwick but 'who cares, its Christmas'. I love that phrase, it the 'one size fits all' answer to all the excessive of Christmas. I have used it on the odd occasion and why not.

Wednesday 21st December 2016 - The shortest day!

Today we turn the corner, from today, the days get longer as it's the shortest day of the year and will be light for 7 hours 49 minutes and 41 seconds in Britain, which makes the day 8 hours, 49 minutes shorter than on June Solstice. But on the downside it's officially the first day of winter and I don't care for that.

I like to run on this symbolic day but alas today, life got in the way and I needed to get to the office. A little disappointing as in the period of all things brown, I love to get out for a run and keep the intake to exercise ratio in some sense of balance, but today was one of them. I look forward to the longer days and the promise of better dawn runs in the sights.

Always a funny time of year and this week in particular is when time plays its nasty tricks. I am sure the clock goes into slow motion as the days although technically the same duration just drag. Every day the attendance in the office reduces and the perceived length of the working day increases proportionally it seems.

Call me old fashioned, but I do miss the days of my youth when the last day was the last day and the dramatic closure to the year was just the best with a few beers thrown in for good measure. I am sure the rise in car ownership and the strict drink driving laws, along with awareness are playing a massive part in the decline of the office party.

Friday 23rd December 2016 - Schools out.

I love the phrase 'Black eyed Friday', I had never heard it until back in 2010 when we were first introduced. The landlady of a traditional guest house in the back streets of Whitehaven had the honours. We stayed in the little place the night before Nigel and I commence our 'coast to coast' bike ride. Over breakfast the friendly almost mother figure lady was making small talk as she served up our full English breakfast complete with eggs floating in a little pool of fat.

Just what you need before a day in the saddle and just for the record, this was the first and last full English of the trip. Together with a hearty breakfast came an English lesson. With the arrival of the food came with an enquiring on how we had spent our evening in the town and port on the west coast of Cumbria asking if the bars were busy. Turning to check her calendar to see if it was 'black eyed Friday', my face must have given away my last of understand of the term.

Payday at Sellafield, you might remember it being called Windscale, a huge nuclear power plant and the biggest employee in the area, was on the last day of the month. Locals, with a pocketful of cash, went on the town and with a belly full of beer, the fights started and with the punches, you have guessed it, black eyes.

The relevance of the phrase, today is the last working day of the year for many and the start of the holiday season and with town and city centres getting busy, the result I guess with be similar to payday in Whitehaven.

Saturday 24th December 2017 - Go hard or go home.

Christmas Eve Park run and I so wanted Santa to bring me a sub twenty seven minute 5 k, but alas this was not going to be the case. I think my Christmas lard jumper had something to do with it, but I had a good run nevertheless.

So many people taking part today and a little muddy. Yet again my nerves kicked in, why oh why I just don't get it. Steve was, as always by my side and great support as always, a top man. I did not want to go into a new year with a target unhit, but still a few days of 2016 to have another go at it, but with Christmas excess but a sleep away that will be a big ask.

It was lovely to see many folks today that I haven't seen for a while and was surprised to see Mitchell and his old dad Richard.

I have known Rich for over twenty years. We first met over twenty years ago when we worked together on Jaguar X type although our main connection is children related having honed our parenting skills at local pre-natal classes together, as we awaited the arrival of our respective first borns.

Mitchell arriving few days later than Libby who chose Christmas day to make her guest appearance, but more about that later.

Christmas Eve is a strange night of the year for me, mixed emotions as just before Christmas, I traditionally make a visit to my parents grave to lay a wreath. It always gets to me and I hope it always will as I will never ever forget my mum and dad. Never far from my thoughts, but as a reader of the book so far you will know that too well.

In the past I always did the wreath run on Christmas Morning and especially in the early days of losing my Mum but it knocked me about too much, so these days I visit the church yard on Christmas Eve. It still gets to me but does make the process a little easier.

One Christmas, a good few years ago when corporate gifting was common place, I remember receiving a bottle of scotch and as not a big spirit drinker, leaving it in the car and returning home after laying a wreath on my mum, I noticed a guy sleeping in a bus shelter so I stopped and handed over the bottle.

I might have killed the poor soul, but happier that twenty years on, I am on the verge of making a difference.

25th December 2016 – The big day!

One of my favourite runs of the year is Christmas Morning, a real tradition and always the same route, a very special time with a very special lady, my first born, Libby.

We always run down to the bridge at Ashow and back down Rocky lane with today's run extra special. Not only Christmas Day but Libby's birthday too and a landmark one to boot.

Twenty-one years since I held that little bundle in my arms for the first time and feels like yesterday. Ashow has always been our spiritual home for many years and Rocky lane has some good memories too.

The bridge over the river Avon by the church has always played a big part in both of our lives, we both found the calming waters our little sanctuary and a beautiful place too. I have always said that if, for what every reason I go AWOL, the bridge at Ashow is where I would tell people to look for me first.

This morning this magical place delivered in spade loads, one thing of note for this year's run was the temperature, 12°C, shorts and t shirts, it's Christmas Day for heaven's sake!

The winter sun made this beautiful place look exceptionally stunning, the greener than green grass even greener and the sky so blue. As we run I hope this place will always remain our special place forever.

However before too long we were heading down along Rocky Lane to the real world and Christmas with all the trimmings. I love the banter on the run, not just with each other but with everyone we meet. Dog walkers, the faithful off to church and the obligatory kids on new bikes or roller blades and the folks just walking, exchanging season's greetings with everyone getting a heartfelt 'Merry Christmas' whether they like it or not (most folk do). Before long we return with a big smile and a sweaty head (I blame the santa hat!)

A very special run, happy birthday Libby x.

Monday 26th December 2016 - And breathe!

Such a beautiful morning, I just had to get the trainers on, and Warwick looked stunning today, blue skies et al and I am still in a T shirt.

A lot of folks out running today and so many new bikes in the park. I love to see the faces of the children with their shining new presents from Santa, new outfits and a lot of new phones today. It was lovely to get out and just live the moment.

Plenty of nice photos to be had and the bridge over the River Avon with that view of the castle seemed to be a mecca for running selfies today. I am saying nothing as I might have taken one or two myself and as a passing runner said to me 'you just cannot get bored with that view can you? ' - so true.

A steady run and then home for a prawn cocktail, a family tradition that always reminds me of my Mum, as she always loved the classic starter at Christmas and I always have one or two in her memory over the holidays.

Merry Christmas Mum X.

Tuesday 27th December 2016 - Is there anybody out there?

Not sure if anyone has woken up this morning as it's is oh so quiet!

After a little lie in I had planned on having a lazy morning, but having been given a less then subtle hint that a run would be a good idea so that the other half could mop the floor.

I never need much of an excuse to get out and about on such a beautiful day and with the temperatures back in the minus figures, it felt a lot more seasonal, but I still kept my legs out! I love the feeling of cold legs – must be mad.

Once I had the cue to vacate the house, I now needed a purpose to run, a destination and as my diary kept reminding me I needed to have a follow up blood test from the little worry back in the summer. So I thought why not, it is Christmas so it will be quiet and I need to get it done.

So armed with a legitimate reason to run and an ageing blood test form, I headed out into the chilly morning air. I wanted to run the long way around to check out the parks of Warwick to see if any fellow runners were about.

Saint Nicholas' park was busy, and the banks of the river Avon dotted with fisherman. I assumed they had had the same instructions to get out from under there wife's feet whist their other half did the housework and reckon Warwick must have a lot of clean floors today.

I skirted Priory Park too. I love this park, very understated and a real hidden gem of Warwick, but unfortunately long gone is the best slide in the county or maybe it is still there, hidden in the undergrowth.

Back in the day, the metal slide had been carefully crafted into the side of a natural hollow and was just great! No high steps to climb and no chance of a long drop to the ground, if you're not a big fan of heights!

I best have a look next time I am in the park, but not today.

I ran an unusual route and very nearly got completely lost on my own door-step which would have been ever so slightly embarrassing. But thankfully I regained my sense of direction and was back on familiar ground and headed to the hospital arriving at the bleeding rooms – that name always gives me the creeps!

I didn't know what to expect and not sure if I was going to be greeted by a huge queue or would I be in and out before the sweat dried, but the answer was neither.

The hospital was like a ghost town, lights out all out it seemed with locked doors a plenty, so the blood tests would have to wait until another day.

On the way home I pondered what to have for breakfast and I settle on poached eggs and a couple of slices of my favourite bread – Cotswold crunch and that made the run home so much more enjoyable with a nice spot of breakfast at the end.

I had been out the house for a while, so I hoped the floor is dry!

Wednesday 28th December 2016 - A little run down Memory Lane.

The conditions were perfect for what I had in mind this morning, cold, foggy with the reduced visibility adding to the drama and sense of theatre.

A very special route for today and something that I have been planning for a while and today was the day!

I wanted to take my first born for a trip down memory lane and with Libby by my side, the only place for the run to officially start was Edmondscote Road, where it all began, well for me at least.

This was where I was born, 30th May 1961 and remained my home well into my early twenties. I loved living here most of the time. The houses have had a bit of a makeover with the addition of brickwork over the poured concrete slabs making the outside look a little less temporary.

Double glazing replacing the steel frames, along with central heating early in the life of these 1940's prefabricated council houses. Our old house has grown since we left back in the eighties with some additions since my childhood, with changes to the front garden and shared path. The former was my Dad's pride and joy and was now off-road parking negating the need for the shared path, the bain of my parents' life, but that's another story.

Generally, the street hadn't changed that much in the scheme of things, but one particular place from my childhood that seems to be lost forever is the little park at the end of River Close.

The area is still there but now an overflow carpark for the sports track and 'the swings' as we called the area and any sign of playground equipment long gone. Although the house where the park keeper lived is still there, but I would imagine that Mr Hebby has departed this life.

Mr Hebby or Mr Hebsworth I think was his real name was, kept watch over the park and the adjacent sports track, with the local kids keeping him busy trying to keep us out of mischief.

Steve Atherton

The alley that ran along the sport track was still how I remember as were the local garages, well most of them anyway. Our old house backed on to a large expanse of grass marked out into a couple of football pitches. It came alive every Sunday when the local Sunday football leagues fought it out for fame and glory, with a lot of F'ing and J'ing became part of the Sunday routine, Father Penny, the local priest adding to the colourfully language with quotes that I cannot recall from either the old or new testaments.

The leather match ball was a regular visitor to our garden. My Mum and Dad were not a big fan of the weekly disturbance and longed for the summer months with no football. I remember my Dad secretly fighting his own battle of wills with the footballers and not sure it ever ended well.

I couldn't work out if the area is still used by the footballers – I should have taken a little more notice as the goal posts might have been a bit of a giveaway. The gardens, I did notice however and more construction at the rear of the house too, making them look very different.

The field, 'the swings' and the banks of the river providing the perfect back drop to my childhood. I loved playing 'war' with my local chums with the spring the signal to start building a new den.

One thing I did notice was the absence of a tree missing from the riverbank. This was once home to the mighty imposing oak, not sure when the tree departed the skyline, but is very much missing from today's view.

The tree in question was never without a rope swing hanging from its lower branches, but I am not sure I ever had the balls to test it out, I was a bit of a wimp as a child and still am.

This end of the field in the shadow of the tree, near the weir provided the location for many a 5th November, the annual celebration of terrorism back in my youth. The bonfire was always a victim of its own arson attacks from rival gangs and local spoil sports and many a time was lit ahead of the day. So in later years its own private guard was enlisted to keep around the clock vigil. Not me though as I would not provide any threat to a would-be arsonist and I needed to be home at a decent time.

Although I was partial to a game of 'torch light tig' in the dusk of the evening before heading to my nice warm bed. Like a lot of these street traditions, the change in family habits now tend to focus more on the home and less on the community with neighbourhood spirit on the decline in a lot of areas.

From my old home, we headed along the banks of the river Leam in the shadows of Mid Warwickshire College of Further Education where I spent the first full year of my working life, kicking off my apprenticeship with twelve months off the job training, i.e. full time at college. We did get paid though, the princely sum of nineteen pounds per week.

The days were long and coming straight from school only a few months before, the change was a massive shock to the system.

The college itself hasn't changed much, a bit of fancy cladding and the temporary classrooms having benefited from a bit of brick work and as my first year 'off the job' training was so close to home, I never able to us the excuse that I had forgotten my homework!

The college featured during most of my apprenticeship, with me returning for day release for the remaining three years and a lot of my friendships still stand the test of time.

The run continued and leaving the college behind us, we continued along the riverbank past the sight of the old Feldon school. The school was demolished in early seventies and only I can only remember the long grassy banks and woodland.

Since the school's departure, some of the site had been developed with Swiss style homes not out of place on the steep wooded bank, but in the shadow of Regency houses they do look ever so slightly odd.

The site of the old school became the headquarters of the Leamington Spa building society and later, council offices.

As a youth, this was THE place to go sledging, very steep and with the added complication of potentially ending up in the river.

The area has always intrigued me and I feel that it might be hiding a secret or two as this is an area which is rarely talked about, so might just have to do a little but more digging…

Climbing the steep hidden path alongside little Switzerland, we emerged at the top of Church Hill and past my old doctors. Dr Taylor was at my birth in the back bedroom of Edmondscote Road and was very nearly named after him. Phew! Alexander Atherton, that was a lucky escape. I do remember Dr Taylor coming to the house back in the day when a doctor would actually come to see you at home even if you were not at deaths door, and always provided intrigue and/or fear for many a childhood pet.

The surgery, a Regency town house with the rear ground floor room converted into a consultation room and the room at the front, a waiting room. As we passed, it was apparent that the surgery has returned to a beautiful family home and is just a few doors down to another regular haunt in my later years, the Woodlands Tavern.

My first local and very popular with the young college students and still is I would imagine.

Just around the corner was Portland Street where my buddy Al had a bedsit in one of the five story town houses, providing the basecamp for our popular pound nights, which equated to two pints of Guinness. No wonder why my liver has had such a hard life!

No trip down memory lane would be complete without a mention of Dormer Place, my Nan and Granddads old house and the childhood home of my Dad.

This is the second official visit this year as you may recall it was the start point of my bike ride to Mow Cop back in the summer. I would love to have a look around the old house and see how much it has changed. I always loved the walled garden and I might just have to bite the bullet and knock on the door one of these days have see if I can have the tour.

Next to my Nan and Granddads house was the Regal Cinema, originally one of two in Leamington. This was the posh one but more about the other place later. The Regal originally had just one screen and the number of films seemed less than today, but I have fond memories of the place, although it has changed hands more times than a dodgy fiver and is now a multi-screen entertainment venue. It will always be the Regal to me.

Opposite my Nan's house stood an eclectic row of buildings, some old terraced cottages next to grand Regency houses. The later now swanky offices but in the past, these buildings had many a government purpose.

The labour exchange back in the 1940's with separate doors for men and women. The doors are still there but no longer accessible. Then later the building becoming the driving test centre back in the 70's and 80's where I, along with many others received the news that I had passed my test and was good to be let loose on the roads on my own, but I realise others stood outside dejected having failed.

Cars have been costing me money ever since. My Dad did warn me, 'if it's got tits or wheels, it will cost you money', I should have listened.

The route from Dormer Place towards the Parade, the main spine of Leamington, a path I have travelled so many times in my life. To the park with my Nan and Granddad when generally the weekly visit to see my Dad's parents would end up in the Jepson Gardens. And maybe some sweeties on the way back from the Linden Café, which had a self-service vending machine on the wall outside! Cutting edge back in the sixties with Sunday shopping was yet to come, so this was groundbreaking, especially for a young boy in need of a sugar fix.

The fog showed no signs of lifting and added to the atmospheric view of the pump room gardens; another well used part of Leamington's green lands.

Libby was already seeing things that she had walked past unnoticed and her eyes bright and taking in the adventure and the new focus. Even in the fog, the shape of the pump rooms against the grey mist was obvious, but I remember it as the swimming baths. This half of the building had been recycled into the library, but no mistaking its original use and on the odd occasion I venture in I can still hear the splashing of the water and smell the chlorine; imagination is great for that. I wonder if the tiled pool still lurks below the bookshelves.

Passing the front of the pump rooms we did take the opportunity to take the waters, a must today as we passed the spa water tap. I do love the quote. *'Drink the water of the crisped spring, O sweet content'* - Thomas Deker.

Sweet it is not, but you have to try it at least once in your life.

The water from the crisped spring as Thomas describes it, was the making of Leamington. The spring water which tastes like old pennies had the rich and famous flocking to the 'Royal Borough', gaining the 'Royal' and 'Spa' additions to the name along the way.

Up until now we have stayed on the north side of the river Leam, but as we crossed over the bridge we headed into the badlands of south Leamington or old town as it is sometimes called.

Passing the Loft Theatre where I discovered my passion for the theatre or the technical side at least, but to be honest it was all about the girl...Kym Dyson who went on to be an actress.

Moving swiftly on and past the majestic All Saints Church, '*the parish church*' as most locals call it. Stunning and almost cathedral like in statue. Although a place of worship has been on this site since the twelfth century, the church as we know it today started to take shape in 1842 when Leamington was a tiny hamlet in the parish of Leek Wootton.

This magnificent church has played its part in our family history. My parents' active members of the congregation for many years and my Dad the editor of the parish magazine.

My Dad loved church music and the organ especially and he did get to play it on occasion to a limited audience of my Mum and the church organist who was teaching him.

In contrast, my mother loved the people, the social side, the Women's Institute, and the church. And there is where she spent the night before her funeral – the other end of the circle of life.

Both my daughters were christened at All Saints which Libby didn't know; she was a baby at the time, so every day is a school day on today's run.

The church was where we held the funeral service for my Mum back in June 1992 before heading to Saint Mary Magdalene to be buried. I find the threads of life amazing, how these significant places keep appearing in the journey.

Heading down Bath Street and getting a glimpse of the other cinema, the Clifton or flee pit as it was called locally. It was always the poor relation to the Regal cinema which we passed earlier.

Closing its doors as a cinema back in 1982 and has been the sight of many a business venture, currently a gym I think, but always looking every bit an old cinema from the outside.

The Chair and Rocket, called the old library now, a shit name if you ask me! The place has never been a library to my knowledge, sorry, the Chair and Rocket. Another home to my mate Al and together with our mate Neil, gave me my first involvement with bands and the lighting there of, as I became part of local up and coming band, Alibi's roadcrew.

Off Bath Street was Bath Street School as a strange coincidence! This School was my Dad's old place of learning back in his childhood but was currently boarded up giving no clue of the future incarnation of this beautiful building. I love this part of town, always feel real.

Turning right under the bridges which takes the railway line across the rooftops of the houses at the bottom end of town, and onto London, skirting the inconspicuous door of the old Bridge Club and past the Crown Hotel, the stories and the memories came flooding back.

This part of town has always had a bad reputation, a far cry from the regency splendour of north Leamington. The bridges, even though there is only one now, there is still evidence of the other second bridge, which was taken down in Sixties with the decline of the railway.

The Crown Hotel has always played a part in the colourful history of this great town, as a music venue and as a drinking establishment launching the careers of many a would-be rock star with some success.

Bob Grant was a local hero as the resident entertainer, where he, night after night, knocked out classic tunes from within a self-built music capsule. It looked like something out of Dr Who surrounded by primitive technology bundled together with wires and tape, strumming old favourites as people drank to excess and local ladies, usually ladies, kicked the shit out of each other. Funny how it was always the women that fought.

My mum hated me going to the Crown and her face used to show the signs of concern when I announce the destination for the evening as I headed on my way out of the door.

I always used to tell her not to worry as it was the friendliest place in town as people came out the windows to meet you! A comment which never helped!

Apart from women fighting, I never saw any trouble; maybe I was lucky or didn't look hard enough, but for me the best thing about the Crown was the music. Artists and bands that became household names, locally at least tailored their craft on that stage.

Chevy, the Mosquitoes and the DT's and Alibi too – who I hear you cry!

This was my buddies band and for a while a big part of my life, but that experience is probably a book all by itself and will have to leave you dangling there a little.

Today, the building remains but it is no longer a hotel and is now flats. Interesting that the old place features in many peoples past and a regular feature on social media in 'memories of .....' groups.

Today's run was like being in an out-of-control time machine with the clock a bit faulty and memories out of sequence, so I needed to get back to the timeline and back to my preschool days.

As we headed across Fords Field up to the back of the old boys' club and on to the Queensway, this is the point where Libby and my memory lanes joined, and memories started to become one.

Libby went to the old boys' club or YC as it is known these days as part of the Challenge or NCS a few years before Millie.

Up Westlea Road, past my old mate Steve house- I haven't seen him since 1972.

I reckon at this point I lost my bearings again unless the little row of shops have been turned back into houses, I think not. Alas I had taken a wrong turn and was a street or two out of position; well it is over forty years ago so I am forgiven if the memory is a little bit jaded.

This is not always the case though as sometimes it felt like the years had rolled back and the memories came flooding back. Running past my Auntie Audrey's house (she was not really my Aunty but my mum's friend and had always be around since I was born, so we always thought of her as an Auntie). My earliest memory was being in my pram in the hall of Elizabeth Road fighting the urge to sleep and keen to get back to my mum, some things never changed.

Turning the corner at the end of the road to see my old school in front of me, it looked pretty much the same, but it had changed its name. Why was I not consulted?

Cashmore School had been renamed the Kingsway Community School and still looked very temporary, but why change the name? Sorry to go on about it.

School came as a bit of a shock for a very timid five-year-old with none of the break you in gradually taster days that are very much the norm these days.

Back in the sixties it was straight in – you started school and eleven years later you came out the other end of the educational sausage machine hopefully knowing a bit more that when you entered.

I have some pretty fond memories of Cashmore and enjoyed most of my primary school years so as we ran off into the mist I had a smile on my face.

It was obvious Libby was loving this and I was too, and very special to share all these great memories together and now with you.

Circumnavigating the perimeter of the school and past the neighbouring school, Saint Patrick's, it was getting time to head home. Enough nostalgia for one day me thinks and both of us ready for a bacon butty at our home on the banks of the river.

So nothing has change really apart from 50 years and only a different river swapping the River Leam to the Avon.

Thursday 29th December 2016. Last dawn run of 2016 the year maybe

I love days like today, ok it's a day off, it's -5°C and its 5:10 in the am. Ding dong ding dong – the alarm goes off and on go the trainers for maybe the last dawn run of the year.

A full house for this morning's outing and a little bit sleepy but the streets of Warwick twinkled with more than just ice, someone had a new toy to show off.

The electric gloves were a thing of wonder and for once, I was stuck for words…

Looking like an extra from the electric parade at Disney Land we would not be going unnoticed on the sleepy streets of town today with Michaela's head torch making her look like a unicorn in the foggy air, but it did illuminate the way pretty well! And so the banter started.

My body was warm enough, but my face was bloody freezing. I guess the clever folks would know the science behind all this, but our voices really carried this morning and it felt like our conversation was echoing around the medieval streets.

As always, some deep and meaningful conversations and complicated 'Boy oh boy when did life get so hard?' With Ian already doing a pretty good impression of Bambi even before we headed off, we took it steady, not wanting to end the year in A&E.

As we continued on our well-trodden winter route the arrival of the Sun seemed a while off yet, even though the days are getting longer, the Sun will not make an appearance until gone eight.

This morning, out of the five of us, only Ian had work today, so for the rest of us, the chance to head back to bed was a definite option and today I took it.

A nice cup of tea with a drop of whiskey and back to bed – don't mind if I do and the reward for a run on a holiday in sub-zero temperatures and worth every step. On arriving back home and after a nice hot shower, I had the rare chance to go back to bed and before long, snuggled under the duvet I was purring like a kitten and there I would have remained it the cats hadn't wanted to get in on the action… just perfect!

Thursday 29th December 2016. Part 2 – Tradition!

As the year comes to an end, one of my favourite days of the year is the post Christmas, pre New Year walk to the 'Case has altered' pub at Five Ways with my buddy Nigel and Alfie the dog.

We walk the same route to the same place every year, it's a tradition; but today was just stunning, 'Makes you realise that there is a God after all!' to quote an old friend of ours.

The ground solid as a rock and for this year, I have new boots. I wore my wellies last year, not a good idea.

We talk of music, old friends, family and past road trips along with some Christmas cake to nourish the conversation – tradition of course!

With our friendship spreading over four decades we are never short of things to talk about and a regular of topic of conversation and ended up on the agenda today was the lack of the big employers. Nigel from Coventry, only eight miles away from where I live, but the employment story much the same as my hometown.

Long gone are the big employers of this city, GEC, Alvis, Massy Ferguson, and the old British Leyland (in many of its incarnations Rover Group etc.), Rootes (another major car company that changed its name over the years) famous for the Hillman Hunter, Hillman Imp, the list goes on. The names Peugeot, Chrysler, Humber, the list is endless!

With Nigel talking fondly of his late Dad who worked at Coventry Climax, another of big employers of the city. The clear conclusion was with the demise of the factories, in parallel went the community, the sports and social clubs, the brass bands, the teams, the soul! - I know I have touch on this before.

In the UK we need to start making things again, relearning the skilled jobs along with the support staff and middle management to put the layers to add depth and structure back into society, all deep and meaningful stuff.

Having done the circuit of the closed pub, it's always closed as we set off too early. We're never around in time for lunch time opening, which is a shame because it is a proper pub that doesn't serve food except for snacks and has the best beer.

I asked once if they did food and 'what flavour would you like' came the reply.

With the traditional lap of the pub done and a bit of Christmas Cake – another tradition, not homemade this year but Tesco's Finest! We started our return and past the landmark for the journey home, the Silver Barrel, a house with the distinctive marker that always begs a comment or two before heading back across the fields.

The mist had cleared and with the winter sun on our backs, gloves off and soon the hat, got to love a sweaty head!

The countryside was stunning and with the rolling views of Warwickshire providing the backdrop to yet more chat on varied subject matter. Never a dull moment and the return journey always seems quicker, and with Kenilworth Castle in sight time to finish of the last of the Chrimbo Cake.

Having had a pretty much people free walks except for the occasional dog walker, the last half mile in the shadow of the castle was rammed.

Families, couples and the odd solo walker enjoying this beautiful day, walking of the excesses of the festivities. Kenilworth Castle is beautiful and would love to have seen it in its heyday before the Parliamentary forces knocked seven bells out of it back in the 1646 during the English Civil War.

Enough of the history lesson, the Almanac beckons with the promise of alcoholic refreshment – tradition!

Friday 30th December 2016 - Where's Daniel Craig when you need him?

Got to love a bit of spontaneity, the original plan was to meet up with an old, sorry young running friend of mine who had headed to London to seek her fame and fortune in the big smoke. Harky is a proper half full person and a great friend.

Not in the original plan for today, we were joined by Libby, Sue and Annie to add to the fun and banter.

Meeting at Striders Club house for old times 'sake and big hugs kicking off the proceedings, the route of choice was out to Old Milverton – always a favourite and I knew Libby would be happy with that, always a nice run. Must be a couple of years since I have ran with H, we keep in touch on Facebook but this face to face catch up was long overdue. Rotating around the group to catch up on the goss, Harky was loving every minute and we carried on from where we left off. I am always in ore of how people overcome past life issues and make life happen.

I was stuck for choice today with not one but two talented graphic artists to bounce ideas off. Reckon I might need some support in the next few months with some of the projects on the burner. H was excited to hear all about the 56notout challenge and with the absence of our old buddy Tracy, I knew the subject would not stray to sports bras, female medical examinations, and big nuts (not related). Yet again the variety of subjects never ceasing to amaze me and then out of the blue came Daniel Craig, not in person but the news that 007 was a neighbour turned the run dynamics on its head. So only one thing to do and that was to pop by and see if he was in.

No car outside but we had to stop for a group photo and a nose over the fence of River Cottage. Such a beautiful place to live and hope if the Craigs do live there, I hope they have time to enjoy it.

Next to River Cottage was the now empty Blackdown Mill. I love it when people I run with run past X or Y and never notice the detail, maybe it because it's never about the run for me and I never miss a trick or photo opportunity or I do not run that fast, a combination of all the above I suspect.

The price we paid for the detour to see Mr Bond was a little longer than planned in the trainers, but this was a real special run, spanning the generations and great to have a proper good natter. Harky has been running in the city too long and didn't care for muddy trainers – what's she like!

Epilogue

Saturday 31st December 2016 – Job done!

So we made it, the last run of the year. I have enjoyed the journey so much and it's been great to have you with me.

When I first put pen to paper some twelve months ago, I had no idea where this book was going to take me.

Running off at a tangent, I certainly did plenty of that and glad I changed the title. The year started out with the bones of a plan and I hope I covered most of the things I wanted too and a few others as well.

I have stayed on plan when I could or maybe not, but New Year's Eve is always a good day for reflection and a time to not only look back but forward too. Gone are the days when I would beat myself up for missing the odd goal and realise that sometimes life just get in the way. Everything will be ok in the end and if it's not ok, then it's not the end....

So there you have it, my running year. Thank you for sharing it with me. I have tried to be honest and open without offending any one and if I have, I am sorry, blame my education.

If you have learnt anything from my experiences that can help you, then great. If you have thought 'What a knob' then that is fine too.

I think I have fulfilled the brief and certainly went off at a tangent and pursued a somewhat related or irrelevant course while neglecting the main subject.

As for me, what am I going to do next, the events of Friday 2nd December 2016 would grow legs and become the '56notout challenge' which would keep me busy during most

2017 and 2018, along with book that followed which hopefully you will read next or maybe you have already.

After that, who knows but one thing I can promise you, I ain't done with this life yet.

ACKNOWLEDGEMENTS

There is always a team and this book would not be possible to a number of special people in my life.

My wife, Julie, always by my side to offer help and support with any wacky ideas I have dreamed up along with being the voice of reason when at times it is required and I can tell you there have been times!

My family and friends, I am fortunate to have an amazing family and great friends and for that I am grateful. It is said that friends are family that you pick yourself.

Thank you to everyone who has helped create those memories, the good times and the not so good times.

Libby, Millie and Tim who painfully took my written words, often alcohol fueled and turned them into English and something that actually make sense to the reader.

Thank you to my great friend Sue Cox who is always on hand for all thing graphical.

And finally I thank my parents, for without them there would be no me.

ABOUT THE AUTHOR

Steve Atherton works in the automotive industry and was born in Royal Leamington Spa. Steve lives in Warwick with his wife Julie along with Louis and Leo the cats.

He has two daughters, two step daughters and three grandchildren.

He is also a founder member of Run England running group *Zero to Hero* which encourages and motivates people to start running. A keen cyclist, photographer and gardener along with public speaking occasionally putting pen to paper.

Running off at a tangent

Printed in Great Britain
by Amazon